T5-BPY-958

Children's Literature Through
Storytelling & Drama

Second Edition

Nancy E. Briggs
California State University

Joseph A. Wagner
Long Beach, California

web
Wm. C. Brown Company Publishers
Dubuque, Iowa

U400757

Copyright © 1970, 1979 by Wm. C. Brown Company Publishers

Library of Congress Catalog Card Number: 79—50353

ISBN 0—697—06212—0

All rights reserved. No part of this publication may be reproduced,
stored in a retrieval system, or transmitted, in any form or by any
means, electronic, mechanical, photocopying, recording, or otherwise,
without the prior written permission of the publisher.

Printed in the United States of America

Children's Literature Through
Storytelling &
Drama

$530 X

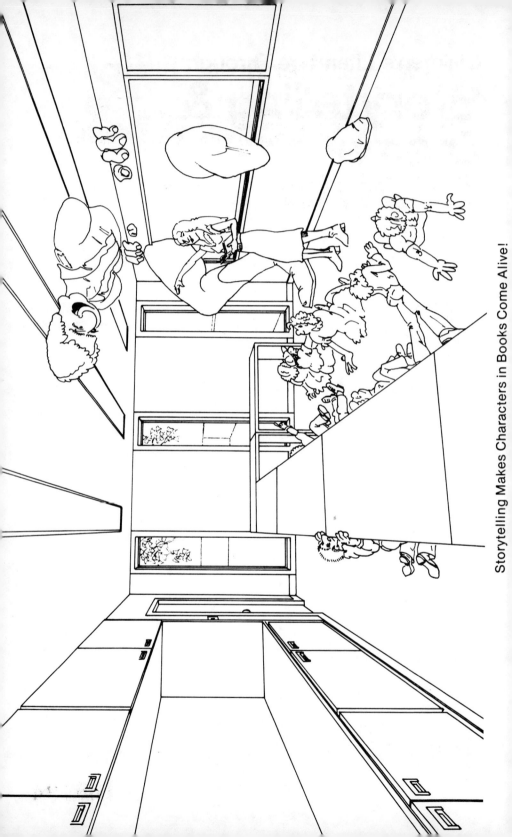

Storytelling Makes Characters in Books Come Alive!

Contents

Preface   xi
Acknowledgments   xiii

1. Storytelling: as Process   1

In the Beginning   1
The Origin of Stories   1
The Dissemination of Stories   4
A Communication Process   6
  Storyteller   6
  The Story   6
  The Channel   7
  Listeners   7
  Environmental Context   8
Storytelling Model   8
Values of Storytelling   8
  Promotes High Ideals   10
  Assists to Reduce Childhood Tensions   10
  Stimulates the Imagination   10
  Entertainment   11
  Assists the Learning Process   11
  Improves Communicative Ability   11
Summary   12

2. Types of Stories   13

Folk Literature   13
  Fables   13
  Folktales and Fairytales   15
  Myths   16
  Legends   18
  Sagas   19
Narrative Poetry   21
  Nursery Rhymes   21
  Ballads   25
  Story Poems   26
  Epics   29
Realistic Stories   30
Biographical Stories   31
Summary   33

3. Selection of Stories   35

The Child   35
  Age of Repetition   36
  Age of Fancy   37
  Age of Hero Worship   40
  Age of Idealism   42
  Every Age: Individualism   43
The Story   44
  Children and Literature   44
  Literary Worth   48
    Universal Theme   48
    Life-like Characters   48
    Effective Word Usage   50
    Logical Plot   51
    Appropriate Setting   51
The Storyteller   53
  Identification With the Story   53
  Purpose   54
  Comprehension Level   54
  Adult and Child Themes   55
  Emotional Dimension   56
  Commitment to Variety   59
    Storytelling Grid   59
Summary   59

4. The Story: Preparation and Delivery   63

Introduction   64
  Attention   64
  Mood   64
  Conflict   65
Body   66
  Attention   66
    Physical Arrangement   66
    Time for Storytelling   67
    Audience Adaptation during the Story   67
  Building Mood   68
    Author's Background   68
    Personal Experiences   68
    Setting   69
    Identification   69
    Clarity   69
    Suspense   69
  Conflict Situation Development   70
    Key Situations   70
    Cue Cards   71
    Cutting   72

Delivery   73
  Conversational Mode and Volume   73
  Correct Speech   73
  Pleasing Inflection   74
  Rate   74
  Gesture   75
Conclusion   75
Reading the Story   76
After the Story   78
Summary   79

**5. Creative Drama and
   Story Dramatization   81**

Definitions   81
  Values   83
  Characteristics of a Story
    for Dramatization   84
  Casting the Story   85
  Listening to the Story   86
  Evaluation   87
Dramatic Play: Getting Started   89
  Dramatic Play Activities   91
Role Playing   92
  Situations for Explorations   94
  Additional Problem Situations   95
Pantomime   95
  Exercises   96
  Games   97
  Music and Mime   98
Choral Speaking   98
  Refrain   99
  Antiphonal   100
  Line-a-choir   100
  Line-a-child   101
  Unison   103
Story Dramatization   104
  Interrogation   104
    Importance of Interrogation   106
  Storyacting   108
  Impromptu Dramatization   115
Story Improvisation   117
Summary   118

6. The Child as Storyteller   119

The Values of Storytelling   120
  Attitudes   120
  Improved Speech   121

Encourages Sharing   121
Increases Exposure to Literature   121
Speaking Presence   121
Management of the Child-told Story   122
  When Children Participate   122
The Child and the Story   123
Criticism of the Child-told Story   125
Participation Stories   125
Choosing Participation Stories   126
Summary   131

7. **Listening   132**

A Definition   132
Its Importance   133
Listening Habits   133
Why Children Do Not Listen   134
Telling and Listening   135
Improving Listening Effectiveness   136
Testing Listening Effectiveness   138
Summary   139

8. **Visual Aids   140**

Purpose   140
Determinants In Choosing Visual Aids   140
General Rules for the Use of
  Visual Aids   141
Types of Visual Aids   141
  Pictures and Chalkboards   142
  Objects Mentioned in the Story   142
  Flannel Boards and Colorforms   143
    Values   143
    Procedures for Use   144
  Puppetry   145
    Values   146
    *Characteristics of a Story for
      Puppet Acting*   147
    Puppet Theatre   148
    Producing a Puppet Story   149
    Types of Puppets   150
      Finger Puppets   150
      Fist Puppets   151
      Glove Puppets   151
      Stick Puppets   152
      Rod Puppets   152
      Shadow Puppets   153
      Hand Puppets   153
      Papier Mache Puppets   155
      Box or Object Puppets   155
      Paper Bag Puppets   156

Sock Puppets   158
Marionettes or String Puppets   159
Summary   161

**9. Creative Approaches
to Storytelling   162**

Contributing Authors
G. Bruce Loganbill   Oral Reading
and Articulation   162
Gloria Hassan   Telling Two Tales   163
Nancy E. Briggs   Creating a
Story   163
Jan Steadman   Stimulating
Imagination   164
Jed H. Davis   Creative Drama
Exercise: The Hijacking   165
Dorothy Skriletz   Outline of
Storytelling Project   165
G. Bruce Loganbill   Poetry   166
Steve Buck   Creating a
Biographical Story   167
Nancy E. Briggs   Follow-up
Story Activity   167
G. Bruce Loganbill   Readers
Theatre for Children   167
Steve Buck   Building a
Repertory of Stories   168
Nancy E. Briggs   Stimulus for
Children Telling Stories   168
Charlotte Wagner   Telling A
"Yarn"   168
Joseph Wagner   Storytelling
Outside the Classroom   169
Charlotte Wagner   Adjective Noun
Drill   169
Joseph Wagner   Visual Imagery   169
Dell Van Leuven   Masks for
Creative Drama   170
Jim Dighera   Stories and Music   171
John Wills   The Original Story   172
John Wills   Stories From Other
Lands or Cultures   172
John Wills   Semester Storytelling
Project   172
John Healy   A Communication
Stress Profile of a Storyteller   173

A Appendix 175
Voice Improvement Exercises

B Appendix 183
Critique Form Suitable for Use in College-
University Storytelling Classes

C Appendix 186
Story Index

Index 199

Preface

The value of storytelling has been recognized over the centuries. During the last two decades there has been a quickening of interest in this timeless subject not only as a means of entertainment but also as an aid to instruction.

The purpose of this book is to give helpful information, methods, suggestions, and guidance to those who wish to share the joys of good literature with children and adults through storytelling and creative drama. Children are encouraged to enter the magic circle not only as listeners but in the storytelling and acting role as well. This approach lends credibility to the concept of storytelling as process described in the first chapter.

This edition has an enlarged treatment of creative drama, which is also viewed as process. Creative drama includes the study and practice of *storytelling, dramatic play, role playing, pantomime, puppetry, choral speaking, story dramatization, and story improvisation.* This edition also includes a unique chapter on creative approaches to storytelling and creative drama. These approaches were contributed by various authors.

The Appendix contains an updated story index including suggested selections for preschoolers.

Acknowledgments

Anna Nix   Typist

Louise Rogers   Typist

Berta Potter   Typist

Paul Richards   Photographer

Michael Joncich   Photographer

Cal Ligh   Frontispiece

Kirk Edgar   Student Assistant

1 Storytelling
as Process

IN THE BEGINNING

One day the great warrior Einu came upon an evil bear that hurt people just by glancing at them. He killed the bear and buried it. When the ground shakes, the bear is angry.[1]

The skin-clad nomads huddled together about a dancing fire as their leader explained why their food search had been disturbed by an earthquake. As the flames died, long shadows flickered across the walls of their cave; a bitter night wind moaned through the forest; silence fell over the group. A hunter asked, "When the ground shook today, Manka died under falling rocks. Where is Manka now?" The leader answered:

One day Man went to Frog and said, "Where do you go after death?" Frog held a small piece of wood on the bottom of the pool, let go of it and it came to the surface. "After death," said Frog, "I rise into the sky." Black Fly overheard their conversation and said, "Watch me." He threw a pebble into the pool and it sank to the bottom. "After death," said Black Fly, "you sink to the bottom of the pool." Man was undecided.[2]

THE ORIGIN OF STORIES

Storytelling may have begun with crude chants and dances thousands of years before the dawn of recorded history. Prehistoric paintings on the walls of caves have been found in some areas. These depict hunters and animals which may describe great hunting exploits. Some petroglyphs also tell stories. As centuries passed, human intelligence gradually recognized the forces of nature as an action outside of themselves. People discovered unexplainable circumstances which frightened and awed him; these reactions found expression in myth and hero tales. These told tales of sacred beings, human heroes who were half-gods, and explained how all living things began. These stories were told and retold many times and in this process changes occurred. Some details that seemed unimportant were dropped and only subjects of universal appeal survived. Emerging, perhaps after centuries, was a folktale of classic literary form. Jacob Grimm (1785-1863) supported this theory relating to the growth of stories. Grimm, who was a German professor, philologist and mythologist also won acclaim as a member of the Germany Academy of Sciences. He and his brother Wilhelm authored *Kinder- und Hausmarchen* which is known today as *Grimm's Fairy*

Tales. The authors believed that today's tales which have survived through the centuries began in crude, fanciful form, were perpetuated by the peasantry and finally became epics in the hands of literary individuals. Brief little stories, such as those which introduced this chapter, may have served as cores for an Homeric epic or an experience of Beowulf. In support of Grimm's theory, some believe that folklore fails to develop when placed in a set form. With freedom it varies continually because it is shaped by the memories, creativity and needs of persons in specific situations. This process of change is known as *oral variation* and it is the very heartbeat of oral folklore. With the introduction of the printing press the growth of some stories was suspended or delayed. It is only when folklore flows back into oral circulation that its development is resumed.

There are many theories that seek to account for the origin of stories. Grimms' version is but one; several others deserve mention. The origin of stories is also attributed to human interpretation of natural phenomena, this theory, which is known as the Sun-Myth position, was supported by Friedrich Max Muller (1823-1900). This German-born British philologist, who exerted a stimulating influence on Oriental studies, contended that heroes of folk tales are regarded as allegorical representations of the sun, rain, storms, etc. In the beginning, people allegedly had difficulty distinguishing between nature and their own personalities. Fanciful interpretations were given to the coming of dawn, dusk, day and night. The weather conditions experienced by storytellers seemed to influence their attitude. Norse stories, for example, seemed more stark, severe and violent than those found in soft, tropical climes. Prehistoric people sought to explain the activities of a volcano by making it a god and offering it sacrifices. The movement of fire made it seem alive to primitives. The sun, for example, was believed to love the dew but in a rage, slew her with his arrows. Early storytellers also held that earth and heaven were married and used to be close together until they were separated by their children who had become cramped trying to live between them. Even a simple child's poem such as "The Song of Six-Pence" is said to have symbolic significance; the pie being the earth and sky, the birds the twenty-four hours, the king the sun, the queen the moon, and the opening of the pie, daybreak. Proponents of the Sun-Myth theory would explain that in "Little Red Riding Hood," the black wolf symbolized night, Red Riding Hood symbolized the sun, and the wolf's act of eating Red Riding Hood symbolized the end of day.

A third group of folklorists believed that all stories began in India and that they may be traced through language to a common Aryan heritage. Joseph Jacobs, (1854-1916), author of the earliest English version of the *Fables of Bidpal*, estimated that at least one-third of all stories common to European children came from India. The close relationship between people and beasts which was fostered by belief in animism and transmigration of souls provided fertile ground for the origin of fanciful stories. Additionally, this theory is supported by the presence of Hindus in ancient times who were sufficiently educated and possessed the intellectual ability to conceive and develop plots.

A fourth group attempted to explain the origin of stories by attributing them to a primitive form of cosmology. These folklorists felt that our ancient ancestors were concerned about his personal origin, how the world was made and why one season followed another. This belief that people always had a thirst for knowledge, has always been concerned about causality, is supported by the discovery of stories throughout the world that end with such statements as, "And that is why a bear's tail is short," or "And that is why a robin's breast is red." The following story is typical of the cosmologist's theory:

BLACKLEG

Back in the days when Man and Deer lived together, man did not have fire. Only Wolf had fire and it would not share it. Many men died trying to get fire from Wolf. One day Deer went to Man and said, "I will get you fire." "How can you do that?" queried Man, "Wolf will eat you." Months passed and Man thought that Deer had forgotten his promise. When winter was coldest, Wolf built the highest fires to stay warm. On a cold night, Deer approached Wolf's camp downwind so its scent would not reach Wolf. Staying behind bushes it walked silently up to the edge of the fire circle and then, with a burst of speed and a mighty leap soared over the roaring fire. As it did so, its hind legs seemed to catch fire. Away went Deer with blinding speed and was out of sight before Wolf realized what had happened. Deer fled in pain back to Man who quickly cut away the burning cedar bark that Deer had tied inside its hind legs. This is why to this day, Deer's hind legs have black on the inside.[3]

What conclusions may be drawn from these various theories? Although there is a basis for each, they in turn may be discounted. Sun-Myth followers run the risk of false analogies and inconsistencies in stories originating in various countries. A large number of these cosmic stories held that the sky was a male and the earth a female. However, a lack of consistency appears in Egyptian stories in which the sky deity is a female. Scholars who believed that all stories began in India have discovered a rival group which contends that the Euphrates Valley is the birthplace of most folktales. Their position is further weakened by the appearance of similar tales in non-Aryan countries. Those who support the cosmologist's approach must admit that some primitive tribes are not concerned about their origin and have not even troubled themselves to formulate a mankind creation myth. It would appear that some folklore researchers have had a tendency to impose their own story interpretations independently of those of native storytellers. The idea that an educated researcher is better able to interpret the allegories of primitive people does not carry much weight. It should be the responsibility of a folklorist to objectively ascertain what a tale means to a native raconteur and to his people in terms of their own daily living, religious habits and customs. A psychoanalyst, for example, should not impose alien Freudian interpretations upon a symbolism that a tribe has repeatedly accepted beyond the memory of its oldest members. Cosmologists, for example, might do well to learn those factors which motivate a tribe individually and collectively, and not assume that it is necessarily moved by the same stimuli that motivates other groups. As far as the foregoing theories relating to the origin of stories are concerned, each has contributed in varying degree to our well-spring of knowledge regarding orally transmitted tales.

THE DISSEMINATION OF STORIES

Estimates on the number of variations of the Cinderella story extant today vary from 345 to nearly 900. What is believed to the first Cinderella story concerns an Egyptian maiden, Rhodopis, who was bathing in the Nile. An eagle swooped down, picked up one of her gilded sandals, and dropped it in the lap of the King who was in the act of administering justice in the city of Memphis. Unlike later versions which had a prince or a king fall in love with the girl, this first version had the King become so impressed with the sandal that he would marry none but the owner of it. The now familiar search for a girl who could wear such a small sandal ensued until finally the King learned that a lovely girl visited the Sphinx each day at daybreak. The King and his entourage journeyed to this point, met the shy and startled Rhodopis, matched his sandal with the one the girl possessed, and not long after a marriage took place. Allegedly, Queen Rhodopis and the King lived happily ever after.

Stories of this kind may have been disseminated by many means. Communication between savage tribes may have begun the process. Warfare with its subsequent seizing of women may have furthered the process. Slaves from Africa

The importance of a circle to storytelling has existed since ancient times.

probably brought stories to the western world. Phoenicians and Viking sailors may have exchanged tales with strangers; the Crusades mingled Moorish and Christian cultures, and the migrations of people from the Orient over the Aleutian land chain to North America could have facilitated story dissemination. Additionally, travelling bards and minstrels who sang and told stories for food and a night's lodging literally carried tales. Once a story became popular, nothing seemed able to contain it. The idea of a one-eyed giant, for example, is found in Greece, Persia, Arabia, Lapland and among the Alaskan Eskimos. Slaves brought to America are believed to have learned tales from the Indians which later became the Uncle Remus stories. Where the Indians learned their versions is problematical. However, one of the slaves' favorite stories, the "Tar Baby," is said to be found in the Ceylonese *Jataka Tales*. Keightly[4] has found equally wide geographic distribution of other famous stories. For example, the *Jack the Giant-Killer* theme is found in Grimm's "The Brave Tailor" and in "Thor's Journey to Utgard" which may be found in the Scandinavian *Edda*. This theme is also present in "The Goat and the Lion" from the Panchatantra. He has also shown relationship in theme in Grimm's "The Fisherman and His Wife" to the *Pentamerone* tale, "Peruonto," to the Russian story, "Emelyan the Fool," and to the Esthonian tale by Laboulaye, "The Fairy Craw-Fish."

Another factor in the dissemination of stories that must be briefly considered is the sophistication of the mode of delivery of the message as man abandoned the hunt and began to establish small communities. Specialization of arts and crafts began and each person shouldered a certain responsibility, i.e. soil preparation, reaping, cooking . . .and even story-telling. Those with the best memories, those who could hold attention, those who identified with the characters in a story became the bearers of exciting history and tradition. Literary form began to develop at this time.

With the exception of today's media capability of carrying a story to millions of listeners in the twinkling of an eye, the greatest period for story dissemination took place from approximately 950 A.D. to the 1500's. Kings and nobles competed to obtain the most proficient storytellers. They were invited to live at the castle and additionally, were remunerated for their efforts. These artists combined music with story themes. They wrote ballads to commemorate important battles, marriages, etc., and would sing them for the King and his guests. In Ireland these storytellers were organized into nine groups and each told a different kind of tale. Germany had its minnesingers who specialized in romantic ballads. The famed meistersingers developed in the 1300's. England had its minstrels, Wales its bards, Scandinavia its skalds, and northern France its trouvers. Such storytellers were named troubadors in southern France. Although some of these "weavers of tales" enjoyed rather long periods in established households, most of them travelled about. Joining this group with their stoires were ordinary travellers, gypsies, crusaders and adventurers of every description. The mingling of these entertainers resulted in the exchange and adaptation of stories to the extent that pinpointing the origin of a story's plot or elements thereof became very difficult. This backward glance at story dissemination suggests that vital nature of the communicative role played by storytellers over thousands of years.

A COMMUNICATION PROCESS

Storytelling is a communication process in which verbal and nonverbal symbols and meanings are exchanged between the speaker and the listener. The ability to communicate efficiently is the key to effective storytelling. From the time of cave dwellers to today, mankind has been translating physical actions and experiences into words to establish social ties and transmit knowledge. For example, a student preparing an assignment in storytelling may find some fascinating material, enjoy it, reflect on it, and still have a feeling of incompleteness *until the story is shared with another.* Storytelling requires interaction with others. It is an elemental social process that includes all the factors necessary for reciprocal communicative relationships with another person or group.

The components of the process include a source of the information, a *storyteller,* and the presentation or encoding under certain circumstances—the environment or the occasion—which might be in a classroom, before a campfire, on a playground, at bedtime, or most anywhere. Additionally, this process must have a message, which is the *story.* The message travels through a *channel,* to the *listeners* or the receivers. Here the message is interpreted or *decoded.* If there is no interference or *noise,* the content of the story may arrive in approximately the same state as it was dispatched. Upon hearing the story, while it is being told, the listener may provide both verbal and nonverbal feedback to the storyteller. Let us briefly consider these components in greater detail:

Storyteller

The storyteller is not only sharing the story, but is reacting to the immediate physical circumstances, to responses from the children which may or may not coincide with the responses sought, and to reasons why the story was told. The latter, the storyteller's purpose may be to entertain, or to explain some arithmetic problem by telling a story of the Arabs who first proposed the idea of arithmetic, or to persuade listeners that more happiness may be found through courtesy rather than discourtesy. With every story there is a purpose that the storyteller wishes to realize. The beliefs, sense of values, interests, desires, and background of knowledge influence the choice of story selected. How the story is shared physically will determine in part the reaction of the listeners.

The Story

The story is the message. In spite of one's best effort, the storyteller may have selected a story that might not mean the same thing to the listeners as it does to the sender. It is helpful to look upon a story as a collection of symbolic stimuli in a communication channel. The meaning does not exist in the words themselves, but only in the minds of the storyteller and the listeners.

The Channel

Simply stated, the channel is the media by which a message is transmitted. In telling a story, the channel used might be the air-waves such as in the case of face-to-face communication, or electronic impulses as in the case of radio, T.V., or telephoned communication. Braille becomes the channel for the blind. It was stated earlier that, under normal circumstances, if noise is not present during transmission of a story, it stands a good chance of being received in the same state as it was dispatched. *Noise* may be defined as anything that detracts or interferes with the presentation of a story or a message. Noise may be attributable to a "bad connection" on a telephone, the floppy, distracting earrings of a storyteller, a mobile swinging from the ceiling, a child whispering to another, a personal concern that prevents a child from listening, a child's tardy arrival in a classroom when a story is in progress, a word that connotes a different meaning to the listener than that intended by the sender, a statement that antagonizes a listener, or the siren of an emergency vehicle. If noise is minimal, a child might strive even more diligently to hear a story; however, if there is too much noise, the child may not be able to listen at all. At best, noise should be eliminated whenever possible in order that a storyteller and listeners may have maximum opportunity to coincide on the meaning of the message.

We can see, then, that the storyteller should be well-prepared, telling an appropriate story properly, in the right setting, to an audience whose interests and objectives are understood, by a storyteller who is able and willing to interpret feedback and thereby improve future presentations. It must be remembered that children are not simply listening to a story. They are reacting to the storyteller's attitudes, voice, nonverbal gestures, and how they perceive the situation in which they find themselves. They have objectives too, and meaning will not occur until they perceive that those objectives are being fulfilled, and until they assign significance to the action taking place in the story.

Listeners

The story comes through the channel to these individuals. Children may sit rather impassively during a story's presentation. Their responsibility is to decode the message and make the story meaningful in their lives. Depending upon their backgrounds, the interpretation of one child might be totally different from that of another. The children bring their own experiences, however limited, and their desires and hopes into play as they decode. How they react to the story will determine the amount and type of *feedback*. Their role vacillates between decoding and encoding as they send signals, either verbal or nonverbal back to the source, the storyteller. The diversity of listener's backgrounds points up the importance of choosing the most appropriate story for them.

Environmental Context

The environmental context involves not only the physical setting where a story is told but also those social aspects which affect oral communication. Physically, a story may be presented before a roaring campfire, beside a quiet pool, in a Sunday school class or at the bedside of a convalescing child. If listeners are comfortably seated, if they are upwind from campfire smoke, if the speaker is easily heard there will be better attention than if these conditions do not prevail. A specific setting or occasion must include the environment of both the storyteller (the source) and the listeners (the receivers). Social aspects of the environment would include attitudes toward the subject of a story. A macabre story would not be told to a nervous, fearful child at bedtime; stories of St. Nick are not popular at a spooky Halloween party and preschoolers would glean little from an adult mystery story. The number of children present when a story is told can influence its reception. Individuals laugh more heartily if many laugh; they applaud more vigorously if many applaud. Children are prone to respond as a unit if they are seated closely together. Evidence of this is found in the reactions of children who listen to a television story alone and then hear the same presentation in the company of their peers. This brief consideration of the environmental context suggests the complexity of oral communication as it affects the behavior of storyteller and listener alike.

STORYTELLING MODEL

The following model illustrates the ways in which all of the components of the communication process interact. It represents the total involvement of the storyteller, the story, the channel, the listener and the environmental context. This interaction may cause effects which the elements separately would not cause. The communication process occurs when the various components exist and are fused into a working relationship. A careful study of the model and its complex interrelationships will assist us to understand why some stories succeed and others are less successful.

VALUES OF STORYTELLING

Several different values may be attributed to storytelling. Some of these are explored in Chapter 7, which provides means of improving a child's listening habits; others are stressed in Chapter 6, which indicates the development which takes place when a youngster begins to tell his own stories. The following values are general ones which may accrue to any child who has the advantage of being exposed to good literature:

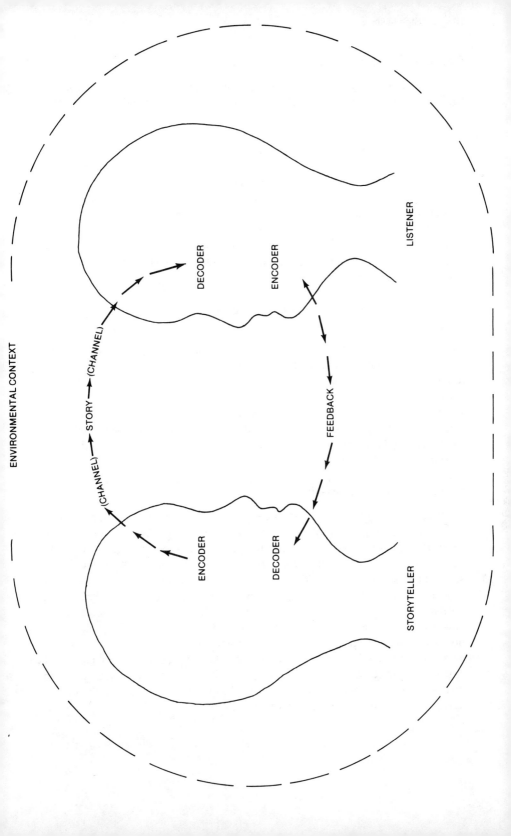

Promotes High Ideals

Characteristically, fairy tales reward good and punish evil. Heroes and heroines are unselfish persons who help less fortunate people and animals. These tales, through fantasy, satisfy human desires for recognition, love, beauty, and courage. Throughout life, the morals imparted by fairy tales may fortify persons faced by adverse circumstances and assist them to cling to their ideals. Human history reveals innumerable instances of religious and patriotic martyrs, for example, who sacrificed their futures and sometimes their lives for what they believed. Our forefathers who had the courage to sign the American Declaration of Independence need not have done so; Nathan Hale might have become a traitor and saved his life; likewise, Joan of Arc might have spared herself torture and death if she had renounced her faith. These individuals are part of our common heritage and storytelling may introduce their strength and beauty to eager young listeners.

Assists to Reduce Childhood Tensions

The fertile imaginations enjoyed by most children sometimes lead to tensions and anxieties. They find themselves in self-created situations which disturb them and which do not seem to lead to easy solution. Fairy tales can come to the rescue under these circumstances. A "transfer" of feeling may occur when the hero or heroine of the story manages to solve her dilemma and thereby provide, vicariously, a tension-relieving solution for the child. It is comforting for the child to discover that story characters also have fears and problems for which solutions may be found. As a result of this association, the child might develop an improved self-concept.

Stimulates the Imagination

Wordsworth believed that in order to appreciate literature fully, there must be a "...willing suspension of disbelief." Through storytelling, children learn to appreciate the value of this position long before they enter a classroom. After being introduced to a world where a frog can turn into a handsome prince, where straw magically becomes gold, where animals can speak, it is little wonder that mother's broom becomes a magic wand, a large packing carton becomes an enchanted castle, and the family dog suddenly discovers that he is a resplendent charger carrying a tousled doll into battle. George Ebers, Egyptologist and novelist, discounts those who criticize the value of fairytales. He explains that, as a child, he could imagine the most marvellous things but, when asked if the experiences were true, he would awaken as if he had been dreaming and immediately separate fact from fancy. Ebers and master storytellers would probably agree with Wordsworth when he wrote:

Imagination, which in truth,
Is but another name for absolute power
And clearest insight, amplitude of mind,
And Reason in her most exalted mood
"The Prelude"

Entertainment

An elderly elementary classroom instructor once stated that in thirty years of teaching, she had *never* had a negative response to her question, "Class, would you like to hear a story today?" Stories are worth their time if only for sheer fun! Who would not like to see an elephant perched in a tree on a bird's nest? How many have thrilled to the excitement of the headless horseman's ride or to Long John Silver's piracy? Although participation stories such as "The Brutal Miner" and "Here We Go On A Lion Hunt" do not conform to the requisites of great literature, they are splendid "ice breakers" when new groups of children gather. Such stories assist to produce social consciousness, group cooperation, and laughter.

Assists the Learning Process

Storytelling is an excellent means of enlivening instruction and making it both enjoyable and more meaningful. One of the most effective ways of doing this is through biographies. In music, for example, before playing recordings from Mendelssohn, Mozart or Bach, the exercise can be humanized with a story from the life of one of these great composers. Art instruction might likewise be embellished. Youngsters might be surprised to learn that as a child, the great Italian artist, Tintoretto, loved to play in boats along Venetian canals. After the children have "accepted" him, a display of some of his great works probably would be more readily appreciated.

In addition to aesthetic stimulation, biographies can also serve as signposts along a child's vocational path. Stories of great industrialists, inventors, doctors, nurses, and athletes could inspire a child to achieve.

Improves Communicative Ability

Listening to stories, telling stories, and dramatizing them with their classmates will assist children to improve in the following aspects of speech arts:

1. To perceive and understand the effects of speaking.
2. To recognize worthwhile ideas.
3. To organize thoughts and feelings.
4. To use appropriate language.

5. To speak with clarity, including:
   a. force or loudness
   b. pitch and inflection
   c. time or pace
   d. quality
   e. articulation and pronunciation.
6. To make effective use of posture and gesture.
7. To adapt to various speech situations.
8. To listen courteously and critically.
9. To help the child become more independent, confident, and creative.
10. To provide an artistic avenue of exciting expression.

SUMMARY

This chapter has listed only four of many possible sources of stories, i.e., stories resulting from human experience, interpretation of natural phenomena, the belief that all stories have a common Aryan heritage, and finally, the theory that primitive people were consumed with curiosity to know their own background and that of their environment so tellers used stories to satisfy this urge to understand. It is evident from this chapter that once a good story was told, its dissemination occurred in spite of geographic and language barriers. While the study of the origin and spread of stories is fascinating, the important thing for today's generation is the fact that these excellent stories have survived countless years and only await the release of their magic influence by those who are willing to share them orally with others.

This chapter has also described storytelling as a communicative process. It has briefly traced the route taken by a message as it travels from the storyteller to the listeners where reaction takes place in the form of feedback to the sender. Noise or interference may hamper the presentation of the story and feedback might be both encouraging and discouraging to the storyteller.

Some of the values of storytelling mentioned were the promotion of high ideals, the reduction of childhood anxieties, stimulation of young imaginations, aids to the learning process, and entertainment. Chapters 5 and 6 reveal further values for children when they tell stories or dramatize them.

---

1. Unpublished Carrier Indian Tale. No Title.
2. Unpublished Carrier Indian Tale. No Title.
3. Unpublished Carrier Indian Tale. "Blackleg."
4. Thomas, Keightly, Tales & Popular Fictions (London: Whittaker & Co., 1934), pp. 34ff.

2   Types of Stories

Literature for today's child includes a vast array of stories written in language that he can understand. It ranges in scope from factual discourses on vocational guidance to suggestions for travel to outer space. Wedged in between may be found the great classics of yesteryear and in addition, there are excellent, beautifully illustrated books on nature, fascinating fiction, and highly educational, biographical profiles. The latter, in the hands of competent storytellers, have added spice to most instructional subjects.

Children's literature is by no means an inferior category of literature. It is a legitimate branch of literature like any other work of art. Children's literature is marked by a consciously planned composition with a subject and theme through which unity and style may be evident.

In an effort to facilitate a choice of stories for telling, material will be considered in four categories: folk literature which includes fables, fairy tales and folktales, myths, legends, and sagas; narrative poetry which is divided into nursery rhymes, ballads, story poems, and epics; realistic stories; and finally, biographical material. Children may progressively experience a richer legacy from *Mother Goose* to the *Iliad,* and from *The Three Bears* to *Phaethon,* each according to their comprehension ability and interest. This classification of stories is meant to be inclusive overall, but not entirely exclusive within categories. For example, the most popular epic of *Robin Hood* was preserved through the oral tradition of the ballad. Moreover, several of *Aesop's Fables* or Andersen's fairy tales may be considered folktales because they were recorded to preserve an oral tradition of a people and to highlight a commoner. *Daniel Boone* may be considered as a saga or a biographical fiction. Parts of the *Volsung Saga* are poetic, therefore some literary critics label it, "epic." Most importantly, the exposure of children to different kinds of literature with appropriate audience adaptation is the key to storytelling variety.

FOLK LITERATURE

Fables

Fables are brief fictitious narratives which attempt to teach a moral lesson. The chief characters are usually talking animals or inanimate objects which behave like humans. The useful lesson, however, is an abstract thought, a maxim or an adage, made clear through the behaviors of particular animals such as the fox, hare, or wolf. From the earliest time, the fable has never ceased to amuse and instruct people.

Several famous fable collections exist. *Aesop's Fables* were supposedly written by the Greek Aesop in the sixth or seventh century B.C. Although the first known collection was made by Demetrius of Phalerum in 320 B.C. Aesop is considered the "Father of the fable." Aesop classified animals, birds and insects according to the good and bad qualities that they seemed to display. For example, the owl represented wisdom, the fox stood for cunning, the wolf for greed, the ant for thrift, the rabbit for pride, and the lion for valor. Of the 350 fables credited to Aesop, approximately fifty are well known. Of these, children are especially fond of "The Shepherd Boy and the Wolf," "The Crow and the Pitcher," "The Hare and the Tortoise," "The Fox and the Grapes," "The Ant and the Grasshopper," "The Lion and the Mouse," "The Country Mouse and the Town Mouse," and "The Wind and the Sun." The latter is a good example of Aesop's storytelling genius:

> The wind and the sun were arguing about which was the stronger. Suddenly they saw a traveler coming down the road. The Sun declared, "I know a way to end our disagreement. Whoever can cause that traveler to take off his coat will be regarded as the stronger. Why don't you start?"
>
> The sun waited behind a cloud and the wind began to blow as hard as he could on the traveler. But the harder he blew the more tightly the traveler wrapped his coat around him. At last, the wind sighed, "I give up."
>
> Then the sun came out and shone with all his might upon the traveler. The traveler soon found it much too hot to wear a coat.
>
> So the sun was the winner. And the sun said, "Gentle persuasion is better than force."

Another valuable collection of fables is from Jean de La Fontaine in the seventeenth century France. He recorded his fables in graceful verses which unfortunately lose much of their appeal when translated into English.

From India, the stories of *The Panchatantra* and *Jatakas* are worth telling. "The Greedy and the Speedy" and "The Hermit and the Mouse" are noteworthy stories.

Many modern stories have fable-like qualities. The truth in an old moral may be rewritten many times and ways and still be entertaining. Consider the following well known morals and their reappearance in contemporary story lines:

1. Misery loves company. (Dr. Seuss, *How the Grinch Stole Christmas*)
2. Honesty is the best policy. (Roald Dahl, *Charlie and the Chocolate Factory*)
3. Don't bite the hand that feeds you. (Katherine Evans, *One Good Deed Deserves Another*)
4. Trouble comes when we least expect it. (Dr. Seuss, *The Cat in the Hat*)
5. One man's meat may be another man's poison. (David McKee, *Lord Rex, the Lion Who Wished*)

6. Familiarity breeds contempt. (Russel Hoban, *Best Friends for Frances*)
7. He who does a thing well does not need to boast. (Jeffrey Allen, *Mary Alice, Operator #9*)
8. He laughs best who laughs last. (Flora Steel, *The Tiger, the Old Man, and the Jackal*)
9. A man may smile, yet be a villain. (Dottie Smith, *101 Dalmations*)
10. A change of scene does not change one's character. (Jeanette Krinsley, *The Cow Went Over the Mountain*)

Folktales and Fairytales

Folktales may be defined as stories of anonymous origin which form a part of the oral tradition of a tribe or people. In contrast to the saga, these tales are the product of peasants and they extol the virtues of the lowly, the ones considered least likely to succeed by their families or their townspeople. In "The Bremen Town Musicians" for example, the rejected animals prove their worth by defeating the robbers. In "Boots and His Brothers," it is Boots, the youngest and the least promising of the brothers who manages to chop down the King's tree and win his daughter and half of the kingdom. These tales possess a rather persistent moral character. The deserving individual or creature, be it Snow White, Cinderella or the Little Red Hen ultimately is rewarded. These tales usually reflect the dreams and unfulfilled wishes of the luckless and downtrodden. Through folktales, those in authority were challenged and made to look foolish. A classic case in point is the emperor and his advisors in "The Emperor's New Clothes." The recipient of the ridicule could be a king or a husband as in the case of the humorous Norse tale, "The Husband Who Was to Mind the House." Stories of this type apparently were told to amuse or instruct and made no effort to record historical matters. Fairy stories, both ancient and modern, are usually included within the larger category of folktales even though the authorship of modern fairy stories is known. Adults may classify the stories as folktales, but children call them fairy tales because of the magic, enchantment, and wonder therein.

There are numerous national groups of folktales. Perhaps the most well known collectors are Perrault's French Fairy tales in 1697, The Grimm brothers German folk tales in approximately 1815, the Norwegian folktales by Peter Asbjornsen, Jorgen Moe, and Sir George Dasent in the 1800's, and the British folktales collected by Joseph Jacobs and published in the 1900's.

American children are familiar with folktales from all over the world. They are exposed to European variants of tales, and folklore from the American Negro such as the Uncle Remus Stories, the North American Indians, and the tall tales of the Paul Bunyan type.

The enchanting stories found in *The Arabian Nights* illustrate the oral tradition of many people in the unique form of a compilation of many manuscripts. Most of the stories are of folk tradition and tend to be rather primitive. The structure of the tales includes full length stories that resemble a saga (The Seven

Voyages of Sinbad), to anecdotes or pious stories and fairy tales. *The Thousand and One Nights* are of Persian (Iranian) and Baghdadian origin and the later stories are Egyptian. Some of the stories show French influence. They reflect the social aura of the medieval Middle East and hence are valuable from a historical and cultural perspective.

Today's form of *The Arabian Nights,* at least in English, is still based on the work of Sir Richard Burton in 1885. Most stories that are revised or adapted for children are also from his texts, expurgated of course. The collection contains 180 full stories not counting the Frame story of Scherezade who kept the sultan, her husband, from killing her by telling these tales over 1001 nights. The stories have exciting plots which make them excellent for storytelling purposes. Other well-known stories include "Aladdin and the Magic Lamp," "Ali Baba and the Forty Thieves," "The Story of the Merchant and the Genie," "The Enchanted Horse," "The Story of the Fisherman and the Genie," "The Poor Man and His Dream," and "Sandalwood."[1]

May Hill Arbuthnot sums up the various explanations for the origins and purposes of folktales: "The folk tale is created by most peoples at an early level of civilization, containing elements from past religions, rituals, superstitions, or past events, and serving to satisfy man's basic emotional needs. It also reinforces our faith in morality and the ultimate triumph of good over evil."[2]

In recent years, there has been an increase in the availability of good folktale retellings for children. This includes publications of collections of tales from many peoples whose oral literature was not previously recorded. Examples are the following: Virginia Tashjian's *Once There Was and Was Not,* an Armenian folktale collection; K. L. Parker's *Australian Legendary Tales;* and Dorothy L. Robertson's *Fairy Tales from Vietnam.* Another welcome trend is the publication of individual folktales as separate books with beautiful illustrations. These include: Arthur Ransome's *The Fool and the Flying Ship,* a Russian folktale; *Why the Sun and Moon Live in the Sky,* an African folktale; and the Irish *Hudden and Dudden and Donald O'Leary.*

Myths

A myth is a story that is usually of unknown origin and at least partially tradition. It ostensibly relates historical events usually in order to explain some practice, belief, institution or natural phenomena. A myth is often associated with religious rites or beliefs and is concerned with gods and supernatural beings. It frequently attempts to explain some basic truth. These stories are imaginative precursors to scientific research. Commenting on the use of myths Herzberg writes:

> Poets and storytellers of all nations use myths for many purposes. They retell them in their own language—in prose and verse, in short story and epic and play. Dante had Ulysses, the Greek hero, tell part of his story in the *Inferno.* Shakespeare reworks certain episodes of the Trojan War in *Troilus and Cressida.* Goethe tells the story of

Iphigenia in *Tauris* and Racine that of *Andromache*. William Morris recounts in a long poem the adventures of Jason in search of the Golden Fleece, and several novels have been written about Helen of Troy and about the adventures of King Arthur's knights.[3]

Myths are appropriate material for storytelling because of the imaginative quality of the tale, the exposure to various cultural backgrounds which prove interesting to the audience, and the unique *language* and descriptive phraseology of such tales. Moreover, this is an advanced type of story that listeners and readers can "grow into" and for which they can acquire a taste. The myth teaches through symbolism and allegory, but it also possesses a beauty and elegance of its own. A great hero or heroine may be presented on which to feed the dreams of youth.

An understanding of mythology will make literature more meaningful and enjoyable to children. Occasionally one hears reference to "opening Pandora's box" but relatively few persons understand this allusion. The following myth would take but a few minutes to tell and Pandora would no longer be a mystery:

So men prospered. And as they prospered Jupiter was more and more displeased. He finally settled on a cunning stratagem to overcome Prometheus. With the help of his son Vulcan (Greek: Hephaestus), lord of the forge, and of the other gods, he devised a most beautiful woman, named Pandora (a word in Greek that means "all gifts"). Upon her each of the deities bestowed some grace or beauty. Her he sent to Prometheus, and with her went a great jar, such as men use for storing oil; and the jar was carefully sealed. Prometheus, suspecting a trick on the part of Jupiter, refused to accept either the woman or the jar; and Jupiter sent her to Epimetheus, who had been warned by his brother against the wiles of Jupiter. Epimetheus, however, won by the beauty of Pandora, accepted her as his wife.

"This is my dowry," she explained when Epimetheus inquired what was in the jar; and together they broke the seal and opened it. Immediately a cloud of evils flew forth—all the diseases and troubles and worries that still afflict mankind. Too late, they tried to put the lid back again. But only one spirit remained in the jar; Hope.[4]

Consistent with the definition of a myth set forth earlier, the basic problem or truth this myth explains is why there is so much trouble in the world.

Another type of myth that is appropriate for children concerns how the gods or the ruling forces wield justice. One of the favorites of children is "King Midas," who wished that everything he touched would turn into gold. This type of myth demonstrates the problem of too much human greed. Consequently, the gods or the forces of nature take their toll. "Jason and the Golden Fleece" is another good myth where the gods reward a just and heroic man. Another favorite is the story of Icarus. Children, in particular those ten and above, enjoy these types of myths.

Greek mythology is enchanting and has captured the imaginations of many children. The storyteller should consistently use either Greek or Roman names in the tales. One excellent myth is that of "Phaethon," the son of the Sun God:

For a few ecstatic moments Phaethon felt he was the Lord of the Sky just like his father, the Sun God. Then suddenly, there was a change. The chariot started swinging out of control. The horses were racing ahead without direction. Phaethon knew his weak hands could not compare to the power of his father's. The horses plunged headlong into the earth and set the world on fire.[5]

A modern adaptation of Greek myths was attempted by Nathaniel Hawthorne in *A Wonder Book for Girls and Boys* and *Tanglewood Tales for Girls and Boys*. In England, Charles Kingsley retold the myths for children in his book titled "The Heroes." Sally Benson's *Stories of Gods and Heroes* is also recommended for age ten and up. Mary Renault's *The King Must Die,* portrays the Theseus myth very well. Robert Graves' *Greek Gods and Heroes* is a tongue-in-cheek adaptation of famous Greek myths. Another excellent source is Mabie Wright Hamilton's *Myths Every Child Should Know*.

Another popular source of myths for children is Norwegian. In "Thor's Visit to the Giants," we find a bold adventure where Thor is dealt with justly. Throughout this episode, Thor's courage is rewarded, but his vanity is discouraged. In this scene he is forced to fight in a battle of the sexes. His opponent, chosen by the King of the Giants, is Elli an old woman:

> She was wrinkled and gray, and her back was bent nearly double with the weight of the years which she carried, but she chuckled when she saw Thor standing with bared arm in the middle of the floor. "Come and be thrown, dearie," she cried in her cracked voice, grinning horribly.
>
> "I will not wrestle with a woman!" exclaimed Thor, eyeing her with pity and disgust, for she was an ugly creature to behold. But the old woman taunted him to his face and the giants clapped their hands, howling that he was "afraid." So there was no way but that Thor must grapple with the hag.
>
> The game began. Thor rushed at the old woman and gripped her tightly in his iron arms, thinking that as soon as she screamed with the pain of his mighty hug, he would give over. But the crone seemed not to mind it at all. Indeed, the more he crushed her old ribs together the firmer and stronger she stood. . . .[6]

This exciting adventure entices the listener to hear and read more of the Norwegian myths.

Legends

A legend is related to the myth. It may be considered a popular myth usually of current origin. It may be a collection of stories that form an account or history of the life of a heroic commoner, or a people or a clan. The story is passed on by tradition and popularly regarded as historical although not entirely verifiable.

Perhaps the most famous of legends is that of "Sleepy Hollow." Near the eastern shore of the Hudson River in New York, about two miles from Tarrytown, Sleepy Hollow is still there. The author, Washington Irving was the first American writer to be acclaimed throughout the world and though he became an important ambassador and historian, his real nature is revealed in his tales, *Rip Van Winkle* and *The Legend of Sleepy Hollow.* This legend is a ghost story that is a funny and rollicking yarn:

As Ichabod approached this fearful tree of Major Andre, he could clearly see in the moonlight that its limbs were gnarled, and fantastic, large enough to form trunks for ordinary trees, twisting down almost to the earth, and rising again into the air. Ichabod began to whistle. He thought the whistle was answered but it was a blast of air sweeping sharply through the dry branches. As he approached a little nearer, he thought he saw something white, hanging in the midst of the tree. He paused and ceased whistling. ''What could it be?'' he thought. Straining to see what it was, he perceived a place where the tree had been scathed by lightning, and the white wood laid bare. Suddenly he heard a groan—his teeth chattered and his knees hugged the saddle. . . .[7]

The skill in building suspense was artistically demonstrated in Irving's works, and a storyteller may have a great challenge in its reconstruction as oral literature.

Sagas

A saga is a prose narrative of the heroic exploits of an individual or of a family. Sagas are written to commemorate some factual matter such as war, heroism during natural disaster, or some other outstanding occurrence. It is a significance, for a later consideration of the characteristics of folktales, that sagas glorify the hero-leader cult in a group. Only persons of good lineage who distinguished themselves, could qualify for literary immortality in a saga. The *Volsung Saga* and those commemorating exploits of the Trojan War are typical of this literary form.

Sagas may be a series of legends that embody in detail the special oral history of a people. The term typically deals with prominent figures and events of the heroic age in Norway and Iceland especially in the 12th and 13th centuries. This series of fictional or historical narratives may be without psychological or historical depth such as the recent winning of the west. But as a matter of fact, the great majority of the oldest sagas preserved are the historical ones, the so-called family sagas, telling stories from the life of the old aristocracy in Iceland.

Sagas are normally used to symbolize the literary works from the Middle Ages which still have appeal for modern listeners. The word ''saga'' literally means ''something said,'' and was in use long before there was any written literature in Iceland. The Icelandic sagas from the thirteenth centuries are still a living literature. In fact, even today a whole library of sagas, approximately fifty, remain popular reading in Iceland in the original language. The art of the saga was the art of telling. Every saga contains a series of events or shorter episodes, and these do not constitute a saga without being linked together into some kind of unity. The real test of a ''saga-man,'' as storytellers of sagas are called, is to make every particular episode or scene of his story as vivid and interesting as possible and be able to combine all single episodes into an interesting whole if need be. He should arouse the curiosity of the listener to make him eager to hear the end of the story.[8]

Expert storytellers may find the challenge of the *Volsung Saga* worthwhile. Difficulties in the names, the text, and the social relationships provide a difficult course to chart. But the violence found in many sagas has the purposes of nobility, self-sacrifice, trust, or idealism. Consider the character of Sigurd of the family of Volsung:

> And they sing of the golden Sigurd and the face without a foe,
> And the lowly man exalted and the mighty brought alow:
> And they say, when the sun of the summer shall come aback to the land,
> It shall shine on the fields of the tiller that fears no heavy hand;
> That the sheaf shall be for the plougher, and the loaf for him that sowed,
> Through every furrowed acre where the Son of Sigmund rode.[9]

Throughout the long and involved prose narrative are woven certain passages from *The Poetic Edda* (900-1050) which is the oldest extant treatment of this story of Sigurd. These few narrative lays are unsurpassed in their kind and are the basis of the *Volsung Saga* written a few hundred years later. Human suffering and adventure in the stories of the gods and heroes of the Scandinavians are exceptionally portrayed in this saga. The story begins with an account of Sigurd's grandfather who is slain by his own son-in-law. Eventually Sigurd recaptures his rights to the realm and then encounters various other problems. The tale of Sigurd's ride through the fire to win Brynhild for Gunnar is an excellent story cutting and there are many others.[10]

Another well-known example of a recent saga is from the account of Daniel Boone. The following adaptation is from the popular *Childhood of Famous Americans* series:

> It was November 2, 1746, and it was Daniel's birthday. He was twelve years old. More than anything, he wanted a gun like his brothers had received on their twelfth birthdays, but the Boones were very poor this fall. Daniel thought to himself, "The gun should be on my chair at breakfast. That's the way it was on his brothers' birthdays. What would he do if it wasn't there? Should he act as if he hadn't expected one? Should he pretend he didn't care?" His mind was so full of these thoughts he couldn't dress. His fingers were all thumbs. He couldn't fasten his leggings.
> "Dan'l," called his mother. "Breakfast is ready! Come quickly!"
> So down the ladder he went with his moccasins in his hand. He looked at the stool. Then he laughed aloud. It was there—"Oh!" he cried. "Oh, it's a gun! I'd rather have it than anything else in the world. You must have given many fine skins for it, Father."
> "Your brothers found the skins." His father replied.
> Daniel just smiled. He couldn't have been happier. He ate quickly and stretched his moccasins to put them on his feet. Daniel was anxious to try out his new gun. "We don't expect you to help with chores today," his brother nodded. And Daniel was off in a flash to go hunting. He was seeking a deer.... (but discovered a wolf as the story continues.)[11]

This series is good for telling particularly because of the realistic and moving dialogue in addition to the simple and clear narration. James Daugherty's *Daniel Boone* also has an excellent narrative for older children with its realistic language from early Kentucky days.

Other national literatures contain various sagas such as Irish sagas about Finn and Fianna, Cuchullin, and the children of Turenn and Lir.[12] The German sagas are also well known such as Gudrun, Dietrich of Bern, Walther of Acquitaine, and Siegfried.[13] Some German tales are based on their Scandinavian counterpart.

NARRATIVE POETRY

Although material of this nature may be read more often than it is told, it should be included in the process of sharing good literature with children. At the beginning of the educational program, children need to be led to the discovery of the beauty contained in poetic lines. This should be achieved not through painstaking scansion but through *enjoyment* of meter, message and sound. Narrative poetry should possess such elements of verse form as imaginative language, movement, rhythm, rhyme schemes, symbolism and appropriate word choice. In a few lines, a good poet can express an idea that might require a page or two to develop in prose. In contrast to lyric poems that simply express an intimate feeling of love, depression, or joy, narrative poetry must possess characters and a plot that moves to a climax through a conflict situation. These are general differences between lyric and narrative poetry although each may contain characteristics of the other. Common examples of narrative poetry are nursery rhymes, ballads, story poems, and epics.

Nursery Rhymes

Amidst the far-ranging gamut of literature, the nursery rhyme has been largely ignored as a means-to-an-end device. When it has been considered at all by literary analysts, particularly in the twentieth century, the form has been treated as a collection of statements that are merely consummatory, having no usefulness beyond their memorization and utterance. The authors suggest a persuasive-consummatory dichotomy in the analysis of the nursery rhyme. Literary analysts may consider the rhyme merely consummatory, whereas expert raconteurs recognize the rhetorical dimensions of the nursery rhyme to the extent that it informs, persuades, cajoles, establishes values, etc. Since the nursery rhyme is too often neglected, the following discussion attempts to be more comprehensive.

The historical origins of the nursery rhymes have been forgotten, and as a consequence, teachers may easily fall into the practice of chanting nursery rhyme messages as meaningless doggerel to hapless children. The historical motives served by the nursery rhyme will be considered later in this discussion.

One of the child's first exposures to subtle forms of persuasion occurs through nursery rhymes which are songs, lullabies, or jingles. The pacifying potential or impact of the nursery rhyme on the tantrums of the restless child is observable. Through rhythm, rhyme, alliteration, and repetition, the nursery rhyme is recited or sung to the child as one would administer some type of "subliminal pill to the subconscious in order to exercise an hypnotic spell."[14]

Apparently, children delight in the charm and incantation of message structures that are reminiscent of the Mother Goose variety. There seems to be, if one listens well, a verve in the concerted chant in an elementary classroom. Alliteration in rhymes such as "Little Boy Blue," "Mistress Mary," and "Little Miss Muffet" appeals to the children's poetic sense. Their need for repetition because of their limited attention span is met by the poetic persuasion of the nursery rhyme's rhythm, rhyme, and alliteration combined in a couplet or a quatrain. Exposure to these elements teaches the child some aspects of literary style.

A substantive message may also be acquired with ease through the rhythmic cadences and rhymed endings. A typical example is the learning of the differences in meaning between the chemical symbols H_2O (water) and H_2SO_4 (sulphuric acid).

> Poor little Willy is dead,
> His face we shall see no more
> For what he thought was H_2O
> Was H_2SO_4.

The message is obvious: if the bottle is labelled H_2SO_4 avoid it. The contents could kill you.

If the substantive message involves prejudicial statements such as "Catch a nigger by the toe," the powerful persuasion of the nursery rhyme may be equally effective in subliminally establishing negative values of human differentiation without justification at a very early age of the listener. Such values may be sustained and reinforced through repetition. Consequently, the mode and content of this kind of speech device is more persuasive than consummatory.

From a developmental perspective—after rhythm, rhyme, alliteration, and repetition have taken on meaning very early in a child's life—memory-testing, counting, and alphabetic distinction become important. These latter aspects of nursery rhymes encourage the child's language recognition, and simultaneously improve his language choices in communicative situations.

Nursery rhymes induce a listener to strengthen and test his sense of memory. A number of them are considered mnemonic learning devices. "Thirty days hath September," dating from 1606[15] may be a child's first hint at abstract calculus. Mother Goose's riddles and tongue twisters challenge the listener to improve his learning and language skills.

Another facet of the rhetoric of nursery rhymes, which is related to memory strengthening and testing, is the involvement of the child in counting numbers or designing letters. The most elementary "counting" rhyme is "Eenie, Meenie, Minie, Mo," used to designate which child of a group shall be singled out as "It." Another example of a rhyme which encourages the acquisition of counting skills is "One, Two, Buckle My Shoe." Alphabet rhymes include "A was an Archer," and "A for Apple." Mastery of the knowledge acquired through such rhetorical devices contributes to both later academic success and improvement in the child's nonacademic power moves.

Still later in a child's learning development, nursery rhymes may contribute through the dimensions of social commentary and cultural condition. Rhymes are rarely said aloud to oneself; the teller usually prefers the company of another person. Thus nursery rhymes promote social facilitation through the techniques of orality, game playing, music, and touching.

"Patty-Cake, Patty-Cake," "This Little Piggy Went to Market," "Rock-a-bye Baby" and other lullabies condition a child early in the sense of touch and therefore enforce more multi-sensory orchestration than is possible in mere oral communication. The warmth and positive reinforcement experienced during such recitation develops a sense of security derived through a feeling of power and love. As the child grows, more social involvement is possible with more advanced rhymes such as "Here We Go 'Round the Mulberry Bush," "Ring a Ring of Roses," and "Here We Go Looby Lou."

As a child grows older, he may also appreciate knowing about the arguments concerning love, politics, and religion which are implicit in the original versions of many nursery rhymes. These rhymes represent an important record of social protest in history, a factor unfortunately largely ignored today. A number of nursery rhymes were written and transmitted as messages through the underground in a manner similar to Negro spirituals. Some nursery rhymes used today probably date back as early as 800 A.D. In context, they represent the cries of the oppressed against the oppressor. This persuasive dimension may stimulate new interest in nursery rhymes among older children.

Let us examine the message-intent of a few of the most commonly known nursery rhymes:

"Bah, Bah, Black Sheep" is a complaint of the common people against the amount of wool that went to the King.[16]

> Bah, Bah, a Black Sheep
> Have you any Wool?
> Yes, merry have I?
> Three bags full
> One for my Master,
> One for my Dame,
> One for the little Boy
> That lives in the lane.

"Ring a Ring of Roses" had its origins in the cry against the Great Plague when the rosy rash of disease required flowers to sweeten the air. Falling down meant death, and ashes referred to the burning of the bodies.[17]

> Ring a ring of roses,
> A pocket full of posies
> Ashes! Ashes!
> We've all tumbled down.

"Pease Porridge" is not a green pea soup but a thin pudding made of pease meal. The feeling which accompanied the original rhyme was that the poor are sick for a want of food, and the rich have an excess of it.[18]

Pease Porridge hot,
Pease Porridge cold,
Pease Porridge in the pot
Nine days old.
Some like it hot,
Some like it cold,
Some like it in the pot
Nine days old.

"London Bridge Is Falling Down" bemoans the destruction of the bridge by King Olaf and his Norsemen in the early part of the Eleventh Century.[19]

London Bridge
Is falling down,
Falling down,
Falling down.
London Bridge
Is falling down,
My fair lady.

"Mistress Mary" is supposed to have been Bloody Mary who imposed her will on the English people.[20]

Mistress Mary,
Quite contrary,
How does your
Garden grow?
With silver bells,
And cockle shells,
And so my garden grows.

Unfortunately, nursery rhymes contain much violence. As social commentary for an older child, some nursery rhymes may be a negative influence in a child's learning development. Just as one may complain today that a number of television programs tend to portray modes of violence and may consequently influence young minds negatively, one may discover that certain nursery rhymes have made similar portrayals. Of the average collection of 200 traditional nursery rhymes, approximately one-half contain unsavory elements such as murder, devouring, hanging, starvation, stealing, dishonesty, drunkenness, cursing, racial discrimination, kidnapping, etc.[21] To be more specific, incidents occur such as dropping babies out of cradles,[22] stealing pigs [23], and saying "last one down is a nigger's baby."[24] Thus, all nursery rhymes may not offer the type of influence one would consciously wish to introduce into a child's environment.

The nursery rhyme attracts and persuades the young child through rhythm, rhyme, alliteration, and repetition. Memory-testing, counting, and the alphabetical distinction learned in the nursery rhyme, when properly introduced, can improve the child's language recognition and general communicative ability. For older children, the social commentary and cultural interpretation offered by nursery rhymes can have meaningful relevance. A child may be sensitized to the themes of social protest, violence, and outdated language in some rhymes. The

nursery rhyme also has a potential for use in teaching meaningless doggerel, prejudicial values, violence, and negative criticism. Like many stories, it must be used discriminately and carefully.

Ballads

Ballads are characterized by rhyme, rhythm and a plot. The story frequently involves tragic, frustrated young love that finds fulfillment after death. They are one of the oldest poetic forms known to the human family and they have survived through the oral tradition. Ballads were told before peasant's hearths and they were also sung by bards in the presence of royalty. They perpetuate the memory of lost causes and lost loves from the West Indies to the range of the American cowboy. Most junior high and senior high school students encounter "Robin Hood and Little John" or Coleridge's "The Rime of the Ancient Mariner." Few of them know that Sir Walter Scott preserved many old tales in verse in his *Minstrelsy of the Scottish Border*. The majority of ballads sung by American colonists were brought here from their native land. "Young Charlotte" is found in the balladry of northern Europe, in Georgia and among Appalachian Mountain dwellers. It is still entertaining folk-song and folktale enthusiasts. Following are selected portions that capture the theme and conclusion of this selection:

1. Now Charlotte lived on the mountain side
    In a bleak and dreary spot;
   There was no house for miles around
    Except her father's cot.

5. How brightly beamed her laughing eye,
    As a well-known voice was heard;
   And driving up to the cottage door
    Her lover's sleigh appeared.

6. "O daughter dear," her mother cried,
    "This blanket 'round you fold'
   It is a dreadful night tonight.
    You'll catch your death of cold."

7. "O nay, O nay!" young Charlotte cried,
    And she laughed like a gypsy queen;
   "To ride in blankets muffled up,
    I never would be seen."

11. "Such a dreadful night I never saw.
     The reins I scarce can hold."
    Fair Charlotte shivering faintly said,
     "I am exceeding cold."

13. Said Charles, "How fast the shivering ice
     Is gathering on my brow."
    And Charlotte still more faintly said,
     "I'm growing warmer now."

17. He took her hand in his—O God!
    'Twas cold and hard as stone.
    He tore the mantle from her face,

    Cold stars upon it shone.

18. Then quickly to the glowing hall
    Her lifeless form he bore;
    Fair Charlotte's eyes were closed in death,
    Her voice was heard no more.

22. Her parents mourned for many a year,
    And Charles wept in the gloom.
    Til at last her lover died of grief,
    And they both lie in one tomb.

The foregoing is a typical example of the ballad and such a tragic theme has been repeated with slight change in both ancient and modern versions of this poetic form.

Several collections are noteworthy for storytellers. Carl Sandburg's "The American Songbag" John and Alan Lomax's "American Ballads and Folk Songs" and "Cowboy Songs and other Frontier Ballads" are well known for railroad songs, cowboy songs, lumberjack songs, etc. Also some story-ballads from Louise Pound's "American Ballads and Songs," and Ruth Seeger's "American Folk Songs for Children: In Home, School and Nursery School," are very appropriate for telling.

Story Poems

Story poems frequently contain dramatic, lyrical qualities. Whereas epics extol the virtues of a heroic person or family and ballads typically are characterized by tragedy, story poems may deal with any topic such as dogs, lovers, war, children or any other subject that makes up the mosaic of life. Robert Browning has contributed richly to the human family's treasury of story poems. The following, "Incident of the French Camp" is typical:

You know, we French stormed Ratisbon: a mile or so away
On a little mound, Napoleon stood on our storming-day;
With neck out-thrust, you fancy how, legs wide, arms locked behind,
As if to balance the prone brow oppressive with its mind.

Just as perhaps he mused, "My plans that soar, to earth may fall,
Let once my army-leader Lannes waver at yonder wall—"
Out 'twix the battery-smokes there flew a rider, bound on bound
Full galloping; nor bridle drew until he reached the mound.

Then off there flung in smiling joy, and held himself erect
By just his horse's mane, a boy: you hardly could suspect—
(So tight he kept his lips compressed, scarce any blood came through)
You looked twice ere you saw his breast was all but shot in two.

"Well," cried he, "Emperor, by God's grace we've got you Ratisbon!
The Marshal's in the market-place, and you'll be there anon

To see your flag—bird flap his vans where I, to heart's desire,
Perched him!'' The chief's eye flashed; his plans soared up again like fire.

The chief's eye flashed; but presently softened itself, as sheathes
A film the mother-eagle's eye when her bruised eaglet breathes;
''You're wounded!'' ''Nay,'' the soldiers pride touched to the quick, he said:
''I'm killed, Sire!'' And his chief beside, smiling the boy fell dead.

Favorite story poems among first, second, and third graders include:

Brown's ''Jonathan Bing''
De la Mare's ''The Lost Shoe''
Howel's ''Going Too Far''
Lear's ''The Pobble Who Has No Toes''
Lindsay's ''The Little Turtle''
Milne's ''Puppy and I''
Putzker's ''Cotton Candy''
Rand's ''Topsy-Turvy World''
Richards' ''The Monkeys and the Crocodile''[25]

Other poets whose writings are preferred by primary children are Mary Austin, Eleanor Farjeon, Rose Fyleman, Theodor Seuss Geisel, Elizabeth Roberts, and Robert Louis Stevenson.[26]

Children in intermediate grades also like story poems related to their interests and experiences especially if they are humorous and demonstrate rhythm and rhyme.[27] They like Ernest Thayer's ''Casey at the Bat,'' written in 1888.

As an introduction, a storyteller might say, ''This is a wonderful poem about baseball. If you like baseball but not poetry, this will help you like poetry. If you like poetry but not baseball, this will help you like baseball. So onto the ball diamond.''

Casey At The Bat
It looked extremely rocky for the Mudville
Nine that day;
The score stood two to four, with but one
inning left to play.

For they thought: ''If only Casey could get a
whack at that,''
They'd put even money now, with Casey at the bat.

But Flynn let drive a single, to the wonderment
of all.
And the much-despised Blakey ''tore the cover off
the ball.''
And when the dust had lifted,
and they saw what had occurred,
There was Blakey safe at second, and Flynn
a-huggin' third.

Then from the gladdened multitude went up a
joyous yell—
It rumbled in the mountaintops, it rattled in the dell;

It struck upon the hillside and rebounded on the flat;
For Casey, Mighty Casey, was advancing to the bat.

Ten thousand eyes were on him as he rubbed his
hands with dirt,
Five thousand tongues applauded when he wiped
them on his shirt;

Close by the sturdy batsman the ball unheeded sped;
"That ain't my style," said Casey. "Strike one,"
the Umpire said.

From the benches, black with people, there went up
a muffled roar,
Like the beating of the storm waves on the stern
and distant shore.

"Kill him! Kill the Umpire!" shouted someone on
the stand;
And it's likely they'd have killed him had not
Casey raised his hand.

He signaled to the Pitcher, and once more the
fast ball flew;
But Casey still ignored it, and the Umpire said,
"Strike Two."

"Fraud!" cried the maddened thousands, and the
echo answered "Fraud"
But one scornful look from Casey and the audience
was awed;

They saw his face grown stern and cold, they
saw his muscles strain,
And they knew that Casey wouldn't let the ball
go by again.

The sneer is gone from Casey's lips, his teeth
are clenched in hate,
He pounds with cruel vengeance his bat upon the
plate:

And now the Pitcher holds the ball, and now he
lets it go,
And now the air is shattered by the force of
Casey's blow,

Oh, somewhere in this favored land the sun is
shining bright,
The band is playing somewhere, and somewhere
hearts are light;

And somewhere men are laughing

And somewhere children shout,

But there is no joy in Mudville—Mighty Casey
has struck out.[28]

(Adapted by Nancy Briggs)

"The Cremation of Sam McGee" by Robert Service, "The Blind Man and the Elephant" by John Saxe, "The Owl and the Pussycat" by Edward Lear, "The Walrus and the Carpenter" by Lewis Carroll are also good story poems for telling.

Epics

An epic is a long narrative poem recounting the adventures of a legendary or historical hero. An epic has a serious theme developed in a unified manner and written in an elevated style with certain formal characteristics such as extended similes, invocation to the muse, etc. From the Greek *The Iliad* and *The Odyssey*, and *The Aeneid*, the English *Beowulf*, the Spanish *El Cid*, France's *Song of Roland*, the Irish *Cuchulain the Hound of Ulster*, and Milton's *Paradise Lost* are classical examples of the epic form.

The length of these works and the difficulty of the language should discourage a teacher from attempting to read them to her children. However, there are stories within the longer selections such as Ulysses' adventures and Beowulf's underwater battles with Grendel that will hold the interest of upper grade youngsters.

According to a critic of children's literature, Sara Fenwick, of all literary forms from the oral tradition perhaps the richest and least familiar is the hero tale. These tales represent the ideals and aspirations of peoples preserved in the exploits of the famous Robin Hood, King Arthur, Guy of Warwick, Charlemagne and Roland, El Cid, Rustem, Lord of Persia, Cuchulain of Ireland, Benkei of Japan and many more. This is difficult literature; the plots are complex and the vocabulary is difficult. If everyone who works with children made him or herself thoroughly acquainted with just one of these cycles of stories for sharing, a rich literary experience could be given to young people aged 10 and up. The experience could encourage further exploration of the literature by students.[29]

The *Iliad* and the *Odyssey* have come to typify this particular literary genre. In them legendary heroes pursue goals, aided and hindered by partisan gods. Unlike the myth, the center of interest has now shifted from the gods to a human hero. The epic is strongly national in its implications. Odysseus may never have lived, but he embodies many Greek ideals. Many individual stories like "Ulysses and Circe" are worth telling. Through the telling of parts of an epic, the listeners discover the moral code of the nation or era involved by focusing on the heroic deeds of a single figure.

> Then said one of Ulysses men, "Let us call to this singer, and see whether she is a woman or a goddess." So they called, and a certain Circe, who was said to be a daughter of the Sun, came out and asked them to go in. This they did, and also they drank out of a cup which she gave them. A cup of wine it seemed to be, mixed with barley-meal and honey, but she had put in it some strange drug, which makes a man forget all that he loves. And when they had drunk, lo! They were turned into pigs. They had snouts and bristles, and they grunted like pigs, but they had the hearts of men.[30]

After this encounter, Ulysses uses special herbs to overcome the power of Circe's drugs. Then as equals they become friends, and he stayed in her palace for a year before sailing.

REALISTIC STORIES

Realism is not a definite form in fiction, rather it is an objective, an endeavor to represent life honestly. Literature is said to be a mirror of life with all its beauty and bestiality. Realistic stories seek to represent it as it is. The desire to create realistic stories has been with mankind for centuries. "The Little Red Hen," "Hans in Luck," and "Why the Sea is Salt" are tales that reflect this desire. Hans Christian Andersen's frustrations with society are found in "The Ugly Duckling" and "The Steadfast Tin Soldier." Charles Dickens' *Oliver Twist* and Tolstoi's "The Death of Ivan Ilyich" illustrate the tragedy of the poor and unfortunate. The forerunners of realism were such books as *Hans Brinker and the Silver Skates, Heidi,* and *Little Women.*

In the United States, Mark Twain accurately depicted river town life through the adventures of Huck Finn; Bret Harte acquainted readers with mining camp life in "The Outcasts of Poker Flat" and Jack London pitted man and beast against nature in *The Call of the Wild.* John Steinbeck captured the poverty and humiliation of economic depression in *The Grapes of Wrath* and in more recent times, Louis Lomax' writing has brought ghetto existence into sharp focus.

Good realistic stories should satisfy some of a child's basic needs—such as a need for security, a love of adventure, the need for love and loving. The stories will give a listener increased insight into his own personal problems and social relationships. Realistic stories include tales about people from other lands, "historical" novels, animal stories, romantic stories, and life in our own country. Another important factor in consideration of these stories is that there is large appeal on all age levels. Realism for the youngest includes Margaret Wise Brown's *Runaway Bunny* and *Little Lost Lamb,* Slobodkina's *Caps for Sale,* Beatrice De Regniers' *The Snow Party,* Marjorie Flack's *Wait for William,* Ruth Krauss' *The Growing Story, The Little Train,* and *The Little Farm,* Robert McCloskey's *Make Way for Ducklings,* and Gene Zion's *Dear Garbage Man.* Tales for older children include E. B. White's *Charlotte's Web,* William Steig's *Sylvester and the Magic Pebble,* Marjorie William's *The Velveteen Rabbit,* Roald Dahl's *Charlie and the Chocolate Factory,* and William Armstrong's *Sounder.*

Like story poems, realistic stories claim a vast range of interests. Animal stories, sports, life with one's family, sea adventure and excursions into outer space all fall within its purview. Realistic stories may help both parents and teachers develop tolerance in their children. Alberta Armer's *Trouble-maker,* for example, explains the plight of a twelve-year-old whose father is incarcerated and his mother is mentally disturbed. Mimi Brodsky's *The House at 12 Rose*

Street develops a sense of appreciation for the trials faced by black Americans in white neighborhoods. *The Hundred Dresses* by Eleanor Estes reveals the savagery of insensitive classmates toward a virtually penniless immigrant girl who lacks proper clothing. This hostility breaks the spirit of the family and they decide to leave the neighborhood.

Literally thousands of stories with a realistic impact await storytellers who possess the energy and patience to match appropriate stories to the needs of their audience.

A librarian shows children different types of stories.

BIOGRAPHICAL STORIES

This form of literature is enjoying a great period of popularity. The flood of biographical books published in this century prompts a reader to wonder why material of this type enjoys such demand. The answer probably lies in the realistic approach being taken by most authors. From the publication of *Plutarch's Lives* to the beginning of this century, biographies were either boringly factual or idealistic to the point that a hero's misdeeds were never revealed. In contrast to this, most authors today strive for accurate reporting of a more comprehensive nature that does not overlook human frailties. Some writers seem obsessed with the latter and apparently take pleasure in defaming cherished national heroes.

Other authors have enhanced their works by using reliable, primary source materials which have provided insight into the motives and emotional reactions of great persons during periods of trial. The style of modern biographies has also contributed to their popularity. Today's accounts are streamlined by sharp imagery, animated dialogue and suspenseful situations that build to a climax. Reputable biographers have not sacrificed accuracy in their efforts to fictionalize events.

Despite their popularity, biographies have been avoided by too many storytellers. Their choices are to condense the life of a person considerably, or to select an appropriate chapter or portion of a biography that fairly represents the person and his character or achievements. Children often cannot and should not have the complete account of a person's life anyway. There are parts of each hero's life that can and should be overlooked or not stressed. There are scandals and tragedies that need not be presented. This may help a storyteller plan his narrative carefully. Benjamin Franklin is an excellent example of one about whom there is too much to record or tell. Therefore, an exciting chapter in his life may become a wonderful story for those listening. Perhaps the cutting is a barrier and discourages some storytellers. However, the motivating factor of exposing a child to literature which one may then finish reading for oneself should be challenge enough for any storyteller, teacher or parent. Storytelling used to encourage reading of biography is a worthwhile educational objective.

The endless variety of subjects available in biographies lends enchantment to this form of literature. From childhood, most adults can recall those early tales of America's discovery by Columbus, John Smith's efforts to provide food for the colonists, Washington's leadership that brought us independence, the winning of the West by men such as Daniel Boone, early explorations by Lewis and Clark, and Sacajawea's guidance of the latter which assisted so materially to the success of their expedition. A biographical approach to the study of history lends a personalized touch to this subject. Children are lifted temporarily from their daily routine and into a heroic realm. Like the realistic stories, biographies provide excellent orientation to problems faced by minority group members. Jackie Robinson's rocky road to fame as the first Negro to play in the major leagues is sensitively described in *Breakthrough to the Big League: The Story of Jackie Robinson* by Jackie Robinson and Alfred Ducket. *Frederick Douglass* by Arna Bontemps describes one of the first successful efforts of a black man to provide leadership for his people. Music will take on added meaning through the stories of Beethoven and Mozart by Reba Paeff Mirsky. Both boys and girls will thrill to the excitement of *John H. Glenn: Astronaut* by Lt. Col. Philip Pierce and Karl Schuon. The role of girls in space exploration is told in *Astronaut's Nurse: The Story of Dee O'Hara* by Virginia McDonnell. Fine stories such as these will inspire children and also help to build a love for literature.

The most important factor in children's biographies when told as stories, is the addition of dialogue. This may be imagined by the author or storyteller in keeping with the attitudes of the characters involved. Dialogue makes the characters come to life. Action and live dialogue are the dynamics of a story. In addition, enough vivid details must be retained in a cutting in order to clarify the images presented. Dialogue is one means of clarifying details. Most biographies for children are considered fictionalized biographies because they are based on careful research, but facts are presented in narrated episodes with conversation. Often a storyteller must add dialogue to liven up the story and yet allow it to remain accurate. Consider the following cutting of a famous biographical story:

> Jack Kennedy was a Boy Scout, a good sailor, and a great swimmer. His father's constant advice was, "Win! Win! Win! It's not good being second or third. It's winning that counts." So at the public swimming races that summer when Jack was twelve years old, he was determined to win a blue ribbon. All the children in his family were racing. They all wore red swimming caps. Mother said, "You must wear the same color so that I can count all five quickly and make sure you're all safe." And so all the children in the contest were ready to push off at the starting line. "On your mark, ready, set, go!" cried the lifeguard. And Jack took off with all his strength.[31]

This story has ample potential dialogue when adapted and children can identify with President Kennedy, the excellent boy swimmer.

Most biographies are written for eight year olds or above. However, the comprehension level far exceeds the reading level, and some biographies are appropriate for primary grades such as Alice Daegliesh's "The Spirit of St. Louis." This is the story of the boyhood and the famous flight of Charles Lindbergh for children too young to read. Jerry Siebert's *Amelia Earhart* is an excellent narrative of the "First Lady of the Air." Opal Wheeler has also written many wonderful biographies about famous musical figures such as *Ludwig Beethoven and the Chiming Tower Bells; Frederic Chopin, Son of Poland; Handel at the Court of the Kings;* and *Mozart, the Wonder Boy.*

SUMMARY

This chapter has briefly delineated and described several of the traditional types of stories suitable for the raconteur. The four categories discussed were folk literature which included fables, folktales and fairytales, myths, legends, and sagas; narrative poetry which embraced nursery rhymes, ballads, story poems and epics; realistic stories; and biographies. It is hoped that this chapter has provided additional background for storytellers which will facilitate story selection from various genres of children's literature.

NOTES

1. Mia I. Gerhardt, *The Art of Storytelling: A Literary Study of a Thousand and One Nights* (Leiden, Netherlands, E. J. Brill, 1963).
2. May Hill Arbuthnot, *Children and Books,* 3rd ed. (Chicago, Scott, Foresman and Co., 1964), p. 255.
3. Max J. Herzberg, *Myths and Their Meaning* (Boston, Allyn and Bacon, Inc., 1966), pp. 4-5.
4. *Ibid.,* p. 15.
5. Edith Hamilton, *Mythology,* (New York, A Mentor Book, 1942), pp. 131-144.

6. Abbie Farwell Brown, *In The Days of The Giants*, (New York, Houghton Mifflin Co., A30), pp. 163-164.
7. Washington Irving, *The Legend of Sleepy Hollow (1880)*, (University Microfilms, Inc., Ann Arbor, 1966), pp. 161-162.
8. Halvdan Koht, *The Old Norse Sagas*, (New York, W. W. Norton & Co., Inc.), 1971.
9. William Morris, translator, *Volsunga Saga*, (New York, Collier Books, 1962), p. 70.
10. *The Saga of the Volsungs*, (London, Margaret Schlaugh, George Allen and Unwin, Ltd., 1949).
11. Augusta Stevenson, *Daniel Boone, Boy Hunter*, (Indianapolis, Bobbs Merrill Co., Inc., 1961), pp. 125-128.
12. Eileen O'Faolain, *Irish Sagas and Folktales*, (New York, Henry Z. Walck, Inc.), 1954.
13. Barbara Picard, *German Hero-sagas and Folktales*, (New York, Henry Walck, Inc.), 1958.
14. Marshall McLuhan, *The Mechanical Bride: Folklore of Industrial Man*, (New York, The Vanguard Press, Inc., 1954), p. 13.
15. William S. and Ceil Baring-Gould, *The Annotated Mother Goose*, (Cleveland, The World Publishing Company, 1967), p. 180.
16. *Ibid.*, p. 33.
17. *Ibid.*, p. 253.
18. *Ibid.*, p. 237.
19. *Ibid.*, p. 254.
20. *Ibid.*, p. 31.
21. *Ibid.*, p. 20.
22. *Ibid.*, p. 224.
23. *Ibid.*, p. 104.
24. *Ibid.*, p. 253.
25. Richard C. Nelson, "Children's Poetry Preferences," *Elementary English*, 43, (March, 1966): Copyright © 1966 by the National Council of Teachers of English. Reprinted with permission.
26. Grace Pittman, "Young Children Enjoy Poetry," *Elementary English*, 43, (January, 1966): pp. 56-59.
27. Ethel B. Bridge, "Using Children's Choices of and Reactions to Poetry as Determinants in Enriching Literary Experience in the Middle Grades," *Dis. Ab.*, May, 1967, 27: p. 3749A.
28. Ernest Lawrence Thayer, "Casey at the Bat," (Englewood Cliffs, N.J., Prentice-Hall, 1964).
29. S. I. Fenwick, "Men's Dreams of Long Ago: The Oral Tradition," International Reading Association Conference Papers. 14 (1970): pp. 42-43.
30. Alfred Church, *The Odyssey of Homer*, (New York: The Macmillan Co., 1951), pp. 16-17.
31. Iris Vinton, *The Story of President Kennedy*, (New York, Grosset and Dunlap, 1966), p. 37.

3 Selection of Stories

Shall we permit our children, without scruple, to hear any fables composed by any authors indifferently, and so to receive into their minds opinions generally and reverse of those which, when they are grown to manhood, we shall think they ought to entertain?

Plato, *The Republic*

Stories possessing the action, clarity and content that are desirable for children are not found in every book store. This chapter seeks to establish guidelines relating to the child, the story and the storyteller which will facilitate an intelligent choice of material.

THE CHILD

A librarian was once asked by a parent, ''What type of story should I tell my six-year-old son?'' Lacking additional information about the child, the librarian could only reply, ''It all depends on the child.'' An introverted boy who knocks game-winning home runs only in his imagination might profit from participation stories. An athletically-inclined child might develop insight into the problem of those who have to struggle to excel physically if he were to read the life story of Theodore Roosevelt or Robert Louis Stevenson. If a story's objective is to be realized, it must be adapted to the individual needs of the child. Teachers and youth workers who tell stories to groups of children of diverse interests will find help in the following delineation of specific characteristics of four age groups. Storytelling parents will also find assistance in the grouping that matches their child's age, maturation, and interests. These categories may overlap, and some stories could belong in more than one category. Moreover, a child does not pass neatly from one category to the next on a given birthday. This classification should not be used literally because of individual differences in children, and some stories appeal to all ages, but the four categories indicate a pattern of growth. Children's response to artistic and imaginative material follows a regular pattern. Storytelling experiences with literature proceed from the simple to the complex in terms of form and content. They proceed from the literal to the abstract or symbolic. Nevertheless, it is important to recognize in any given group of children some variations from the norm.

Age of Repetition

This group includes children from three to six years old. Stories which contain concrete, familiar objects, talking animals and a repetitious plot will appeal to this age group. "The Three Little Pigs," "Chicken Little," and "The Gingerbread Boy" are examples of such stories. Plots should be simple with a repetitious story line. Plots that demand abstract thinking should be avoided. Tales with characters whose counterparts have been seen by children on trips to the zoo and the countryside will find ready acceptance. Included in stories for this age group should be familiar objects such as dogs, kittens, balls, toys, boats, airplanes, etc. In *Another Here and Now Story Book,* Lucy Sprague Mitchell indicates in detail how to develop skill in building stories from the immediate environment for ages two to six. The young child is interested in everything in the immediate environment which is experienced first-hand.[1]

A child's experiences during the age of repetition is heavily dependent upon his five senses. Objects that one has felt, tasted, smelled, heard or seen will be welcomed in stories. Children in this group are well-acquainted with their own pattern of play activity. Consequently, they respond favorably to stories about themselves or the activities of other children of their own age. Children's sensory experience is critical to the selection of stories at this early age.

Ruth Tooze in *Storytelling* discusses in some detail the importance of younger children's responses as being largely motor. They may respond to a story with moving hands, heads, and feet. They love repetition in a recurring refrain or word pattern and may often repeat it along with the storyteller. A child is clearly interested in his own movements and everything around that moves such as animals, wagons, trucks, trains, etc.[2]

Since youngsters do not enjoy the attention span of an adult, the same picture must be flashed upon their mental screen frequently. The following repetitive taunt of the Gingerbread Boy is enjoyed by three to six-year-olds because of its reassuring and rhythmic nature:

> I ran away from a little old woman,
> I ran away from a little old man,
> I ran away from a barn full of threshers,
> I ran away from a field full of mowers,
> I ran away from a cow and a pig,
> And I can run away from you, I can! I can!

As these lines are repeated, a child is quickly oriented to the sequence of the story. One is subtly pleased and flattered by recognition of what has happened to the Gingerbread Boy. The child feels secure because he anticipates which action follows another. The youngster not only enjoys repetition within the story, but also through repeat performances of the same tale. Commenting on this characteristic, Gesell states that a five-year-old "...shows preference for certain stories which he likes to hear over and over."[3]

According to Jed Davis and Mary Watkins in their study of children's audiences under five, rhythm and repetition are essential. Funny names, animal characters with human traits, nonsense rhymes or jingles are all appealing. Melodrama such as people or animals who are splashed with mud or paint, or who are chased, or who are sad, or who are very silly-acting are perfectly acceptable to this young group. Such story action avoids the signs of boredom and restlessness in an audience.[4]

For the youngest listener, the stories should be short, with vivid or realistic pictures or visual aids, and plots involving situations and emotions that are familiar to them. Realistic stories appeal to this age; therefore a story in which animals or machines behave like people, which represents their anthropomorphic way of looking at things, is "reality" to two and three-year-olds. *On Mother's Lap, Inch by Inch, Roar and More, Whose Mouse Are You, Angus Lost, Angus and the Ducks, The Very Hungry Caterpillar, Goodnight Moon,* and *My Hopping Bunny* have been successfully introduced and used at Story Hour (20 minutes in reality) at several libraries.[5] The measure of success may not be a rapt, hushed audience, but an involved moving group of youngsters who cry for "more" at the end of a story. Many librarian storytellers and preschool teachers for this early age often abridge the stories. This process is an anathema to purists, but adaptation of materials to the audience is common to the storytelling and the communication process. More details on adaptation are in Chapter 4.

Children in the Age of Repetition will accept talking animals, trees and rivers without question. This latter characteristic is by no means limited to children in this group. The message of the talking animal, insect, or bird is the important element. *The Jatakas,* for example, are ancient animal fables sacred to Buddhists. These describe the rebirth of Buddha in various animal incarnations. In the story of *Charlotte's Web,* a loquacious spider provides action for a six-year-old, emotional appeal for a third grader and a lampooning of the shallow values of today's society that will delight high school students. Other talking animals which appeal to more mature listeners and readers may be found in *Dr. Doolittle's Travels, The Wind in the Willows,* and in the mirth-provoking story of Amos, the talking mouse, in *Ben and Me.*

Older youth must be prepared for flights of fancy. One children's librarian, who was faced with the assignment of telling stories to mixed groups ranging in age from five to eleven years, began her story by saying, "Children, we are going to take a journey to the Land of Make-Believe and visit a sister and brother who own a magic horse." This approach called for a willing suspension of disbelief on the part of the older children and also served to eliminate any doubt as to whether the ensuing story was going to be fact or fiction.

Age of Fancy

This group includes children from six to nine years of age. It is a magical period for storytellers and children alike. Creative thinking can be stimulated and desirable character traits strengthened by such tales as Grimm's "The Golden Goose," Filmore's "The Twelve Months," and the Vietnamese tale, "The Sparrow." According to Davis and Watkins, the child usually embarks into a realm of the fairy tale as soon as they feel secure in the world of reality. A lot of unsavory characters and actions can be tolerated when children reach the point where they feel safe with unreal and frightening characters and are aroused by "delicious fear." This generally occurs by age six or seven.[6] Arbuthnot agrees that children reach the peak of interest in fairy tales when they are around seven to nine years old, not four or five.[7] Benjamin Spock speculates on the use of fairy tales with children. He maintains that the younger children are—two or three years old—the more they are upset by violence or bad characters. As they mature they can distinguish better between what is real and what is not. A child who is active and outgoing does not have a strong impact from a troubling experience many times because the child turns passive into active. Instead of feeling like the victim, they quickly become the aggressor. For example, if a witch puts a child in the oven, the child may grab his doll and put it in the oven. Whereas the quiet, intent child may be too sensitive to frightening material at any age and may remember it for a long time. By acting out angry, aggressive, or hostile feelings, a child copes with those feelings on the surface and feels guilty only to the extent that their parents show disapproval of the expressed hostility. Authority figures can keep hostility at a minimum by admitting the naturalness of anger and encourage the use of words instead of actions.[8] By allowing the child to handle his most powerful thoughts and feelings in the form of emotional words, an adult allows the child to eventually sort out the word from the deed. Close observation of your audience will reveal acceptance level and maturation of the child.

The strong interest in wicked characters at this age may exist because the child expects justice to come to those who are evil. Davis and Watkins explain that lines of battle are clearly drawn in the fairy tale. The child recognizes that good overcomes evil and the bad are punished and the good are rewarded.[9] Stories of this period in the fairy tale category should reward generosity and punish evil-doing and selfishness. Although the immediate effect of a fairy tale is to entertain, the long-term effect of such stories may have moral significance. The child's reaction of approval or disapproval during these vicarious experiences assists him to develop a sense of values.

Child psychologist Bruno Bettelheim in his book, *The Uses of Enchantment: The Meaning and Importance of Fairy Tales,* makes convincing arguments aboust using fairy tales with children for an invaluable education as to good and evil. Like all great art, fairy tales both delight and instruct. Children have rich fantasies with fears and anxieties and fairy tales may guide the child toward reassuring solutions. Fairy tales nearly always contain evil figures who are properly punished, and good is always rewarded. Based on personal experience, Bettleheim argued that even in the Nazi concentration camps, the basic message of fairy stories stayed with him. In life we encounter terrible events, but if we cling to our values, we might survive and be better it. The happy endings are not unrealistic because they teach the value of independence, risks, good friends, and perseverance.[10] In effect, the lessons of fantasy can be a key to helping a child unlock the mysteries of reality.

In *Twentieth Century Children's Books,* Frank Eyre remarks that when scholars or writers for adults set aside their customary work to write something for children, they usually write some form of fantasy.[11] In fantasy, of course, the strangest characters, irrational behaviors and concepts of the unconscious may be expressed. Many people of all ages enjoy fantasy, and certainly it occupies a central position in children's literature. Ravenna Helson in *The Horn Book* indicates that fantasy is not only enjoyable but important to the discovery of self and all its potential. She presents a comprehensive Jungian point of view on the significance of fantasy for children. Our primitive fears and awe of nature, our spiritual development, deeper hidden meanings, gratification of our wishes, and pure imagination are expressed in the name of fantasy and are sanctioned.[12] Bettleheim adds that adults who outlaw tales with threatening monsters miss the monster the child knows best and is most concerned with: the monster one feels or fears oneself to be. Without such fantasies, the child fails to know the monster better, and is not given solutions as to how to gain mastery over it.[13] It is interesting that many new books are being published about "monsters" in keeping with this trend: *One Monster After Another, The Monster at the End of This Book, Where the Wild Things Are.*

Delightful fantasy may also be found in modern fairy tales such as the *Wizard of Oz, Alice in Wonderland, Winnie the Pooh* and *Peter Pan.* Geeslin's study of

The teacher and the children acting like big monsters.

current book choices of pupils revealed that *Winnie the Pooh* was the most consistent preference of third graders interviewed.[14]

This study was updated by Briggs a few years later, and again *Winnie the Pooh* was a favorite of third and fourth graders. Surprisingly, it was also a favorite of kindergartners. However, the particular version of Pooh was not indicated.[15] This variable is important because the difference in Disney's version and Milne's version is considerable. This holds true for the numerous versions of fairy tales and myths also. Margaret O'Connell indicates that we send our children to school to learn the realities of the world, past and present. Therefore, in the use of folk and fairy tales, storytellers must carefully select which version of Grimm they want. It depends on how you want to start a child's literary breakfast: with the porridge of the hardworking peasant, with the pancakes of an enterprising middle-class family or with crepes at a sophisticate's table. Collections of fairy tales vary greatly. A wise choice should satisfy the teller and the listeners.[16]

In addition to fairy tales, children in this age group enjoy stories about air travel, science, primitive times, children's classics and religious stories. Most nine-year-olds will also respond to mysteries, biographies and travel adventure.

Age of Hero Worship

This group includes children from nine to twelve years of age. Youngsters in this period like to experience danger, daring, and action from a vicarious vantage point. They will be more attracted to the dashing action of Joan of Arc than to the quiet laboratory experiments of Madame Curie, though both women are heroines. The exploits of a World Series pitcher seem more important than the computations of Albert Einstein. However, both Madame Curie and Albert Einstein belong to the world of storytelling but they demand older audiences. The physical exploits and adventure found in the tales of Robin Hood and King Arthur have timeless appeal. The stories surrounding Tom Sawyer and Huck Finn also belong in this category. Added to these may be the adventures of Beowulf, Hercules, Sir Walter Raleigh, William Tell, Robert the Bruce, Kit Carson and many other heroes of yesteryear. More recent heroes include Lou Gehrig, George Washington Carver, Florence Nightingale, Clara Barton, Charles Lindbergh, and Amelia Earhart.

The opportunity to identify with a hero is one of the most valuable experiences for every human being. Historical fiction for children is one means of meeting this need. F. J. Monjo commented on this need for planting the seeds of greatness in children's character:

> So much for the line between fact and fiction. Even more important are the needs of the present times. We need to inspire our gifted young people to make an attempt at greatness. We need to make them want to reach out after that splendid, elusive, brass ring known as achievement and make it theirs. Our age is more tawdry than we wish it to be, and we yearn for some heroes and heroines for ourselves and for the future. I

have not yet utterly abandoned the Western world. It has produced many men and women who still make my skin prickle. I have not yet abandoned the American experiment, for it has produced large numbers of people whom I wish I might have emulated. That is why I would like my books to arouse young people. To make them understand that all great human beings were once uncertain children, unaware of their powers. I want my books to incite children to dare to do something marvelous.[17]

Monjo's *Poor Richard in France* is an exciting adventure about Benjamin Franklin, his seventeen-year-old and seven-year-old grandsons who went to France to try to persuade the French to help the Americans with the Revolution in 1776.

Ruth Tooze explains that one means of identification that leads to increased self understanding is to become acquainted with great people, with their actions and motivations through stories, with what the listener is because of what heroes did and with the potential of all people to be great.[18] Early hero tales and recent heroes provide this chance for identification.

Another reason exciting historical themes have appeal to this age group is that they have a fairly well developed concept of time. The past could be yesterday or last month until young people have had enough experience to form an image of its relationship to life and growth. The relationship of one period of time to another and progression from age to age is oriented to the inquiring minds of this age group.[19]

In addition, Gessell has found that ten-year-olds are attracted to stories that have "secret," "mystery," or "horse" in the title.

> Besides horse and dog stories, even sad ones that are going to come out good in the end. Ten likes biographies of famous people, adventure and mystery. Some restrict themselves to stories of their own age and time. Others like to experience children of their own age growing up to become famous people. Historical books are interesting but sometimes they lack enough adventure.[20]

Listening to children's needs and interests is imperative to good storytelling. Marion Garthwaite, a librarian in charge of Story Hour, testified that she was often requested to tell horse stories such as *The Humpbacked Horse, Bellerophon and Pegasus, The Tangle-coated Horse,* etc. However, one girl complained because she wanted to hear a story about a girl on a horse. Garthwaite in desperation wrote one called *Sally's Ride for the Pony Express.* The children asked for it again and again. Later it was published in *Story Parade* and a dozen school texts and has been paying dividends ever since. Garthwaite contends that in storytelling—selection, preparation and presentation are important, but the most important of these is selection.[21]

Children of this age welcome changes of routine in the school day. Starting with a story, rather than a formalized approach is appreciated. Perhaps a chapter from *Huckleberry Finn* or *The Voyage of Ulysses* would begin the day successfully. Biographies should personalize great persons and make them seem real. Youngsters welcome incidents that depict their hero's failures as well as his successes. Most children, for example, will sympathize with Herbert Hoover on the occasion when he discovered that he had failed his composition examinations.

Recent research has shed some interesting light on children's literary interest and characteristics in this age group. Steirt designed an inventory to investigate recreational reading interests of pupils in grades five and six. She learned that girls read more books than boys and prefer fiction to non-fiction. Boys, in contrast, choose non-fiction over fiction. Comic books were not mentioned as a reading choice by any of the 285 children studied.[22] Burgdorf found that scores on drawing inferences from literary selections were significantly higher when children listened to stories than when they read the stories themselves. The effect of maturation is suggested as the children's ability to draw inferences was significantly higher both in grade five as compared with grade four and in grade six as compared with grade five. There was no significant difference between the scores of boys and girls.[23]

Storytellers may also benefit from the findings contained in Peltola's study of the literary choices of fourth and sixth grade boys and girls. A sex difference was discernible in the type of favorite characters chosen. Most frequently, the children named characters of their own sex. In second place, boys named animal characters most frequently. Girls named as many male characters as animal characters. Real stories were preferred by more children in both grades than make-believe stories. However, the proximity of fourth graders to the Age of Fancy is probably responsible for their naming make-believe stories as their favorites more often than sixth graders. More children in both grades named recommended books in preference to non-recommended books. However, the sixth graders named fewer recommended books than the fourth graders. This latter finding may suggest the establishment of more independent reading habits by the older children.[24]

The conclusions found in the foregoing research will facilitate an intelligent selection of stories for children in the Age of Hero Worship. Many teachers find that the urge for adventure is further satisfied by creatively acting out scenes and short stories. Chapter 5 explains the value of this activity for all ages.

Age of Idealism

This period begins at age twelve and, ideally lasts for the rest of one's life. Stories of adventure which are replete with action, suspense and excitement continue to be popular at this age. Both sexes will show interest in stories which explore vocational and professional areas. Biographies of John Fitzgerald Kennedy, Dwight Eisenhower and Martin Luther King, Jr. are typical materials. Boys will listen to stories about boys but they are cool to *Little Women,* for example. Girls, in contrast to this, will listen to stories about boys and they also enjoy stories of family relations and romance. Girls of thirteen continue to be fond of animal stories, especially those that involve horses. Stories about athletes, with emphasis on fair play, are prized by twelve-year-olds and those in early teens. Stories of primitive peoples, mystery stories and tales of intrigue will also prove popular.

Stanchfield has concluded an enlightening study on the reading interests of eighth-grade boys. Her subjects varied in reading ability from superior to poor. Out of the twenty characteristics of stories, excitement, suspense, unusual experiences and surprise or unexpectedness were preferred most frequently. Family love and closeness and familiar experiences were least popular. The most preferred subjects were stories of explorations and expeditions, and outdoor life. These adventure stories tied for first place. Tales of fantasy, life adventure of boys, historical fiction of their own age, sea adventure, sports and games and war followed in that order. Family and home life, plays, art and poetry were last. This study did not bear out the belief that boys at the same grade level with differing reading abilities, will have different reading interests. There were no significant differences in the preferences of superior, average, and poor readers. The boys showed little interest in such qualities as anger, hatred, cruelty, fighting, brutality and sadness. Stanchfield explains,

> War stories had a great appeal for the boys, but only in the idealized sense; they did not care for the brutality, fighting, and horror of war. It was evident that they were highly interested in unusual experiences and not very much interested in familiar, commonplace happenings.[25]

As young people become sex-conscious, both boys and girls normally gravitate toward stories involving boy-girl relations. Teachers, parents and youth workers are faced with the problem of choosing stories for young people in whom elemental passions have begun to stir, yet who lack the self-control and judgment that comes with maturity. A wholesome development of the boy-girl theme takes place in *High Trail* by Vivian Breck. The author portrays the doubts, curiosity, bewilderment and pain of young love and still manages to preserve its rare beauty. Storytellers should be alert for materials that represent the natural attraction of the two sexes within the confines of social acceptability.

Every Age: Individualism

Many conditions affect the development of children and their storytelling experience and expertise. It is dangerous to generalize about a group to the exclusion of individual children's rights, tastes, and cultural backgrounds. There is a new emphasis in our society on freedom for all. These new freedoms include sexual freedom. Two interesting studies have helped reform sexist textbooks and develop a trend in children's literature free from restrictive stereotypes.[26] The cruelty of stepparents, mean parents, blind beggars, the aged, the inferiority of any race are all questioned as appropriate topics in children's literature. The teller should carefully examine the story selected and be aware of the complaints and sensitivity of the new generation.

According to Martha Dallman, one of the outstanding characteristics of the intellectual and social development of the primary grade child is the existence of striking individual differences. The variations in intermediate grades are even more pronounced.[27] Adaptation to the individual is essential to good storytelling. Listening to the child's request and reaction helps the storyteller's interpretation of appropriate material for a particular age level. Donnarae MacCann reminds storytellers that a child has little free choice in the selection of stories because the accessibility is almost entirely limited and controlled by the adult book purchasers: librarians, teachers, and parents.[28] Good stories cannot survive artistically if the teller exists in a vacuum. The teller needs to establish a complete process of communication including considerable feedback from the child. Then, and only then, will the raconteur be assured that the selection of material is appropriate to the interests, background, and maturation of the child listener.

THE STORY

Children and Literature

When today's great-grandparents were children, a more leisurely manner of living provided storytelling occasions around cracker barrels in neighborhood stores, in classrooms and within the family circle as its members gathered around a potbellied stove or a crackling hearth fire for an evening's activities. Mark Twain remembered sitting around Uncle Daniel's fire at John Quarles's farm:

> I can see the white and black children grouped on the hearth, with the firelight playing on their faces and the shadows flickering upon the walls, clear back toward the cavernous gloom of the rear, and I can hear Uncle Dan'l telling the immortal tales which Uncle Remus Harris was to gather into his books and charm the world with, by and by; and I can feel again the creepy joy which quivered through me when the time for the ghost story of the "Golden Arm" was reached—and the sense of regret, too, which came over me, for it was always the last story of the evening and there was nothing between it and the unwelcome bed."[29]

Today's expanded curriculum, children's organizations, radio and television all compete for the precious moments that used to be devoted to reading and listening to stories. Witty reports that in 1965, children spent about twenty hours weekly in front of television sets. In the first grade the average was about fifteen hours; a peak of twenty-five hours was reached in the fifth grade. Pupils in the second grade stated that they spent about three hours each listening to radio; in the fifth and sixth grades the weekly average was about eight hours. He adds.

> It is clear from our studies that the amount of reading of children today is a little greater than in the past. But there are many pupils who read less now, and many others who read very little. Moreover, we should bear in mind that the time devoted to TV, as compared with that given to reading, is very large—about three hours daily to TV and only one hour to reading. The picture is not a bright one in so far as the first "R" is concerned.[30]

Liebert and Anderson in 1973 also comment on the effects of television on youth. By the age of 18, children have spent more time watching television than any other activity except sleeping. The effects of television on our society are becoming more profound. Heavy users have a distorted view of the world in accepting more violence and a resultant fear as the norm. Light watchers have more realistic views.[31] Storytelling as an alternative presents an advantage to children, teachers, and parents.

Although television is criticized for the inroads it makes into a child's day, it has also earned praise as a means of stimulating viewer's interest in literature. In recent studies, about 25 percent of the elementary school children interviewed claimed that Walt Disney productions had encouraged them to read certain books. Middle grade students credited television and movies with their interest in Tom Sawyer, Mary Poppins, Helen Keller, Little Women, Robin Hood, Heidi and Treasure Island.[32] In a television experiment in London, publicity given to twelve authors resulted in increased reading of their works in public libraries.[33] The foregoing research suggests that television is capable of lending increased impetus to interest in good literature if a larger percentage of youngsters could be encouraged by their parents to view the most helpful programs. Unfortunately, there seems to be little supervision. Hess and Goldman's research reveals that in the majority of families, the young child watches almost as much as he/she wishes, and, for the most part, views programs of his/her own choice. In the majority of families, the mothers make little effort to supervise either program selection of the child or the amount of time devoted to viewing. The father, likewise, exerts little influence in guiding the television behavior of his child.[34]

Ray Brown's *Children and Television* is an excellent source of information on the adolescent television audience including preschoolers.

The task of placing good books in the hands of children is further complicated by the large numbers of young people that must be served by classroom teachers and librarians. Individual guidance that would lead to children's classics and other quality literature is in short supply. Too few parents are equipped to assist professional educators with this problem. They are prone to accede to their children's pleading for a poorly-written, easily acquired, gaily-colored book from a supermarket's book section without bothering to look between its covers. Peltola found in her study of children's book choices that the jacket or cover influenced children's selections. As an example, youngsters selected Syd Hoff's *Julius,* on the basis of its cover, before they even opened the book.[35] Parents who are in doubt as to which story to select for their child may do well to begin with the time-tested tales that appealed to them when they were children. The wisdom of this procedure is evidenced by Wilson's poll taken of two hundred and seventy-two young children who were interviewed to determine their preference for stories. "The Three Bears" and other children's classics such as "Mother Goose", "Little Red Riding Hood", and "Cinderella" topped the list.[36] Geeslin's study of current book choices of pupils disclosed that *Tom Sawyer, Huckleberry Finn* and *Call of the Wild* were among titles popular with older children for forty years.[37] Wilson further indicated that factors which influenced the children's responses might have been parents' knowledge of the ability to purchase books combined with the presence or absence of desirable books.[38]

A number of studies of stories preferred by children have been accomplished in the past twenty years. For example, D. H. Geeslin's research covered children's interests in three grade levels in 1967.[39] Nearly thirty years ago, the last comprehensive study of children's favorite stories was undertaken by Frank Wilson.[40] In light of previous studies, it was thought an updated comprehensive survey would be valuable to educators, grade school teachers, storytellers, and parents alike. The author's research was financed by the National Science Foundation. The primary aim of this survey was to discover the current story favorites of pupils from kindergarten to grade six.

In 1971, approximately 2000 grade school students in the Los Angeles area were surveyed in the present study of story favorites. The following results lists *in order of preference* the top ten names of stories discovered as favorites for each grade level.[41]

Kindergarten: *The Three Bears, Winnie the Pooh, Snow White, Cinderella, Jack and the Beanstalk, Red Riding Hood, Cat in the Hat Comes Back, Three Pigs, Rumplestiltskin, Charlotte's Web.*

First Grade: *The Three Bears, The Three Little Kittens, Cinderella, Ten Apples Up On Top, Snow White, Black Beauty, Ticky Ticky Thimble, Hansel and Gretel, Alice in Wonderland, Raggedy Ann.*

Second Grade: *Charlie and the Chocolate Factory, Three Bears, Wizard of Oz, Cinderella, Ramona the Pest, Peter Pan, 100 Hats, Snow White, Davy Crockett, Curious George.*

Third Grade: *Charlotte's Web, Winnie the Pooh, Charlie and the Chocolate Factory, Henry Huggins, Snow White, Born Free, Cinderella, Mr. Poppin's Penguins, Charlie Brown, Clifford and the Big Red Dog.*

Fourth Grade: *Charlie and the Chocolate Factory, Charlotte's Web, James and the Giant Peach, Winnie the Pooh, Tom Sawyer, The Iron Arm, Brighty of the Grand Canyon, The Hobbit, Nancy Drew Mysteries, Tower to the Moon.*

Fifth Grade: *He's Your Dog Charlie Brown, Ramona the Pest, Charlotte's Web, The Table and the Chair, King of the Wind, Nancy Drew Mysteries, The Bear Story, Happiness Is a Warm Puppy, 101 Dalmatians, Cotton in my Sack.*

Sixth Grade: *Swiss Family Robinson, Charlie and the Chocolate Factory, 101 Dalmatians, Alice in Wonderland, Born Free, Wizard of Oz, Huck Finn, Jungle Book, Charlotte's Web, A Wrinkle in Time.*

If parents cannot afford to budget for some of the fine collections of children's stories available on today's market, perhaps the best alternative is to depend on their local library and the reliable advice pertaining to book choice that awaits them there.

Alice Hackett and James Burke in an examination of best sellers from 1895 to 1975 discovered those books with accurate sales records of a million copies or more. The following titles listed in order include most books published in the first quarter of this century: *Green Eggs and Ham; One Fish, Two Fish, Red*

Fish, Blue Fish; Hop on Pop; Dr. Seuss's ABC; The Cat in the Hat; The Wonderful Wizard of Oz; Charlotte's Web; The Cat in the Hat Comes Back; The Little Prince; The Little House on the Prairie; The Little House in the Big Woods; My First Atlas; Love and the Facts of Life; Egermeier's Bible Story Book; Go Ask Alice; Benji; The Little Engine That Could; Stuart Little; Freckles; The Girl of the Limberlost; Sounder; Harry, the Dirty Dog; Seventeen; Where the Wild Things Are; Laddie; The Big Book of Mother Goose; The Golden Dictionary; A Friend Is Someone Who Likes You; Rebecca of Sunnybrook Farm; Love Is a Special Way of Feeling; The Real Mother Goose; The Pigman; Better Homes and Gardens Story Book; Trouble After School; Better Homes and Gardens Junior Cook Book; Pollyanna; Le Petit Prince; Mary Poppins; Winnie the Pooh; Pollyanna Grows Up; Little Black Sambo. In addition, series books that sell in great quantities numbering over one million include the *Frank Merriwell* books; *Doctor Dolittle* books; *Oz* books; *Raggedy Ann* books; *Little Colonel* books, *Nancy Drew* stories, *Bobbsey Twins* series, *Tom Swift* series, *Elsie Dinsmore,* and the *Five Little Peppers.* [42] Many of the longer narratives in the books listed may be used by some teachers and librarians as "book talks" in which they use a version of storytelling which introduces a book to a point where children will desire to read the book. The aim is to stimulate interest in a variety of good books which otherwise children might not be encouraged to enjoy because the cover or title did not catch their interest. Many teachers have had success with this and find these books have a higher library check-out than other books.

In selection of appropriate stories, librarian Marion Garthwaite argues that teachers need sources first of all. They need to know where to find good stories before they begin the difficult task of preparation. They need more than a list of anthologies. They should know where to find stories for the interest level of the children and stories for given purposes such as holidays, stories for periods of history, family stories, tales of minority groups, stories about lions, courage, or whatever. [43] There are numerous anthologies for the teller to consult. Those indices to children's stories which are annotated are very helpful. For example, *Building Bridges of Understanding* is an index which indicates stories about various races, age level interest, and some annotation on content of story. The *Children's Catalogue* indicates age level, price, and a review of the story. The *Subject and Title Index to Short Stories for Children* includes subject, author, title, grade level, and text summary. Jeanne Hardendorff's *Stories to Tell* is another interesting index. Various indices are available. The teller should be familiar with several in building a repertory of tales.

Two very well known awards in the field of Children's Literature include the Newbery Medal and the Caldecott Medal. The former was first given in 1921 by Frederic Melcher as an incentive for better quality in children's books. Named after John Newbery, the famous 18th century publisher and seller of children's books, it is now donated annually by Daniel Melcher, son of the original donor, to the author of the most distinguished contribution to American literature for children published during the preceding year. The Caldecott Medal, like the Newbery Medal, is also awarded annually by the Children's Services Division of the American Library Association. In 1938, the first Caldecott medal was awarded to the artist of the most distinguished American picture book for children published in the United States during the preceding year. According to Sara Innis Fenwick, The Newbery Medal in particular has had considerable influence over the years in recognizing and encouraging the publishing of good books for children, and in publicizing the books and standards by which they are judged to alert the attention of both children and especially adults.[44] The Medal winners are well known in every library and perhaps the storyteller will find them excellent choices of material for telling with some adaptation, perhaps as "book talks."

Although there is no simple solution to the foregoing problems of selection they do reinforce the need to present good literature to young people whenever a storytelling opportunity presents itself. Teachers and parents cannot hope to tell *all* of the children's classics, fairy tales, myths, etc., to their young charges. However, by choosing interesting material of literary worth, they may introduce young people to good stories and whet their appetites for more of the same fare. How can one determine if a story is worth telling? Perhaps one of the most satisfactory means of determining the merit of material is to evaluate it according to literary standards.

Literary Worth

Great stories which have survived centuries of appraisal may be found to contain a *universal truth* . . .a message that applies not to one little village or a country but to all of mankind. *Cinderella*, for example, is translated into many languages for it reminds the world that goodness is its own reward; the *Steadfast Tin Soldier* stands firmly in the presence of adversity; *Sleeping Beauty* demonstrates the power of love over evil; and *The Emperor's New Clothes* reveals man's frailty to speak the truth for fear of breaking with convention. A more contemporary example of the powerful use of a universal truth is found in L. M. Boston's *The Stranger at Green Knowe*. A child who had been imprisoned as a refugee identifies with a gorilla which had escaped from a zoo. Both had experienced the frustration of incarceration and both sought freedom . . .a goal which is common to both man and beast. Universals flow like deep rivers through fine literature.

A story possessing literary worth should also have *life-like characters*. "Life-like" does not mean that the characters have actually lived, but they must be convincing. Characters such as Jim and Della in "The Gift of the Magi" are realistic; the husband and wife in "The Three Wishes" are pure fantasy, yet all four are life-like. Storybook personalities may use "cockney" English, slang, or precise, correct grammar depending on their station in life. They must "fit" into the era into which they are cast. The jargon of teenagers does not belong at the conference table of King Arthur and his knights. Parents in stories should react as parents normally do. An unrealistic, highly idealistic portrayal of family relationships is found in "Moving Day" by Earl M. Rush. The father maintained his composure in spite of the trying circumstances that are usually associated with furniture moving. Milk is spilled on his suit, one bedroom slipper is lost, he is constantly questioned by his sons about when the moving van would come, and he caps his performance by lending his wristwatch to his little boy for the balance of the day. The mother permits her children, ages eight and nine years old, to choose and pack kitchen dishes that wouldn't be needed for some time. Children who had never cooked were expected to make these judgments. The moving men were the epitome of patience as the children collided with them and interfered with their work. No one seemed concerned as little sister unpacked boxes that had been carefully packed. Strangely too, the children seemed happy to leave their friends and move to the country. Peterson observes that a normal family would experience fatigue, tension, annoyance, homesickness, etc. during a family move. She also notes that a child reading this story cannot help but wonder why his father does not do such an adequate job of fulfilling his children's fantasies. She states,

> A picture with a few shadows may be healthier and perhaps even less threatening than a blindingly bright one. It should be reassuring for children to realize that a family can remain a solid unit in spite of occasional disagreements and that parents who love their children will still be annoyed with them at times. If we constantly expose children to idealized images of family relationships, most of them must sometimes make an unfavorable comparison between the model we present and the reality of their own home situations. Although we hope many of our students can avoid patterning their adult lives after the unstable or disturbed patterns of their present environment, it is unwise to present them with models which deny a large segment of human experience.[45]

Storytellers should select stories that portray the weaknesses and strengths of characters in a life-like manner. This will facilitate the listener's identification with persons in the story.

Advice on examination of lifelike characters in children's literature is helpful. Virginia Wolf, an instructor of children's literature, explains that lifelike character is the root out of which the story grows. What makes a story convincing when it is cast in the realistic mode? First, the hero or heroine is a growing, changing person with believable development. Second, character determines action; the action must be consistent with the hero's age, experience, and personality. Third, each character and the pursuant story must be unique. Finally, a major prerequisite to all the above, is the fact that the listener must be able to identify with the hero's point of view.[46] When such character development is possible for whatever age level, the story is likely to be a successful choice of literature.

Norma Ainsworth in *Writer's Digest* summarizes how to create live characters in a juvenile short story. The necessities are action, a strong point of view, liveliness and plenty of dialogue within the vocabulary of the average third grader. Some familiar places and objects and natural sounding dialogue quickly establish character.[47] Simply stated, every word counts, which leads us to the next consideration of word usage.

Another means of judging a story's literary worth is through an examination of an author's *word usage*. Although a storyteller usually does not repeat the identical words of an author when telling stories, an examination of the story will reveal the author's skill at describing accurately, vividly and imparting a smoothly flowing action. Consider Wordsworth's splendid employment of verbs, adjectives, and adverbs in the following excerpt:

I WANDERED LONELY AS A CLOUD

I wandered lonely as a cloud
That floats on high o'er vales and hills,
When all at once I saw a crowd,
A host, of golden daffodils;
Beside the lake, beneath the trees,
Fluttering and dancing in the breeze.

Continuous as the stars that shine
And twinkle on the milky way,
They stretched in never-ending line
Along the margin of a bay:
Ten thousand saw I at a glance,
Tossing their heads in sprightly dance.

Word usage of this nature kindles a child's imagination and deepens his sense of appreciation of nature's wonders.

Word usage in terms of dialogue to make the characters come to life is also critical to good storytelling. Direct discourse clarifies the situation and allows greater expression for the character and the teller. Compare these two adaptations of Beatrix Potter's *Tale of Peter Rabbit:*

1. Once upon a time there were four little rabbits, Flopsy, Mopsy, Cottontail, and Peter. One day their mother needed to go shopping so she warned the little rabbits to play in the fields or down the lane, but not to go into Mr. McGregor's garden. Then she took her basket and left.

2. Flopsy, Mopsy, Cottontail, and Peter were the names of four little rabbits who lived under a big fir tree with their Mother.

One morning, Mother Rabbit explained, "I'm going to the baker's to buy some bread and your favorite raisin rolls. Now I want you to be good little rabbits and stay out of trouble."

"May we pick some berries?" asked Mopsy.

"Yes, you may go into the fields or down the lane, but don't go near Mr. McGregor's garden," warned Mother Rabbit.

Word usage in the second adaptation is more clear, lively, and interesting particularly in terms of dialogue for character development. In addition a good storyteller also avoids overuse of the word, "said" in the dialogue development.

Theodor Seuss Geisel has written and illustrated a children's library of thirty-two amazingly fanciful and cleverly worded books which sell around the world. *The Lorax* is one recent example of a hard-sell ecological allegory with a rippling imagery of words and pictures. I have observed a preschool class and a class of eight-year-olds equally enchanted by the rhythm and rhyme displayed in delightful word usage of *The Lorax*. Few critics would deny that Seuss understands the magic of words for children. As Davis and Watkins explain, rhythm is one factor which can be relied upon to establish a common ground among children of all ages.[48]

To be worthy in a literary sense, a story must also possess a *logical plot*. A plot is a story's plan of action, a synthesis of the incidents which happen to the characters. A good plot will produce clear character development and a sequence of action that partitions into distinct episodes. Stories with digressions, subplots, and flashbacks should be avoided for young audiences because of their confusing effects. Following is an example of concise plot construction:

The Fisherman and His Wife

I. Introduction: A fisherman and his wife live in a pigsty close to the sea. The fisherman catches a magic fish, which was actually an enchanted prince, and returns it to the sea.

II. Rising Action: A. Wife has husband request a cottage from the fish.
B. Wife has husband request a castle from the fish.
C. Wife has husband request that she be made king.
D. Wife has husband request that she be made emperor.
E. Wife has husband request that she be made pope.
F. Wife has husband request that she be made lord of the sun and of the moon. (climax)

III. Conclusion: The fisherman and his wife are reduced to living in a pigsty as they were originally.

This story introduces its conflict situation after a short introduction, it marches directly toward the final resolution of the conflict and concludes quickly after its climax or denouement is reached. The story line consists of a short introduction, a conflict situation, a rising action, a climax, a denouement (falling action) and a conclusion. In children's literature the climax and denouement are almost simultaneous. Stories such as the foregoing that present harmony in their emotional tone, structure, content and word usage are said to have *unity*.

In addition to containing a universal truth, life-like characters, effective word usage and a logical plot, a story must have an *appropriate setting*. Mention was made earlier regarding the inadvisability of mixing modern jargon with the vocabulary of King Arthur's knights. Vocabulary must be appropriate to the setting. Similarly, the setting should be consistent as far as place is concerned. If a story begins in a land of make-believe, its mood would be shattered for children if the locale shifted to the Santa Ana Freeway. Stories should be examined for the artistry proper setting may provide. In the foregoing tale of ''The Fisherman and His Wife,'' Grimm skillfully adjusted the condition of the sea to the mood of the fish. The sea was calm when the cottage was requested but with each subsequent demand, more turbulence was introduced to the setting until, "...all the heavens became black with storm clouds, and the lightenings played, and the thunders rolled; and you might have seen in the sea great black waves, swelling up like mountains with crowns of white foam upon their heads." Effect through setting is also achieved in "Snow White and the Seven Dwarfs" wherein the queen's chemistry laboratory contributes to the feelings of evil surrounding the witch, while the simple, white cottage suggested the innocence and goodness of Snow White and the dwarfs.

A happy blending of literary worth is embodied in "The Elves and the Shoemaker":

I. Introduction: A destitute cobbler and his wife have leather left for but one pair of shoes. He prepares the leather for sewing and retires for the night.

II. Rising Action: A. Cobbler finds completed shoes in the morning. He sells shoes and is able to purchase leather for two pairs, which he cuts.

B. The next morning two completed pairs of shoes await him. The shoes are sold and leather for four pairs of shoes is purchased and cut.

C. Shoemaker and wife sit up and see two elves complete their shoes. They resolve to make clothing for them.

D. Christmas Eve finds the shoemaker and his wife in their hiding place watching the elves as they complete more shoes and find their gifts.

III. Conclusion: Elves dance happily away and the cobbler and wife prosper.

The universal theme in this tale is the power of love. The characters are kindly and generous. They contrast sharply in attitude. The elderly cobbler seems to feel the cares and poverty of a long life but the elves, though threadbare in appearance, seem spritely, spirited and happy. The use of image-producing words make the four characters seem life-like. The plot is crisp and it is easily followed by children. The mystery of how the shoes were being made is introduced early and the suspense continues even after the elves are observed. The action is cast in the barren, cheerless shop of the shoemaker. This serves as a foil for the prosperity engendered by the elves. The climax is appropriately staged on Christmas Eve...a time when many children have thrilled to both giving and receiving gifts. How will the elves react to the surprise planned by the shoemaker and his wife? The ending is happy as the elves dance away into the night.

The foregoing discussion of literary worth of material for storytelling has indicated the importance of a theme that possesses a universal appeal, of characters that seem natural, of word usage that is accurate, smooth and vivid, of a plot that is logical and concise with clear development, and finally, of a setting that is appropriate to the action. Stories with these characteristics contribute to the total effectiveness of a storyteller.

One effective means of collecting stories is to prepare a story file made up of abstracts of the stories much like the previous references to *The Fisherman and*

His Wife or *The Shoemaker and the Elves*. The storytellers should write whatever is needed to refresh their memory concerning the story line. The Story File is usually kept on 3'' by 5'' cards, or 4'' by 6'' cards, which cite the complete source of the story, the outline of the plot, key words or phrases, character's names and various scenes. These cards can be consulted quickly before the teller meets the audience. The concept of a story file is discussed further in Chapter 4. Once the file is started, raconteurs soon develop their own list of ''Best Stories for a Particular Age Level.''

THE STORYTELLER

Identification With the Story

A tale chosen for telling must ''fit'' both the storyteller and the audience. A raconteur must *identify* with the story. Some material may seem appropriate to one storyteller and foreign to another. Some women feel, without adequate justification, that it takes a man to relate war or sporting-type stories. Preference for tales can frequently be traced to a person's experiences and aptitudes. Followers of the sea will probably be inclined to tell sea stories; foresters and mountaineers may find wilderness tales their *forte*. Whatever the choice, the storyteller must feel at ease with the material. The storyteller must enjoy the story and must

The storyteller and the listener should identify with the story.

desire to share it with others. The storyteller should select a story which suits the teller's personality. Telling a story which is considered interesting will soon result in a flat bland tale instead of an enthusiastic one. Neophyte storytellers will do well to begin with folktales and read at least a half dozen before attempting to make a selection. The story enjoyed most on first reading will probably be a safe choice for telling.

Purpose

Stories are usually selected for a *specific purpose*. All stories should entertain but some are selected solely for that reason. Others are selected to meet the interest level of the audience, to meet an educational need, or for their worth as literature. Purposes and motivations often overlap and are complicated. A teacher may wish to instruct by telling the class about the discovery of radium. The teacher may wish to stir interest in professional pursuits by relating the biographies of Dr. Walter Reed, Henry Ford or Clarence Darrow. An instructor may wish to inculcate ideals by describing the character traits displayed by Lou Gehrig, Martin Luther King or Nathan Hale. A teacher might find that children learn obedience more quickly by listening to "Peter Rabbit" than they would by stern admonitions; cleanliness may be incorporated into their behavior patterns more painlessly through hearing of *Angelo, the Naughty One* than through rules, and fear may be dissipated through *Call It Courage*. According to author and teacher, Marguerite Jensen, teachers are often admonished to humanize learning experiences and storytelling is just one way to do that effectively.[49] For example telling *The Giving Tree* is sharing a humanistic experience of generosity, greed, and love.

Comprehension Level

All who choose stories for young audiences should be alert to the problems that have resulted from a confusion of reading and listening comprehension levels. In an effort to meet the reading needs of youngsters, stories have been categorized into graduated degrees of difficulty known as "reading levels." While there is no intent to criticize the techniques of teaching reading, the result of classification of stories by grade has led to confusion between what a child can read and what a child can listen to successfully. Children have been deprived of many stories within the range of their listening comprehension because these stories have been classified in groups beyond their level of reading comprehension. For example, "Rip Van Winkle" is fascinating listening fare for children in the third grade, and "The Three Sillies" is highly amusing to an audience in the second grade; yet both of these stories are beyond the average reading comprehension of these groups. According to Markowsky, even at age 2, children have a speaking vocabulary of 200 to 300 words, although they can comprehend much more.[50]

Children of today comprehend a great deal more orally than their peers did fifty years ago. Those who work with children should avoid a tendency to "talk down" to them. Youngsters in the kindergarten-primary range watch, in addition to children's television programs, travelogues, documentaries, newscasts and adult movies. According to Nicholson, the vocabulary of kindergarten children in 1967 differs from the vocabulary of the 1926 kindergartner in that the former's vocabulary reflects a wide range of words related to space science, technology and social class values. This research on the oral vocabulary of kindergarten children disclosed that social class was a significant determinant in contrast to sex and race which were not significant determinants of oral vocabulary used by children of this age.[51] An earlier study by Sheehy found similarly that children in 1964 have shifted toward adult responses and norms far more than they did in 1916.[52] The implications for the storyteller are obvious. Not only must vocabulary be geared to a social class generally, but it must challenge six-year-olds who are capable of comprehending far more than their years suggest.

Adult and Child Themes

One of the most common errors of story choice is that of selecting a tale that appeals to an adult with little thought to the interest level of the child. A child may comprehend an adult theme but not be interested in it. A well-meaning individual, swayed one way or the other on a racial problem, for example, might seek out a story on this subject for pre-schoolers or kindergartners. At this age, most children are "color blind" as far as choice of playmates is concerned. Furthermore, at this age, children would probably prefer "Goldilocks and the Three Bears" to a theme of racial discrimination. Mary Fulton's *My Friend,* 1974, is a good choice for preschoolers on the subject of interracial friendship. For older children, Judith Thompson and Gloria Woodard argue that better books such as *Gabrielle and Selena* by Peter Desbarts, lead children naturally to the conclusion that differences in personality, abilities and background are desirable among people.[53] Carole Parks in "Goodbye Black Sambo" discusses how black writers forge new images in children's literature in tasteful appropriate ways in order to build egos, not destroy them. "Positive" is the key password.[54]

In the story-poem, "Little Boy Lost", the same problem of lack of children's interest may prevail. The story is about a child but it is not for children. Longfellow's reminiscent "The Children's Hour" is appropriate for elderly persons who have raised their families and who enjoy reverie and contemplation of parental experiences. This material should not be force-fed to third graders who crave fairy tales. Many researchers attempt to prove the popularity of particular children's books by asking children their favorites or by noting how often a story is requested. These two queries may help storytellers distinguish between adult and child themes.

Emotional Dimension

Most literary researchers agree that a story's emotional dimension assists listeners and readers to identify with the characters. However, there is a division of opinion as to what constitutes an appropriate act to evoke this emotional response. Kingsley has conducted a critical analysis of the depth and strength of characterization in American children's drama. He contends that some authors espouse happy endings because of the fear of a negative audience reaction to an unhappy ending. Some feel that children need to escape their own sordid surroundings and enter a world of happiness. There is also concern over stunting children's emotional growth due to exposure to adult material. Some educators, allegedly, cling to highly idealistic conditions in stories in their desire to preserve and nurture children's natural moral superiority. Some theologians support the concept of poetic justice and happy endings because of an assumption that a universal and deified system of unerring justice is constantly operating in ultimate reality. Finally, it is believed that some authors and playwrights soften their characterizations because of society's abhorrence of violence and aggression.

In response to these positions, Kingsley explains that new and strange material may be introduced gradually rather than with shocking abruptness. He suggests that it is not so much what is presented but rather how it is done. If children find escape in a world of happiness, they may also find escape in the troubles of others. Most children are believed to be too adaptive to become stunted emotionally by exposure to adult material and their innocence is said to be due to a lack of technique rather than an abundance of virtue. Efforts to depict "rightness" collides with society's conglomeration of confused and conflicting value systems rather than one unified moral code. He further contends, that, theology to the contrary, there are other deities far removed from the deities that children's authorities envision. He points out that happy endings and poetic justice do not happen as often in real life as they do in children's plays and seeks to justify a more realistic approach to this matter:

> It may be that children manifest fright at sudden representation of horror, suffer bad dreams, and for a long time afterward remember the terrifying experience. It also may be that children gain a reinforced pleasure out of imitating the violence which allows them to express their hidden aggressive desires. In any event, the children find the viewing of both pleasurable. However, children's fright need not go unattended, nor must their imitation of aggression become an unfortunate and sometimes deadly carbon copy of the original violent act. It can be rather a "talking out" of the child's fears or a verbal reenactment of the aggression—preferably to the parent who will provide the much needed haven of security the child so often needs.[55]

The results of other research indicate that viewing crime and violence on television is not a crucial determinant of behavior nor of attitudes which might be manifested in behavior. In support of the foregoing, there are indications that such viewing may serve special functions for those who are already socially maladjusted.[56]

In terms of the new realism, some children's authors contend that there are no longer any taboos in children's books except that of bad taste. Jane Yolen explains the existence of this trend in terms of three instrumental factors: the change in readership with children in all classes of society having access to books; the rise in mass media in every household including brightly colored magazines discussing drugs, death, divorce, etc.; and finally the advent of television in which a child has easy access to almost all subjects. Books like *Sounder* discuss white man's brutality to blacks; *My Darling, My Hamburger*—premarital sex, pregnancy, and abortion; *I'll Get There: It Better Be Worth the Trip*—homosexuality; *The Pigman*—senility. But at the same time, these "relevant" books may exploit or explore problems. A sensitive exploration may lead juveniles into deeper insight and knowledge of problems, some of which he or she may share directly. They may provide avenues of problem solving.[57]

Julius Lester, Newbery runner-up for *To Be a Slave* and author of *Black Folktales,* argues that some children need relevant books. Too often the kinds of books given to children are an indication of what we think of them. Perhaps too much fantasy, nonsense and fairy tales are emphasized, and they do not represent the totality of a child's world. Lester was never able to find any relationship between the children's books and the slum in which he lived. He looked for violence and violent deaths in order to understand and adjust to his environment, but his parents wanted to "protect" him through education and books when in fact his real life was obsessed with violence and violent deaths. He maintains that children are not as frightened of reality as adults are.[58]

On the other hand, a study that produced conclusions which contradicted Kingsley's findings was conducted by Bandura. His experimentation involved nursery children who were divided into three groups. One group watched models perform aggressively, both physically and verbally, toward a large, plastic doll. Another group witnessed subdued behavior of the model toward the doll, while a third group, the control children, were not exposed to the model. Bandura reports:

> Children who observed the aggressive models displayed a great number of precisely imitative physical and verbal responses, whereas such behavior rarely occurred in either the non-aggressive model group or the control group. Children who had observed the aggressive models exhibited approximately twice as much aggression as did subjects in either the nonaggressive model group or the control group. By contrast, children who witnessed the subdued, non-aggressive models displayed the inhibited behavior characteristic of the model and expressed significantly less aggression than the control group.[59]

There has been continued research and the evidence supports Bandura's point of view. Some research has also shown that adults are also influenced by exposure to violence. The effects of television are daily becoming more pronounced. Children who watch shows with heavy violence content or with slanted views are assuredly worse off than those who watch no television, whereas children who watch heavily educational or socially positive programs are better off than those who watch no television. Guidance from parents is imperative.[60]

During the time children listen, they visualize only within their own experience and vocabulary, so they may not get the full impact of a story's cruelty. Even though all children have not personally experienced violence, today's children have observed television violence and thus have vicariously experienced violence. When they hear a book which includes violence, those children with experience react differently emotionally and visually than those children not exposed to violence. Those children already exposed to violence adjust more readily to violence portrayed in children's books. This could be a factor in choosing books. Again the teller should adapt to the audience.

It is evident from the foregoing that there is need for additional research on this subject. What should be the position of the storyteller in regard to the use of emotional material? How realistic should he be and what influence, if any, should the listener's age have on the selection of material? Perhaps there is a common sense approach to this problem. As far as bedtime storytelling is concerned, most parents put their children to bed to sleep . . .not to toss and turn. Intelligent parents who possess enough courage to supervise their child's TV viewing will not permit horror-type TV programs, especially in the evening hours. Neither will bedtime stories be the nightmare-inducing variety. Admittedly, all TV viewing cannot be supervised and it seems inevitable that some programs will be watched that are probably not in the child's best interests. Parents might also do well to recognize that there is a difference between being horrified and being "properly" frightened. Walter de la Mare, in retrospect, senses the fun and the anticipation of a harmless, scary tale which never lost its emotional flavor for him:

> . . .A very small boy may go shivering to bed after listening to the teeny tiny tale of the teeny tiny little woman who found a teeny tiny little bone in the churchyard. The very marrow in his bones may tremble at that final "Take It." Mine used to; and yet I delighted to have told me again and again by my mother.[61]

Fear is not an emotion to avoid in storytelling, even for the very young. Fear, or perhaps it should be called "respect", for the results of running into the street after a ball, is the reaction that serves to keep many youngsters alive. Stories containing appeals to fear may be chosen but they must be employed with the consummate skill of audience adaptation demanded of successful storytellers.

The amount of sobbing done by preschool children suggests that they are aware that life is not all sweetness and light. However, a liberal representation of stories with happy endings and poetic justice is appropriate from nursery school to the third grade. This is a highly impressionable period during which a child indulges in little abstract thinking. Causal reasoning is at low ebb. It has been indicated that a legitimate aim of storytelling is to instruct. If society is to have order rather than anarchy, youngsters must be conditioned to understand that policemen subdue robbers, and not the reverse of this. Law must be respected.

During this period, stories should be told that represent life as it *should* be. Of course, the starkness of reality must be faced by older children both within and without the story. Such books as *The Railroad to Freedom* by Hildegarde Swift, *Southtown* by Lorenz Graham, and *Johnny Tremaine* by Esther Forbes help children to come to grips with life as it is without excessive idealism or didactic moralizing.

Commitment to Variety

Numerous teachers know the value of storytelling when using a variety of types or forms of literature in a school year's program. Even if the teller polishes only a few stories each year, the exposure of children to different kinds of stories is essential to their literary and communication development. Fenwick reminds tellers, the oft-repeated phrase that "children know what they like" can profitably be accompanied by the response that they do not always know all the books that they might like. Therefore it is important that the storyteller provides this availability and understanding which establishes a confrontation between child and story.[62] Storytellers have a personal obligation to familiarize themselves with a variety of stories in order to reach as many children as possible. Perhaps an adaptation of the following Storytelling Grid may be utilized by tellers in order to encourage self-exposure to different kinds of literature whatever the age level.

Storytelling Grid

	Repetition 3-6	Fancy 6-9	Hero Worship 9-12	Idealism 12-
Folk Literature	Gingerbread Man	Sleeping Beauty	Aladdin and the Magic Lamp	Legend of Sleepy Hollow
Narrative Poetry	Hickory Dickory Dock	How the Grinch Stole Christmas	Casey at the Bat	The Cremation of Sam McGee
Realistic Stories	What Mary Jo Shared	Mary Alice Operator Number 9	Berries Goodman	Gentle Ben
Biographies	The Columbus Story	Abraham Lincoln (Doubleday)	America's Mark Twain	Johnny Tremain

SUMMARY

This chapter has explored guidelines relating to the child, the story and the storyteller which will facilitate appropriate choice of stories for telling. It has indicated that children from three to six years of age prefer stories that contain concrete, familiar objects, repetition and talking animals. Six to nine-year-olds enjoy fairy tales especially, but they also will listen attentively to children's classics and stories about elementary technology. Children from nine to twelve years of age prefer mysteries, biographies and travel adventures. From twelve on, youngsters continue to enjoy adventure, sports, biographies, and with maturity, romance. In addition, tellers must consider the individual and his or her particular needs and development.

Storytellers are urged to examine material for its literary worth. Stories possessing the latter contain a universal truth, life-like characters, imaginative, accurate word usage, logical plot and an appropriate setting. Storytellers are encouraged to compile a story file and are urged to choose stories which they enjoy personally. Selection should be made with a definite purpose in mind whether it be to entertain, instruct, or inculcate ideals. Stories should be chosen on the basis of the child's listening, not his reading ability. During children's early years, stories should be selected that represent life as it should be, not as it frequently is. Emotional dimensions of a tale should be appropriate to the mental age of the listeners. Commitment to a variety of types of children's literature for storytelling is important to both tellers and listeners.

NOTES

1. Lucy Sprague Mitchell, *Another Here and Now Story Book,* (New York, E. P. Dutton and Co., Inc., 1948).
2. Ruth Tooze, *Storytelling,* (Englewood Cliffs, N.J., Prentice-Hall, Inc., 1959), p. 55.
3. Arnold L. Gesell and Frances L. Ilg, *The Child From Five to Ten.* (New York and London; Harper & Bros., 1946), p. 371.
4. Jed Davis and Mary Watkins, *Children's Theatre,* (New York, Harper and Row, 1960), p. 26-28.
5. Juliet Markowsky, "Storytime for Toddlers," *School Library Journal.* 23, (May, 1977): p. 31.
6. Davis and Watkins, *Children's Theatre,* p. 27.
7. May Hill Arbuthnot, *Children and Books,* 3rd ed., (Chicago, Scott, Foresman and Co., 1964,) p. 284.
8. Benjamin Spock, "Are Fairy Tales Good for Children?", *Redbook.* 141. (June 1976): 22-23. Copyright © 1976 by John D. Houston, II, Trustee.
9. Davis and Watkins, *Children's Theatre,* p. 28.
10. From *The Uses of Enchantment: The Meaning and Importance of Fairy Tales,* by Bruno Bettelheim. Copyright © 1976 by Bruno Bettelheim. Reprinted by permission of Alfred A. Knopf, Inc. Portions of this book originally appeared in *The New Yorker.*
11. Frank Eyre, *Twentieth Century Children's Books,* (London: Longsman, Green, 1952).
12. Ravenna Helson, "Fantasy and Self-Discovery," *The Horn Book,* Vol. 46, No. 2. (April, 1970): pp. 121-134.
13. Bettleheim, *Meaning & Importance of Fairy Tales.*
14. D. H. Geeslin, "A Descriptive Study of the Current Book Choices of Pupils on Three Grade Levels: A Search for the Effects of Reading Age upon Interests," *Dissertation Abstracts.* 27, (1967), p. 875-A.
15. Nancy E. Briggs, "A Survey of Favorite Stories of Pupils From Kindergarten to Grade Six," *The Speech Teacher,* (March, 1972): pp. 140-141.
16. Margaret F. O'Connell, "Children's Books," *P.T.A. Magazine* 68, (April, 1974): pp. 8-9.
17. F. N. Monjo, "Great Men, Melodies, Experiments, Plots, Predictability and Surprises," *The Horn Book,* vol. 51, No. 5, (October, 1975): p. 440.
18. Tooze, *Storytelling,* p. 68.
19. Davis and Watkins, *Children's Theatre,* p. 29.
20. Gesell, *Child From Five to Ten,* p. 59.

21. Marion Garthwaite, "Stories to Shorten the Road," *Elementary English*, vol. 49, No. 4, (April, 1972): pp. 601-602.
22. Katherine Steirt, "The Designing of an Inventory to Investigate Recreational Reading Interests of Pupils in Grades Five and Six," *Dissertation Abstracts*, 28, (1967), p. 148-A.
23. Arlene Bernice Burgdorf, "A Study of the Ability of Intermediate-Grade Children to Draw Inferences from Selections of Children's Literature," *Dissertation Abstracts*, 27, (1966), p. 2003-A.
24. Bette Jean Peltola, "A Study of the Indicated Literary Choices and Measured Literary Knowledge of Fourth and Sixth Grade Boys and Girls," *Dissertation Abstracts*, 27, (1966), p. 609-A.
25. Jo M. Stanchfield, "The Reading Interests of Eighth-Grade Boys," *Journal of Developmental Reading*, (Summer, 1962), pp. 256-265.
26. Women on Words and Images, "Dick and Jane as Victims: Sex Stereotyping in Children's Readers," 1974, P. O. Box 2163, Princeton, New Jersey, 98540; Lenore J. Weitzman and Diane Rizzo, "Images of Males and Females in Elementary School Textbooks in Five Subject Areas," 1975, Resource Center on Sex Roles in Education, 1156 15th St., N.W., Washington, D.C. 20005.
27. Martha Dallman, *Teaching the Language Arts in the Elementary School*. (Dubuque, Iowa, Wm. C. Brown Co., 1972), pp. 20-24.
28. Donnarae MacCann, "A Valid Criticism for Children's Books," *Wilson Library Bulletin*. 44, (December, 1969): p. 394.
29. Mark Twain's Autobiography, Vol. 1, *Harper's*, (New York, 1924): p. 112.
30. Paul Witty, "Children of the Television Era," *Elementary English*. (1967), 44: 529-531.
31. Robert Liebert and Daniel Anderson, *The Early Window: The Effects of Television on Children and Youth*. (Elmsford, N.Y., Pergamon Press, 1973). (Used by permission).
32. Witty, *Children of Television Era*, p. 530.
33. *Times* Editorial Supplement, 2710:1435, "Television and the Reader," April 28, 1967.
34. Robert D. Hess and Harriet Goldman, "Parents' Views on the Effect of Television on Their Children," *Child Development* 35, (June, 1962): p. 424.
35. Bette J. Peltola, "A Study of Children's Book Choices," *Elementary English*. (November, 1963): 690-695.
36. Frank T. Wilson, "Stories That Are Liked by Young Children," *The Journal of Genetic Psychology*. 63 (1943): 68-69.
37. D. H. Geeslin, "A Descriptive Study of the Current Book Choices of Pupils on Three Grade Levels: A Search for the Effects of Reading Age Upon Reading Interests," *Dissertation Abstracts*. (1968), 28: 875-A.
38. Wilson, *Stories Liked by Young Children*, 68-69.
39. Geeslin, *Descriptive Study*.
40. Wilson, *Stories Liked by Young Children*.
41. Briggs, *Survey of Favorite Stories*.
42. Alice P. Hackett and James H. Burke, *80 Years of Best Sellers*, (New York: R. R. Bowker Co., 1977), pp. 45-47. (Used by permission.)
43. Garthwaite, Stories to Shorten the Road.
44. Sara Innes Fenwick, "Which Will Fade, Which Endure?" *Wilson Library Bulletin* 47, (October 1972): p. 184.
45. Barbara G. Peterson, "Life Maladjustment Through Children's Literature", *Elementary English* 40, (November, 1963): 718.
46. Virginia Wolf, "The Root and Measure of Realism," *Wilson Library Bulletin*. 44, (December, 1969): p. 409.
47. Norma Ainsworth, "How to Create 'Live' Characters in A Juvenile Short Story," *Writer's Digest*. 49, (December, 1969): pp. 36-39.
48. Davis and Watkins, *Children's Theatre*, p. 34.
49. Marguerite Jensen, "Tell Me a Story," *Instruction*. 82, (January, 1973): p. 89.
50. Markowsky, *Storytime for Toddlers*, p. 30.
51. Elsie Mae Nicholson, "An Investigation of the Oral Vocabulary of Kindergarten Children from Three Cultural Groups with Implications for Readiness and Beginning Reading Programs," *Dissertation Abstracts*. 27, (1966), 710-A.
52. Sister Mary Serena Sheehy, "A Developmental and Normative Study of Word Associations in Children Grades One Through Six," *Dissertation Abstracts*. 26, (July, 1965): 484.

53. Judith Thompson and Gloria Woodard, "Black Perspective in Books for Children," *Wilson Library Bulletin*. 44, (December, 1969): pp. 420-421.
54. Carole Parks, "Goodbye Black Sambo," *Ebony*. Magazine, November 1972. (Used by permission.)
55. W. H. Kingsley, "Happy Endings, Poetic Justice and the Depth and Strength of Characterization in American Children's Drama: A Critical Analysis," *Dissertation Abstracts*. 26, (1965): 3534-3535.
56. Joseph T. Klapper, *The Effects of Mass Communication*, (Glencoe, Illinois, The Free Press of Glencoe, 1960).
57. Jane Yolen, "It's Not All Peter Rabbit," *The Writer*. 88, (April, 1975): pp. 12-15.
58. Julius Lester, "The Kinds of Books We Give Children: Whose Nonsense?" *Publisher's Weekly*. 197, (February 23, 1970): pp. 86-88.
59. Albert Bandura, "Behavioral Modifications Through Modeling Procedures", L. Krasmer and L. P. Ullman, *Research in Behavior Modification*, (New York: Holt, Rinehart and Winston, 1965).
60. Nancy Polette and Marjorie Hamlin, *Reading Guidance in a Media Age*. (Metuchin, N. J., The Scarecrow Press, Inc., 1975), p. 32.
61. Walter de la Mare, *Animal Stories*, (New York: Scribner, 1939).
62. Sara Innes Fenwick, *Which Will Fade*, p. 185.

4

The Story
Preparation and Delivery

A famed American industrialist, Charles M. Schwab, once gave this description of the plight of a new prisoner in the prison dining hall. After lunch one of the inmates stood up and yelled, "Sixty-two!" The men roared with laughter. Then he called out, "Eighty-seven," and the prisoners were hilarious. "Thirty-four," and they rolled in the aisles.

The new prisoner was puzzled and turned to his neighbor for an explanation. "It's simple," he was told. "We have the same jokes in the prison library, which we all know. So we give each joke a number, stand up and tell it, and the men recognize it and laugh. Saves time and effort."

So the new prisoner, seeking popularity, went to the library and memorized all the better jokes. The next day he stood up after lunch and called out, "Forty-one!" Not a laugh.

He tried again. "Seventy-five!" Dead silence. Once more, "Twenty-nine!" The men didn't crack a smile.

He sat down dismayed, and turned to his neighbor, whispering: "I don't understand it. I picked out some of the best in the book, and yet nobody laughed. What do you suppose is the trouble?"

"Well, you know how it is," the other man patted him on the shoulder consolingly. "Some people can tell a story, and some people can't!"

Like the sympathetic prisoner, many persons believe that storytelling is a rare ability reserved only for the artistic few. The authors of this book are diametrically opposed to this position. Any person may become an effective storyteller if enough determination to excel is present. Persons deprived of hearing have been known to "speak with their fingers" and hold deaf audiences spellbound with their "signing". Careful attention to the requisites of careful preparation combined with animated identification with the story compensated for the absence of voice. The pleasure of bringing delight to an audience through a well-told-tale may be experienced by all.

A student-teacher once visited the office of her storytelling professor in a depressed state. She explained that she selected a story for her class very carefully . . . .it was one she liked. She read it several times before practicing it aloud; she visualized each scene and determined where the action arose; she felt as if the characters were "alive" and yet, the story "fell flat". What went wrong? Her second graders continued to whisper, fidget, and look about the room as she spoke. Should she give up the idea of telling stories and simply read to her class?

An examination of the student-teacher's story revealed that a key consideration had been overlooked, i.e. that of commanding her students' attention. The latter is an integral part of a story's introduction.

INTRODUCTION

Attention

It follows from the foregoing that an effective introduction must motivate children to listen. Additionally, it must establish the mood of the story and present the conflict situation.

In practice, a story usually has a "pre-introduction" and then the actual introduction to the story itself. A typical classroom audience may consist of a child who is sleepy, perhaps one without breakfast, a third admiring new shoes, a fourth watching a bird in a bush by the window, a fifth deeply troubled by an argument his parents had had at breakfast, a sixth deeply resentful of a classmate who had struck him on the playground, etc. How can this diversity of attention be brought into common focus? How can a storyteller command attention? Reference to the familiar and commonplace is one of the easiest ways to accomplish this. A teacher may ask, "Did you notice the new snow on the mountain when you came to school today?" or, "How many know which holiday is next?...Raise your hands!" or, "How many of you own a dog or a cat? Raise your hands." Let the lead-in or pre-introductory attention-getter tie-in to the story to be told. Reference to snow could signal the telling of Roy Cottrell's short story "Snowbird"; if Christmas were just around the corner, the question about the holiday could usher in "Why the Chimes Rang." A device which assists children to concentrate their attention is to permit limited participation following interrogation. After children had raised their hands in response to the pet question the teacher may say, depending on the size of the class, "Would you like to tell me the name of your pet?" In a small group this could be accomplished quickly, in a large classroom, the teacher could permit limited participation with the promise that with the next dog or cat story, others could share. Once attention is captured, the teacher could get directly to the story's introduction with, "All of us have problems, don't we? Today I would like to share a problem faced by a boy named Freddie. You have probably had a similar problem to face. Let us see if Freddie's solution is the one you would have chosen."

Mood

Next, the mood of the story must be established. The brevity of story introductions places most of the mood development in the body of the tale but the storyteller may create mood by her attitude. Listeners will be prone to believe that a story is funny, adventurous, serious or tragic if the narrator reflects such attitudes. In addition to the storyteller's facial reaction and voice pattern, mood may be created by reference to time. Children may be wafted off to the land of yesteryear by saying, ''Once upon a time, long before there were automobiles, telephones, radios or television sets, a little boy was born in a log cabin in Kentucky.'' Emotional appeal will also set mood, e.g. ''once upon a time there lived a little girl who was so poor that she had neither shoes on her feet nor a warm coat to shield her from a bitter wind.'' There must be a consistency of mood throughout the story. Children feel betrayed if the story begins with, ''Long, long ago in the magic land of Persia. . . .'' and they suddenly find the plot depositing them on the chaotic corner of Hollywood and Vine.

Conflict

In addition to developing the audience's desire to listen and building mood, the introduction should pique interest by presenting the problem, the conflict upon which the story must grow. Note, in the following examples, how concisely and quickly the authors introduce the conflict and make the listeners a part of it:

Grimm ''The Twin Brother''
There were once two brothers, one of whom was rich and the other poor. The rich brother was a goldsmith and had a wicked heart. The poor brother supported himself by making brooms, and was good and honest.

Perrault ''Red Riding Hood''
Once upon a time there lived in a small village in the country a little girl, the prettiest, sweetest creature that ever was seen. Her mother loved her fondly and her grandmother doted on her still more.

Hans Christian Andersen's ''The Pea Blossom''
There were once five peas in a pod. They were green and the pod was green, and they thought all the world was green.

Hans Christian Andersen's ''Thumbelina''
There was once a woman who had the greatest longing for a little tiny child, but she had no idea where to get one; so she went to an old witch and said to her. ''I do so long to have a little child, will you tell me where I can get one?''

In ''The Twin Brother'', Grimm quickly establishes his ''good-evil'' theme without any lost motion; Perrault purposely gives us a quick minimal description of the child which serves as a splendid foil for the loathsome wolf. The action in both of Andersen's introductions is swift; he quickly establishes the ignorance of the peas and the desire of the woman to have a child. The clarity and brevity of these opening lines make immediate identification with the characters possible. The children should feel as if they are a part of the action. A storyteller will not say, ''When Robert Louis Stevenson was a boy. . . .'' but rather, ''Once upon a time there lived a boy about your age whose name was Robert.'' Children wait expectantly for action and they must be given it. Not all stories have introductions as ideally suited for storytelling as the foregoing examples. However, through a judicious elimination of unnecessary material, storytellers may create introductions that command attention, set the mood of the story and present the conflict situation.

BODY

The body of the story must move directly toward the climax without any betrayal of what the latter is going to be. It enlarges on the sound foundation layed in the introduction. Attention must be maintained, and mood enhanced, and the conflict situation developed to its conclusion.

Attention

Some storytellers feel that attention is a self-perpetuating thing. . . .Not so! They make the same error as the Greek orator who was speaking to the people of Athens on a hot day. The speaker's arguments were dry and the audience became inattentive. He realized he had lost his audience so he turned to this story for help:

> There were once two travelers on their way from Athens down to the Piraeus to take ship. One of them, having a great deal of baggage, had rented a donkey to transport it for him. At the noon hour, the two travelers paused for rest. The one who had the donkey led it to one side of the road and lay down in its shade. The other traveller insisted that he be permitted to share the shade. The man who had rented the donkey contended that with it he had rented its shade. The other denied this and a heated argument began.

At this point, the speaker abruptly walked off the platform. The audience began to shout, "Come back, come back, and finish the story." After a few minutes he reappeared and said, "Oh men of Athens, when I speak concerning the salvation of our city, you fall asleep. But when I tell you the silly story of two men and an ass, you are all ears!" A speaker astute enough to recapture his audience with a story should not have lost their attention earlier. Storytellers must bear the responsibility of holding their listeners' interest and if they cannot, they will fail their purpose. The importance of choosing an appropriate story has previously been explained. Even though a wise selection of material has been made, other factors may handicap its presentation. The physical arrangement of the room, the time the story is told, and the ability of the raconteur to adapt material during the presentation must be considered.

Physical Arrangement

Once a good story has been chosen and thoroughly prepared, every effort should be made to insure easy reception by children. The storyteller must be certain that room lighting is adequate. She should place the children so that window light is to their backs and not in their faces. Every child should be able to see the speaker without having to peer around the head of the boy or girl in front of him. Chairs need to be spaced to prevent the backs from becoming footrests. If children remain at their desks during the story, every item of school work should be cleared away before the story is told. Pencils, crayons, paper, books and scissors should be left behind if the group moves to chairs or mats for the occasion. As a wise teacher once said before starting a story, "Leave everything behind except your imaginations." Environmental distractions should be avoided. If a jet plane passes over a school at a regular time each day, that period should not be used for storytelling. Eye catchers should be eliminated from the presentation. For example, a story should not be told in front of a bulletin board with brightly colored posters. If a chalkboard is behind the storyteller, it should be erased before beginning the story. Another distraction might well be clothing or accessories worn by the storyteller. Excessive makeup, inappropriate apparel, flashy jewelry or dangling earrings are capable of shifting a child's attention away from the story and to the storyteller. The narrator should seat the audience in front of her, using short, crescent-shaped rows with staggered chair arrangement. Sitting in a circle poses the problem of placing the teacher in a position where she cannot be readily seen by children on either side. Children with behavior problems should be seated near the teacher. The magic of the story may be enhanced by creating a "story corner" in the classroom. Formal seating arrangements would be left behind as the group assembles. As long as behavior is appropriate, friends may sit with friends during the journey to make-believe land. The "story corner" needs only chairs and a table or a shelf for the children's favorite books. This rather barren environment provides the best atmosphere for concentration on the storyteller's message.

Time of Day for Storytelling

A good story, well told, will have an eager audience at any hour of the school day. Some children have requested that their day begin with a story. Teachers have found the following times advantageous: (1) just prior to, or immediately following recess; (2) just prior to or immediately following lunch; and (3) just prior to the end of the school day. Stories presented immediately before recess, lunch, or the close of the school day provide relief from fatigue. Stories told just after recess or lunch provide a means of bringing children to attention quickly and these stories also facilitate classroom control. The foregoing suggestions do not relate to stories employed for instructional purposes. Of necessity, the latter would be told during the regular period of subject matter instruction.

Audience Adaptation During the Story

Earlier in this book, the importance of choosing an appropriate story for a given age group was stressed. During storytelling, audience adaptation continues and it may be defined as the storyteller's adjustment to responses of the audience. It includes a continuing evaluation of whether an audience can hear what is being said, whether it can identify itself with what is taking place. Because a teacher usually knows her class members well and because she practices adaptive techniques in her teaching of subject matter, only two suggestions for increasing rapport during storytelling will be made: (1) Danger signals in the form of unrest and mischief may indicate that a story is not "getting through" to a pupil. Sometimes a distracted child can be "recaptured" by saying, "And Johnny, at that moment a wonderful thing happened!" This approach personalizes the story for Johnny, flatters him and regains his attention. The narrator is able to pick up the thread of the story with the minimal amount of correction. (2) Storytellers are urged to use rhetorical questions as attention getters provided they do so wisely. If, in a story, Mary is established as one who assists her mother with house cleaning and baking, the storyteller may inquire, "Mary was a helpful girl, wasn't she?" with little danger of irresponsible or negative chorus answers. However, general questions can lead to disaster. Difficulty awaits the teacher who asks, "Now, what do you suppose Tom received on his birthday?" The likely avalanche of divergent responses would consume the balance of the period and destroy the value of the story.

If more than one story is told during a session, stories should be adapted to the prevailing mood of the children as closely as possible. An excellent example of this is found in youth camps where storytelling takes place around a campfire. When the fire is high, lively, humorous stories are in order; when the flames sink low, when the group quiets, when noises from the forest occasionally penetrate the campfire ring . . . then bring on a mystery story!

Building Mood

In earlier pages it has been recommended that beginning storytellers will find their storytelling debut easier if they select a story that they enjoy and one that deals with a subject they understand. Following its selection, the story should be reread for thorough comprehension. Knowing the story implies more than simply scanning the material. It indicates that the criteria for choosing stories has been applied. Every character and every scene is visualized clearly. The more effectively mood is built when preparing a story, the easier it will be to recapture the proper feelings when telling the story. Mood can be developed in the following ways:

1. An understanding of the trials and joys in an author's life may strengthen one's storytelling ability. Knowing the circumstances that prompted an author to write a selection frequently results in a more sympathetic identification by the teller. Edgar Allan Poe's various afflictions haunt his writings. Milton wrote authoritatively on blindness because he had been blind. Robert Frost knew the sound of whining wood saws and the appearance of birches "ridden down" by a young boy because he had lived on a farm and knew the life intimately. In a mysterious and exciting way, the building of atmosphere and mood begins with the author.

2. Recalling personal experiences that demanded or elicited the same mood as those evidenced in the story will help speed the storyteller into a

proper frame of mind. If the mood is light and fanciful, it will help to think of a happy time such as a party, a humorous situation, or the moment when a cherished gift caused delight. Transfer of that mood to the reading of a story will enchance its presentation.

3. Understanding the setting is mandatory. An appreciation of Switzerland's topography and her customs will help one make Heidi's experiences come alive. If one plans to tell a sea story, it might prove helpful to visit the docks and the seashore to "absorb" atmosphere.

4. Identification with situations and characters in a story may be hastened by acting out as much of the tale as possible. This may be done in the privacy of one's study. The storyteller might simulate digging for pirate gold until the shovel strikes a metallic object or perhaps "dancing" with a prince will turn "Cinderella" into a more believable character.

5. All meanings must be clear. Mood is dependent upon understanding every paragraph, every sentence and every word. Only then may the author's words be paraphrased with accuracy.

6. Suspense has been mentioned as an indispensable ingredient in almost every worthwhile story. Nothing creates more immediate suspense than a calculated pause by a storyteller. Pauses should be observed during rehearsals in precisely the same manner that they will be employed when children sit expectantly before their teacher. In the familiar story, *Ferdinand,* the principal character has a marvelous entrance into the bullring. The crowd is in a state of frenzy, the trumpets blare and the matadors march. Then an expectant hush falls over the stadium as Ferdinand is released. Here the teacher may pause as the children wonder, "What is Ferdinand going to do?" "Will he get hurt?" Ferdinand charges into the ring. The picadores and the matador eye him warily . . . At this point the tension and suspense will be heightened by another pause. The subsequent action by Ferdinand becomes all the more ludicrous because of the intense build-up which had been dramatized and sharpened by pauses. From the foregoing, it is evident that a pause before an idea or an action builds suspense. What is the effect of a pause after an idea or action has been expressed? Pausing after an idea strengthens the effect of the thought and enables listeners to adjust to approaching dramatic events. For example, one may say, "A manned space craft has just landed on Mars." A pause at this point will magnify the importance of this pronouncement. Listeners may be prone to ruminate, "What have they found?" "Is there any indication of life?" "Can the ship return?" The pause has dignified the idea and captivated the attention of the audience. Use of a dramatic pause before and after ideas, when done artfully, lends enchantment to storytelling. A storyteller must remember that a pause may seem like an eternity when relating a tale but to children hearing the story, the period is but a twinkling. Practice will reveal the importance of this technique.

A prepared storyteller.

Conflict Situation Development

Key Situations

Following the preparation of the introduction, a storyteller should reread the story to seek out the ideas that belong together. When the reader begins to see a relationship of thought groups, the story's *key situations* become evident. Key situations are actually minor climaxes which lead to the high point or the main climax of a poem or story. Each key situation has a purpose. It may build character, intensify tragedy, provide relief from tension, or speed the tempo toward the climax. Following are the key situations in Russell Herman Conwell's "Acres of Diamonds":

    a. A Buddhist priest visits Al Hafed, the wealthy one, and describes a diamond.
    b. Al Hafed is determined to find diamonds.
    c. Al Hafed disposes of property and family.
    d. Al Hafed searches for the precious stones.
    e. Al Hafed, in poverty, commits suicide. (key situation which is also the climax)
    f. New owner finds diamonds on the farm which Al Hafed had sold him. (anti-climax and conclusion)

After it has been determined where a climax occurs, a teacher should keep this uppermost in mind as she practices the story aloud. She should subordinate key situations to it but continue to build tension and suspense until her preparation reaches the point where listeners are startled by the high point in a story. In "Acres of Diamonds," an audience would know that Al Hafed's fortune is on the downgrade but the story keeps alive the possibility that the once-rich Al Hafed might stumble upon wealth. This hope is dashed at the high and terrible moment when the luckless one hurls himself into the sea and ends his quest. The body of the story develops the conflict situation established in the introduction. Key situations carry the listeners with mounting interest to the climax which signals the conclusion of the tale.

The climax loses its impact if children can "see" the end of the story. Robert Louis Stevenson observed, "The one rule is to be infinitely variable—to interest, to disappoint, to surprise, yet still to gratify." Hans Christian Andersen was faithful to this position in his suspenseful climax to "The Ugly Duckling". Children being told this story would know the duckling only as a persecuted, maligned little bird which had fled its barnyard persecutors only to find sanctuary with a kindly old man and woman who nursed it back to health in the winter. With the coming of spring it was attracted to a flock of swans—

> And he flew toward the beautiful swans. As soon as they saw him they ran to meet him with outstretched wings. "Kill me," he said. But as he bent his head he saw reflected in the water, not a dark, gray bird ugly to see, but a beautiful swan.

Andersen had carefully concealed this rather shocking and delightful conclusion. The mood of children hearing this tale turns from pity to joy as they learn of the magnificent transformation.

Cue Cards

Many storytellers find a cue card beneficial. It is a skeleton outline of a story which includes the title, author, source, the time required for telling, the names of the separate characters, the scenes to indicate change in time and/or place and a brief synopsis of the plot. The use of cue cards is usually preferred to the painstaking memorization of stories that involves a prodigious amount of time. For most individuals, memorization stands in the way of a spontaneous, uninhibited presentation. It limits immediate adaptation to an audience which is one of the primary virtues of storytelling. Furthermore, the verbatim method of preparation also increases the possibility of speech fright in a storyteller. If the teacher concentrates on the specific language of an author, a momentary lapse of memory becomes infinitely more upsetting than if the plot and characters had been the primary items of study. Cue cards will encourage teachers to tell stories they normally would be inclined to read to their classes. They should be used inconspicuously so as not to detract from the story. Storytellers are urged to develop card files of useful stories which may be quickly reviewed for telling. 4" x 6" cards are a functional size for this purpose. Following are typical examples of cue cards:

Title: "Talk" (African folk tale)
Author: Harold Courlander and George Herzog

Source: *The Bookshelf for Boys and Girls,* The University Society, New York, 1958, IV, p. 85.
Time: Five Minutes
Characters: The farmer, the fisherman, the weaver, a man bathing, the Chief.
Scenes: Farm, road, river, house of the Chief.

Synopsis: Once, in the country of Guinea, a farmer went out into his garden to dig up some yams to take to market. One of the yams said, "Leave me alone." The farmer looked around to see who had spoken, and his dog said, "The yam said to leave him alone." The farmer became angry and cut a branch from a palm tree to whip the dog. The palm said, "Put that branch down." The farmer was about to throw it away when the branch said, "Put me down gently." He put the branch on a stone, and the stone said, "Take that thing off me." This was enough—the frightened farmer started running for his village. He met a fisherman carrying a fish trap. He told his story, and the fisherman was unmoved until his fish trap said, "Well, did he do it?" Then they ran together toward the village. They met a weaver carrying a bundle of cloth. They told him their story. The weaver couldn't understand their fright until his cloth said, "You'd be frightened too!" All three men ran until they met a bather in the river and told their story. The bather couldn't understand why they were running until the river said, "You'd run too!" They all ran to the house of the Chief, who brought his stool out, sat down, and listened to their story. When they were through he scolded them and sent them back to work. He said to himself, "Nonsense like that upsets the village." "Fantastic, isn't it? his stool said. "Imagine a talking yam."

Title: "The Baker's Neighbor" (Peruvian folk tale)
Author: Translated by Frank Henuis
Source: *The Bookshelf for Boys and Girls,* The University Society, New York, 1958, IV, p. 218.
Time: Five or six minutes.
Characters: A baker, his neighbor, a judge.
Scenes: A bakery, a street, a courtroom.

Synopsis: Once in Lima, Peru, there lived a very industrious baker who loved money. His neighbor was the opposite, and each morning loved to smell the freshly baked bread. The greedy baker thought he should pay for this daily aroma and asked him to do so. The man laughed and before long the whole town was laughing. The baker took the case to court. The judge ordered both men to appear and told the neighbor to bring a bag filled with 100 gold coins. It appeared the judge was going to make him pay. In court, the baker told his story and the neighbor admitted that he did enjoy the aroma. The judge took the money and handed it to the baker, asking him to count the money to be sure it was all there. Then the judge arose and announced his decision: "I hereby declare that this case is now settled, baker. Your neighbor has smelled your pastry, and you have seen and touched his gold. The case is dismissed."

Cutting

Storytellers find material, occasionally, that lacks appropriate construction, contains irrelevant ideas, or is too lengthy for the amount of time allotted for the story period. Under these circumstances, it is permissible to eliminate portions of a story provided the *intent of the author is not changed.* In "The Little Red Hen," for example, the goose or the duck could be eliminated. The time spent describing the trip to the mill and details of the miller's conversation could be condensed without changing the moral of the story. Similarly, if the teacher were taking a portion of Irving's "Legend of Sleepy Hollow" for telling, she might eliminate or compress many of the author's lengthy, involved descriptions of the landscape without altering the mood of the story or its plot. Facility in cutting stories comes with practice. Storytellers are urged to perfect this aspect of story preparation because it will admit literature into the story hour which otherwise might go untold.

Delivery

Conversational Mode and Volume

The spoken word may indicate the level of one's education, the degree of friendliness and sincerity, and it may also suggest the amount of time and effort expended in preparation. When a story is practiced aloud the first time, a hesitant, stilted presentation is to be expected. The speaker gropes for words and struggles to remember the sequence. However, with practice, clumsy phrasing and unnecessary repetitions disappear and fluency is achieved. Through love of children and enjoyment of materials chosen for telling, teachers should strive for the cultivation of a warm, friendly, confidential tone. The latter indicates to every child in the class, "This is just for us." Storytellers occasionally misinterpret the meaning of the confidential tone and as a result, tell tales in a semi-whisper. A half-heard story is a strain for youngsters, as well as adults. It is comparable to a television set with its volume turned just below the level for easy listening. If a story is to be fully enjoyed, it must be easily heard.

Correct Speech

In addition to using proper volume, storytellers should strive for distinct, correct speech. A teacher's articulation and pronunciation is more likely to be imitated by her pupils than any characteristic of her speaking. A model of good speech is not one who carefully and accurately enunciates and isolates every syllable of a word. Excessive precision has no place in any classroom because it does not constitute standard speech. On the other hand, the teacher who constantly says, "an" for *"and,"* "git" for *"get,"* "jist" for *"just,"* "gonna" for *"going to,"* "didja" for *"did you,"* and who connects her sentences with "an uh" or vocalizes every pause with "uh" constitutes a threat to the healthy speech development of elementary grade children. Additionally, a storyteller's grammar must be correct. Words used and the manner in which they are applied are measures of a speaker. Saying, "I done," "They was," or pronouncing "modern" "modren" has a detrimental effect. Applied to storytelling, an awareness of these practices places a teacher on guard against articulatory omission, substitutions and inaccuracies. To promote desirable speech habits does not mean that all dialect, colloquialisms, or "street articulations" should be excised from stories. As long as these traits are identified with story characters they may be retained.

Pleasing Inflection

Storytellers should also strive for a pleasing, expressive, inflectional pattern. Monotony of inflection must be avoided. The latter may be of the "plateau" type which runs along without appreciable inflectional change or it may be the "bishop's tone" type which repeats the same inflectional pattern over and over again. Monotony of either kind will destroy a presentation of the finest story ever written. Unless a person is habitually monotonous both in everyday conversation as well as in a storytelling situation, monotony may be traced to an emotional indifference to what is being said. Basic to the development of variety in storytelling is an appreciation of the importance of full identification with material being presented. Suggestions made earlier for mood development will assist to combat monotony. A key to variety in speaking is found in the statement, "Impression precedes and determines expression." A reader's impression from the idea on the printed page comes first. This is followed by the reader's mental reaction expressed inflectionally which influences children when a story is told. An expressive voice puts life into a story or poem.

Rate

Finally, storytellers should monitor their rate of speaking to be certain that it is appropriate to content. Events within a story are the prime determinants of the speed of delivery. The mood and action of a tale will stimulate a teacher who is sympathetically identified with her material to respond appropriately. A story which depends upon pathos for much of its effectiveness will be delivered more

Gesture.

slowly than a story which is fundamentally comic in theme. Individuals usually speak more slowly when they are sad than when they are happy . . . .because something has stimulated them to *feel* that way. "Cinderella," "The Fir Tree" and "Sleeping Beauty" are three stories that will be characterized by periods of rather slow delivery. In contrast to these, comic tales such as "The Tale of Peter Rabbit," "Pelle's New Suit" and "The Husband Who Was To Mind The House," depend for their effectiveness upon a buoyant interpretation. The storyteller's reaction to events in the story result in a spritely rate of presentation.

Gesture:

In order to have rehearsal periods prepare storytellers as fully as possible, it is recommended that final practice be conducted before a full-length mirror. The latter will provide a reasonable amount of distraction which is comparable to that caused by an audience and it will also let a speaker see herself as children will. "How much should I gesture?" is a question commonly asked by beginning storytellers. This question may be answered in part by explaining the relationship of the storyteller to characters in stories. A raconteur should *interpret* a tale. She does not have to act the role of the several characters. Her primary role is to convey an author's intended impressions in such a manner that her audience always sees the story . . .not the storyteller's performance. More simply stated, she will not simulate tree climbing, riding a witch's broomstick, talk like a squeaky mouse, or drop to her knees in prayer if story characters do these things. Any overt action which transfers attention from a story's content to a storyteller is to be avoided. Speaking before a mirror will also assist to eliminate any nervous, non-meaningful mannerisms such as fingering a necklace, earpulling, needlessly adjusting clothing, and the tiresome, one-arm pump handle gesture. All stories should have gestures but the latter should be subtle. When preparing a story, a teacher may not want to write such instructions as "Smile here," "Raise voice," or "Clench right fist," in the margin as guides to storytelling. Such reactions must arise with spontaneity and sincerity from the stimuli found in the story. Included would be appropriate facial reactions, perhaps a slight shrug of the shoulders to indicate indifference, or a circular motion of an upraised hand to describe a staircase in a mystery story. If gestures are so much a part of the story that an audience is unaware of them, then a storyteller has made use of them effectively and desirably.

Use of a tape recorder during rehearsal periods usually proves advantageous inasmuch as it gives a raconteur some idea of the aural impression she is going to make on her audience. Exercises found in the appendix may also prove helpful when used with a tape recorder.

Conclusion

Like the introduction, the conclusion should be characterized by brevity. At this point, the climax has been reached, audience interest has peaked and begun to wane and prolongation only serves to lessen the impact of the story. Note how quickly the following stories have been concluded after their climax has been reached: "How the Coyote Danced with the Blackbirds" is a Zuni legend which ends immediately after the coyote's failure to fly, with the statement, "Therefore, you will often meet coyotes to this day who have little black fringes along the rear of their forelegs, and the tips of their tails are often black. Thus it was in the days of the ancients." In "Gudbrand on the Hillside" the husband commits the grossest of errors only to be praised by his wife. The folktale concludes immediately thereafter with Gudbrand opening his door and saying to his neighbor who had been a silent witness to the scene, "Have I won the hundred dollars now?" The neighbor was obliged to confess that he had. The apex of interest in each of the foregoing stories had been reached, the impact had been made on the listeners, and prolongation with moralizing by a storyteller would only lead to a laboring of the obvious.

READING THE STORY

Some stories depend so completely on their language for their effectiveness that they should be read, not told to children. Unless a teacher is willing to devote many hours to perfecting dialects, she will probably do better to read such stories as the Irish Fairy Tale, "King O'Toole and His Goose," and Harris' "Adventures with Uncle Remus." There are also stories by authors with inimitable styles such as Kipling and Scott. Tales by these authors sometimes lose their appeal when they are told instead of read. Lastly, there is a vast supply of story poems which can serve many different purposes in a classroom. Unless a teacher has time to memorize, she will do well to read "I Hear America Singing" to illustrate the American heritage; "King Robert of Sicily" to supply an example of humility; or "The Walrus and the Carpenter" to share just for fun.

Many of the suggestions for preparing and presenting stories apply to reading stories as well as telling them. However, story readers are faced with problems that are unique to this activity. The following additional suggestions should prove helpful:

1. A teacher must encourage the concept of sharing mentioned earlier. The book must not be a barrier between a reader and her listeners thereby causing a teacher to read *to* her children and not *with* them. It is helpful to pretend that the book is held aloft before the children by some magical means, with words pouring mysteriously from it. Where would the teacher be? She would be seated with her children, enjoying the story. The concept of sharing the material permits a teacher to laugh or be sad with the children when a story prompts these reactions. Although a reader must sit or stand before a class and make a printed page come alive by her re-creation of characters and vitalization of scenes, mentally she is in the audience enjoying the story.

2. The manner in which a book is held during oral reading may have considerable influence on the interest and attention of those listening.

A book should not be held so high that it obscures all or part of the face, neither should it be held so low that the reader's chin rests on her chest. A teacher should hold her book at such an angle that eye contact is made easily without excessive up-and-down head movement.

One of the obvious disadvantages of story-reading is a loss of some of the eye contact enjoyed by storytellers. This can be compensated in part if a systematic approach is used to establish visual contact with listeners. Looking from book to audience should not be a furtive, slipshod, catch-as-catch-can procedure but rather a well-formulated technique. A reader should develop the habit of looking up from a page upon completion of a thought. This usually occurs at a semicolon or a period. This procedure is rule-of-thumb and must be tempered with common sense. Some story poems, for example, are composed of many short, four-or-five word sentences. When presenting material of this sort, it would be acceptable to look up at the end of every other sentence. Frequent bobbing of the head to establish eye contact is distracting. Eye contact with an audience should be made approximately four or five words from the end of a sentence. This procedure will eliminate looking up, in random fashion within a line. Looking up indiscriminately may be likened to writing commas in lines where they do not belong. *Underlining* in the following sentence is an example of the point at which a reader's attention might leave the printed page and communicate directly with her audience.

The old man gathered his meager possessions, closed the cupboard, walked from the cabin, and *left his boyhood home forever.*

When a reader looks up from a book her glance should be meaningful . . . .she must want to communicate directly. It should grow out of her desire to share an idea upon its completion. Eye contact should not be a fleeting, furtive action from the book, to the audience in general, and then back to the book. Instead, as a reader looks up, ready to utter the final words of a sentence, she should pick *one* member of the group and complete the thought to him. A different child, seated in another part of the room will be singled out to receive eye contact each time the latter is effected. This procedure personalizes the presentation and makes children feel as if they were being read to individually. Eye contact of this type also helps to "steady" restless or mischievous children. Readers also find that looking up at the end of a sentence systematically, rather than looking up randomly, facilitates finding one's place easily upon glancing back to the book. Additionally, eye contact at the end of a sentence, when accompanied by a pause, permits a reader to collect herself for presentation of the idea contained in the next sentence. Finally, if a reader is prone to have stage fright, this systematic method of eye contact will prove reassuring. Indecision of any kind in a speaking situation is conducive to fright and confusion. Knowing when contact is to be made and practicing this techinque until it is accomplished automatically will assist a teacher to develop poise and confidence.

Rhythm is a characteristic of all literature, both prose and verse. In prose, the pattern of movement results partly from the idea and partly, but to a lesser degree, from the arrangement of words. In verse, the meter determines rhythm and the idea provides the basis for variety. One of the besetting fears of some readers is that their presentations will be "sing-song." When reading to kindergarten and primary grade children, a reader should not worry if rhythm is prominent and strong. Rhythm is probably the first characteristic of verse that attracts children. They like its swing. Their appreciation of rhythm would probably continue if, when they begin to read, they were not criticized for being "sing-song." When reading the following Mother Goose rhyme, the beat should predominate.

> Ride a cockhorse to Banbury Cross
> To see an old lady upon a white horse;
> Rings on her fingers and bells on her toes,
> She shall have music wherever she goes.

Children will sit and sway in rhythm if material such as this is presented enthusiastically. A life-long love for literature may develop if youngsters are favorably impressed with poetry and prose during the Age of Repetition.

Listeners must not lose their appreciation of rhythm's value, but they must make it secondary to content. In Browning's "How They Brought the Good News from Ghent to Aix" the rhythm, figuratively speaking, puts a listener into the saddle:

> I sprang to the stirrup, and Joris, and He;
> I galloped, Dirck galloped, we galloped all three;
> "Good speed!" cried the watch, as the gatebolts undrew;
>
> "Speed!" echoed the wall to us galloping through;
> Behind shut the postern, the lights sank to rest,
> And into the midnight we galloped abreast.

Additionally, an oral reader must give consideration not only to the overall fundamental rhythm of a story-verse, but she must also recognize the value of specific words that contribute vitally to the movement. The duration of given vowel sounds provides the key to action. Observe the effect of prolonging and shortening vowels in the following underlined examples:

> The avalanche smashed and ground down the mountain.
> His fist splattered the outlaw's nose.
> Fluffy, white clouds dotted the azure sky.

Prolongation of vowels would assist action in the first two sentences. Rhythm, however, would be impaired in the third sentence if vowel sounds were lengthened. "Fluffy" sounds fluffier if the vowel is soft and short. Adept word handling enhances the imaginative quality of poetry and makes excursions into the realm of literature more enjoyable for children.

AFTER THE STORY

The type of story and the purpose for which it is told will determine the action a storyteller should take when the tale has concluded. Children should have a brief period at the close of a story to reflect upon it. This will reinforce the story's message. In general, a story with a serious theme should be followed by a longer pause than one with a whimsical mood. The length of reflection will depend upon the level of control enjoyed by the teacher. In some situations, a moment of silence would be the signal for some children to create disorder. Following a period of reflection, a teacher may ask if there are any questions or observations class members might want to make. Discussing a story's implications or having children share personal experiences similar to those in a story provide an excellent means of developing communicative facility.

Having children tell back a story is an excellent means of reinforcing the tale. This may be done by outright recall by various members of the group or the teacher may show pictures from a well-illustrated book and let the pictures remind the children of the story's sequence. Another feedback technique is to give flannel board objects appropriate to a story to members of the group. As the story is retold, the children will apply their objects to the flannel board at the proper moment.

Art work may also follow storytelling. Children may draw, color and cut out silhouette pictures depicting some aspect of the story. These may be assembled into a composite scene from the tale or they may be retained by the children for their own pleasure. The latter course of action is probably preferable if there is danger that less gifted children will come to dislike storytelling because their subsequent artistic efforts to draw or paint do not compare to work done by more talented classmates.

Story acting is another excellent follow-up activity. Details on this form of educational endeavor will be found in Chapter 5.

SUMMARY

This chapter has recommended procedure for the preparation and presentation of stories. The section devoted to story preparation has stressed the importance of maintaining a lively audience interest by presenting a short introduction, a body characterized by action and suspense that moves directly toward a climax and a quick conclusion that follows immediately upon the climax. Story preparation will be facilitated by studying the author's life, associating personal experiences with situations in a story, studying a story's setting, "acting" out its scenes and mastering the meaning of every word, sentence and paragraph. Storytellers are urged to seek out a story's key situations and then prepare cue cards that will facilitate delivery. Use of a tape recorder will assist a teacher to develop appropriate volume, articulation, pronunciation and rate of delivery. This section reminds the raconteur that the story is the primary consideration and the teller is secondary. Storytellers will suggest action, interpret the conversation of various characters, but will not literally act out the parts.

The actual telling of a story must be preceded by physical preparation that insures comfort for children and cuts distractions to a minimum. The teacher must be easily seen and heard during her presentation and she must be capable of adapting to her group as her story unfolds. Stories may be read as well as told.

Some materials lend themselves to the former mode of delivery because of their vocabulary or form. Read stories are enchanced when good eye contact is demonstrated by the reader, when rhythm is appropriate to the age level of a group and when a reader is fully identified with an author's work.

Follow-up activity after a story may take the form of tell back, art work of various types and story acting.

The following model provides a succinct summary of the foregoing pages. It illustrates the intimate, overlapping nature of each aspect of story telling. For example, preparation literally begins during the process of selection of a story; the latter is "matched" to a certain group of listeners, some portions may be cut and others amplified. No sharply defined line may be drawn between selection and preparation of a story. Likewise, preparation involves careful synthesis of the introduction, body and conclusion. Follow-up efforts of listeners reveal their reactions to a story and facilitate its evaluation by both the raconteur and the listeners.

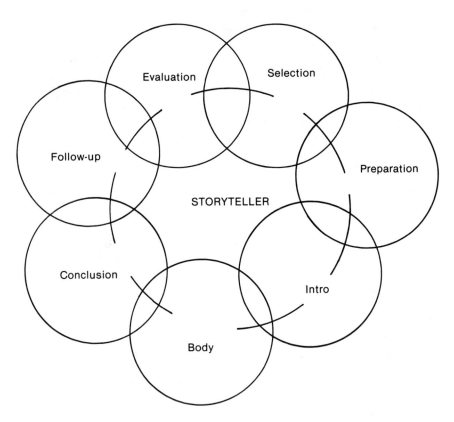

5 Creative Drama and Story Dramatization

DEFINITIONS

Effective storytelling leads directly to story dramatization. When children identify with the various characters in the story, it is natural for them to want to imitate those characters. Story dramatization is the re-creation of part or all of a story with the emphasis on spontaneity, cognition, action, identification, dialogue and sequence of events. Greater appreciation of the literature may then occur. According to research with a variety of students from different grades and socioeconomic backgrounds, through expression of feelings and thoughts in story dramatization and creative drama, self concept is improved.[1] This is an important educational value to be achieved in the schools. If story dramatization is the process to achieve that end, then more teachers should become familiar with basic principles of such expression. Winifred Ward, the founder of creative drama as a discipline, argues that its greatest value is in speech training.[2] This makes it an invaluable tool in the field of speech communication, storytelling, and language arts.

Story dramatization is considered an integral part of creative drama. Many authorities in this discipline believe that there should be a developmental progression of activities leading to story dramatization and improvisation. Creative drama includes dramatic play, roleplaying, pantomime, storytelling, puppetry, choral speaking, story dramatization and story improvisation.

Creative drama like storytelling is a process of communication. It is ongoing, flexible, fluid and an unfinished art form. It is more of a process than a finished product. All of the previous experience and data related to storytelling and drama that children have encountered, they bring to story dramatization. Even after the technical end of the session, the skills gained, the influence on personality and the socialization continue to have an impact. Such an art provides an outlet that may have hidden rewards unexpected by the teacher. The process of humanization and sensitization is a slow and difficult one at times. Value orientation takes time and experience to develop. Action and a variety of creative and imaginative practices in the classroom motivate students to discover new frontiers of learning and values.

Moreover, creative drama of which story dramatization is central, is a process of doing. Billy Tyas in *Child Drama in Action* suggests the term "draosophics," from the Greek words "drao" meaning I do, and "sophiskos" meaning wisdom.[3] In other words, learning by doing may be reflected in an official Greek term. Professor Patricia Grasty goes one step further. She argues that teachers should be trained to use the technique of draosophics because it is such a successful method of teaching.[4] This is because children are directly involved and active. Story dramatization provides a unique experience for the teacher to learn about the individual children in her class, and their interaction in group communication. It also provides a tool which correlates various subject areas to language arts.

Within creative drama, as an educative form of drama, the players are supreme. Their feelings and thoughts in terms of re-creation of events are the focus of attention. Dorothy Heathcote, a well known English authority in creative drama, emphasizes that educational drama is both creative and coping work.[5] Creative drama, especially story dramatization, is both imaginative and cognitive in terms of developing skills to cope with a changing environment, new perspectives and problem solving skills. All of the forms of creative drama lend support to acquisition of skills in story dramatization techniques. In this chapter some emphasis will be placed in every category of creative drama with the major focus

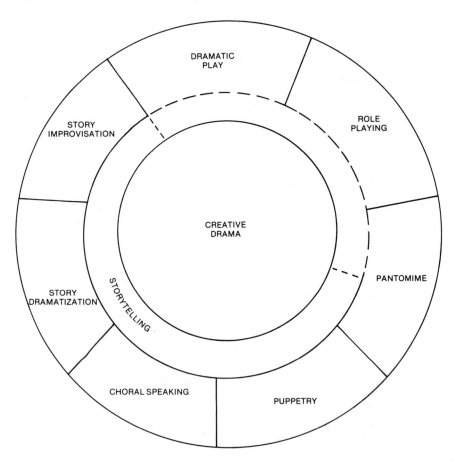

on story dramatization. There will also be a discussion for the teacher who wishes to proceed directly from storytelling to story dramatization through story acting. However, the Child, as Storyteller, is covered in Chapter 6 and puppetry is included under Visual Aids in Chapter 8.

Storytelling is related to almost all forms of creative drama. In dramatic play, role playing and pantomime, storytelling or similar imagery is a fragmentary part of the activity. Each may contain elements of narrative, characterization, gesture and a message. Indeed these three forms of creative drama may include all elements of storytelling on occasion including structure, audience and evaluation. However, the other forms of creative drama have a story as the foundation of the art. Pantomime may be physically acting out a story while it is being read as in Dance-a-story records. Puppetry, choral reading, story dramatization and improvisation clearly involve a narrative with structure and an evaluation after they have taken place. In effect, storytelling is pivotal to the function and success of creative drama in its many forms.

Before various types of creative drama are discussed, elements common to all forms will be considered. These include value, characteristics of an appropriate story selection for dramatization, casting, listening and evaluation.

Values

The values of this activity are many and varied. Storyacting develops the art of communication and as mentioned previously, self concept of the child is improved through story dramatization and creative drama. Children may say what comes naturally in the re-creation of a tale, or utilize a simple script. Either approach increases the ability of children to express themselves. This stimulates their imaginations, emotions and cognitive development. The feelings of success and adequacy that results from this activity are conducive to self confidence.

Through creative drama, children soon discover that in order to be appreciated, they must be understood verbally and nonverbally. Speech patterns may improve as performers are motivated to correct defects of pronunciation and articulation.

In addition, other worthwhile goals which may be achieved are the ability to think on their feet and to easily express themselves. These improve children's adaptation to their environment now and in the future. A certain amount of problem solving is taking place and children are at the center of their own solutions. Story dramatization gives opportunity for quick thinking in contrived and real situations.

Story dramatization permits children to choose the scene they wish to play, the length of time they wish to perform, the number of characters required and the number and kind of "props" to be used. They may evaluate their own effort if they choose and seek to improve it. This activity is a good example of democracy in action. It is a form of self-government in the realm of creative activity.

Social adjustment and unity may be a valuable by-product of creative drama as it provides an opportunity for children to work together in cooperation whatever their socioeconomic background or sex differences. Creative drama provides an invaluable opportunity to grow in group cooperation, consideration and understanding. In terms of personal adjustment, children may experience a healthy emotional and physical release and at the same time receive the amount of attention they need.

Finally, the value of creative drama as pure fun must not be overlooked. The routine that is so characteristic of classrooms, Sunday School classes, youth meetings and playgrounds can be enlivened by this activity.

Characteristics of a Story for Dramatization

Stories for acting must be popular with the group and easily understood by them. There should be an abundance of conversation of an uncomplicated nature. For example, stories for acting on the pre-school level should contain such simple conversational sequence as ''Not I,'' said the duck and ''Not I,'' said the pig. The element of repetition is very acceptable for young children. Eastman's *Are You My Mother?* is a good example of a simple story with many characters, simple dialogue, sufficient action, and emotional appeal for the very young. Children who are old enough to read, may be assisted by having a brief sequence of events listed on the chalkboard. This list may be elicited through appropriate questioning by the teacher. Therefore the discovery of information is student-oriented. Interrogation is discussed at length later in the chapter. In order for a story to be thoroughly understood by the children who participate, the story should be easily understood. Relatively few incidents or a repetitious plot is helpful.

The structure of the story for dramatization should be clear. The introduction, body and conclusion should be distinguishable for both the teacher and student. By reproducing an art form with an easily identifiable structure the student may understand the importance of form itself and reinforce learning on the nature of art.

The story must have an abundance of action. The latter, however, must be feasible for dramatizing. A Paul Bunyan tale, though desirable for telling, would fall short as an acted story because the children could not approach the exaggerated nature of the action demanded. Likewise, a tale from the Arabian Nights that required a flying carpet may be difficult unless the children agree that a rug on the floor will be the imaginary flying carpet. A dramatized story should be as effective or more effective for the child when it is acted than when it is told. If certain aspects of the tale make it impossible to enact satisfactorily, the participants will feel disappointed.

Stories for acting should have numerous characters. This permits greater group participation and enables more children to feel the thrill of adequacy that comes from this activity. The teacher should avoid a story such as Dinah Mulock's ''The Little Lame Prince'' in which one child is alone most of the time. In contrast, ''The Bremen Town Musicians,'' ''The Little Rabbit That Wanted Wings'' and ''The Boy Who Cried Wolf'' permit many children to join in the fun. A story may be dramatized several times with different casts in order to use the entire class.

Part of the class may be sufficiently involved by organizing or creating the props or scenery for the dramatization. The props, scenery design, or costumes should be imaginary or managed by the class members as part of their own re-creation of the story. The children interested in these positions should be able to do the job with a sense of contribution to the whole. In other words, children may serve in many different ways in order to make the play a reality. Elaborate props should be avoided however.

Stories for acting should also have appropriate emotional appeal and contain worthwhile ideas. The former permits more ready identification with the plot and its characters. The emotional response to an exciting climax may be very satisfying to youngsters. A suitable story will exemplify desirable social conduct and confine itself to a single plot. A compounded plot, replete with digressions, may frustrate and confuse even the most attentive and conscientious child actors. The story should also qualify as good literature as described in Chapter 3, Selection of Stories.

To sum up, essentials for good story dramatization include a well liked and easily understood piece of literature, an easily identifiable structure, an abundance of action, numerous characters, simple student-oriented props, emotional appeal and worthwhile ideas. These characteristics are appropriate for all stories used in creative drama except that numerous characters are unnecessary in dramatic play, role playing and puppetry. If a story possesses all of the above characteristics, it will most likely be successful as story dramatization. Even if all the characteristics exemplify a story, some story adaptation will probably be necessary. Story adaptation is discussed in Chapter 4.

Casting the Story

Ideally, a child who needs play-acting experience would volunteer for the part that would benefit him the most. When introducing story acting to a class, expediency may demand that the most dramatically-capable child, not necessarily the most needful, be placed in key roles until the group orients itself to the process of dramatic play. Since children often clamor to reenact the same story several times, the less gifted child may assume a key position in subsequent performances. This order of selection will give a less talented or introverted youngster the benefit of learning appropriate action by watching others perform. Although imitation is not creative, it is preferred in the case of a slower child because it helps to prevent inappropriate actions which might further stigmatize him before his group. Teachers should be alert for various signals which indicate a child is "volunteering." A shy student, by a nod, a half-smile, or other signs, may be saying, "I am too afraid to raise my hand, but I would like to be in the story." Bashful children might be cast as trees, rocks, signposts, flowers, or birds, until a series of successful experiences emboldens them to try a "talking" role. A word of advice on type casting should be considered. Sometimes it has strong disadvantages. A teacher may be encouraging a shy child to remain shy and a bold child to maintain his boldness. Variety and use of children in unlikely parts has its rewards in new learning experiences for the participants.

Listening to the Story

Children engaged in story acting have a right to perform without disturbance from non-participating members of the class. Motivating the latter to listen critically during dramatic activity will lessen chances of disruption. Chapter 7, "Listening" will assist the development of listening habits. The following specific suggestions should prove helpful for story acting:

One or more children may be assigned to each participant for the purpose of listing helpful suggestions that can be shared after the story or scene has been acted. All listeners will be expected to observe all actors, but special attention should be given to assigned buddies by non-acting class members.

Another helpful device is to double or triple cast a scene. This intensifies the interest of the observers in the roles they are going to play.

Children are usually happy to listen if they have developed standards of appreciation. The following questions relating to story acting will sharpen their listening ability and evaluation of creative drama.

Speech

"Were voices loud enough?" "Could you hear without effort?"
"Were all words clearly pronounced?" "How did you know?"
"Could you hear clearly when the actor's back was turned?" "How did he make himself heard under these conditions?"
"If you could not hear him, how can we help him?"

Identification with Role

"Did you forget that you knew the boys and girls and feel that they were the characters in the story?" "Why?"
"Did the actors' expressions look the way you think the real characters in the story might have?"
"Did the actor's voices sound as if they meant what they said?"
"Were they sad or happy when the characters were sad or happy?" "How did they show it?"

Plot

"Was the purpose of the scene or story clear to you?" "How?"
"What was the most important point in the scene?"
"Did you like the story better when it was told or acted?" "Why?"
"Were you satisfied with the ending of the story?" "Why?"

Cast Relations

"Did the characters seem to belong together?" "How did they show this?"
"Did the father and mother bear act as parents should toward each other?" "How did you know?"

"Was the baby bear obedient to his parents?" "How did he show it?"
"Do you think Goldilocks was friendly?" "Did she have good manners?"

Other questions should be framed with a compliment and reference question to elicit a positive response. Any negative responses may stop the freedom children have to try on characters. Statements and questions could be:

I liked the way Eric looked sad when he was unhappy. How did he let us know he was sad?

Eric's voice sounded excited when he found the surprise. How did his voice tell us he was surprised?

This group had a good ending to their story. How else could we end the story?

One will try developing positive questions that will elicit only positive responses and find it is much more difficult to develop the positive questions than to ask a negative question. The point of questioning is to develop growth for another day of acting rather than breaking down a particular acting scene.

The audience should be de-emphasized in creative drama productions. The emphasis on vocal loudness and clarity should be related first to the other players and second, to the listeners. Players must speak in such a way that other players can hear in order for the dialogue to flow. Thus, the sharpening of listening and the use of effective communication by the players should emphasize how a particular character would talk and communicate. This is a different aspect than whether an audience can hear.

Good listening habits will be encouraged if children are convinced that their teacher respects their opinions. If they feel that their suggestions have helped to make the group's effort a successful experience, they will listen more attentively in the future. Formulating constructive judgments will assist them to develop a positive attitude toward story acting.

Evaluation

After each presentation it will prove educationally worthwhile to discuss the dramatization done by the cast. This period must be one of encouragement, not discouragement. The following suggestions have proved helpful when evaluating:

Praise should characterize the opening remarks of an evaluation. *Nothing succeeds like success.* Minor roles could be acknowledged by such remarks as, "Good work, Jackie! You rolled yourself into a ball and appeared to be a rock." "Class, did you notice how gracefully the trees waved in the breeze? We could almost feel that soft summer wind." "The father bear certainly became fierce when he discovered that someone had entered his house without permission! That is the way to act, father bear!" Referring to the name of the character rather than the actor's name is preferred when praising or criticizing "talking parts."

Following a period of tempered, deserved praise, most children will profit from tactful, constructive criticism. Cast members will indulge in self-evaluation when their leader asks, "What could the actors do to be heard more easily?" "Did any parts of the story confuse you?" "Why?" "Was the mother bear tender to her little bear?" "What would you say to the little bear to make it stop crying when it found its broken chair?" "Did you get excited when the bears approached the house?" "Why?" "Did the actors seem excited when the climax was reached?" "How did you know?"

Kindergartners and first graders generally can do little more than manufacture enough lines to keep a story moving. Evaluation of the efforts of these little ones should be limited to praise by other class members. The teacher may ask, "Boys and girls, what did this group do well?" or "Which part of this story did you especially like?" These comments could be followed by a few constructive criticisms by the teacher. From the second grade on, dramatization should begin to reflect the emotional reactions of the characters. This ability is concomitant with the group's mental age. Joy, fear, disappointment and the like, should begin to become evident through situations which demand these reactions. The more mature the group, the more searching the constructive criticism may become.

The teacher must be prepared to "cushion" remarks made by class members if suggestions become too pointed. For example, a non-participant may say, "I thought Goldilocks was too quiet when the bears found her. She didn't get scared." The teacher might soften this criticism by saying, "Goldilocks might have acted more frightened but did you notice how quickly she leaped from the bed and ran away? That is how a frightened girl would act." Here the teacher agrees with the critic and yet leaves Goldilocks with a feeling of accomplishment. The evaluation by a group provides an excellent opportunity for creative play which can grow out of the criticism. A child might say, "I don't think Goldilocks acted as if the porridge were too hot when she tried to sip it." The teacher might reply, "Mary will you show us how you think Goldilocks might have acted?" A problem is only directed back to the proposer when the teacher is certain that the child is aggressive enough to try. If a shy child thinks she will be asked to demonstrate the sampling of porridge when she justifiably disagrees with the way it was done, she will not participate in criticism. When a shy child makes the aforementioned comment, the teacher should turn to the class and ask, "Would someone like to taste the hot porridge for us?" She might also turn to the child who played Goldilocks and say, "Goldilocks, would you like to try the porridge again?" The joy of accomplishment leaves a child's heart when derogatory comments go unchallenged by a teacher or when too much constructive criticism, however justified, is heaped upon the participant. A teacher should *never permit too much criticism of a child or a cast.*

Appraisal of the child's development through creative drama should be examined by the adult. The adult may ask these questions in order to determine what progress has been made:

1. Is the student increasing his self confidence individually and in front of listeners?

2. Are the child's speech patterns and use of language improving?
3. Are the child's vocal quality and projection improving?
4. Is the child better able to speak extemporaneously?
5. Is the child demonstrating creativity and use of imagination?
6. Is the child cooperating and sharing ideas and materials with others?
7. Does the child recall sequence of events in a story?
8. Is the child's identification with characters, physically and mentally, more complete?
9. Is the child's problem-solving ability improving?
10. Are the child's psychomotor activities improving?
11. Is the child learning to react with words rather than physical violence?
12. Does the child appear to enjoy participating?
13. Does the child appear to enjoy listening?

DRAMATIC PLAY: GETTING STARTED

Dramatic play is characteristic of childhood. Young children imitate the mannerisms and actions of older children and their parents. They pantomime floor sweeping, book reading, car driving, lawn mowing and other activities that fall within their sphere of experience. The whistle or bell-ringing from ice cream vending trucks brings a "toot-toot" or a "ding-dong" from children on the sidewalk. As children grow older, they seek the company of others in dramatic play. They learn the valuable concept and interaction of sharing. Dramatic play progresses from individual play, to parallel play where children play independently alongside each other, to interaction which involves some sharing—advancing to more cooperation and more sharing later. Peter Slade in *Child Drama* presents a detailed discussion on the importance of dramatic play to all facets of development in the young child.[6]

Dramatic play is a child's natural means of acting out or pretending a role in life with which he or she is familiar. For the most part, the play is unrehearsed, spontaneous, and inspired by experiences in the child's environment on his journey toward a concept of reality. Dramatic play is common from early years until approximately age seven. Actually "let's pretend" is a form of play that continues throughout life. It is an excellent place to begin dramatization experience with almost any age level. A simple form of dramatic play is sufficient involvement for the very young on one hand, and an excellent introduction to further dramatic skills to be learned for any age. Rigidity must give way to freedom of expression in this form of drama. Structure may not be clear or necessary. A definite beginning, middle or end is not necessary. Emphasis is upon growth in the process of make-believe.

Another important concept for adults to remember is that dramatic play is "hard work." In such a statement, the authors hope to emphasize that dramatic play is a worthwhile and necessary endeavor for the healthy growing child. A young child does not distinguish work from play. He or she works equally hard at both. Essentially the same characteristics of adulthood are utilized by the child in dramatic play: thinking, moving, judging, feeling, reacting, expressing and changing. Dramatic play is a door to a bigger drama and greater experience in life.

Dramatic play may be as simple as playing "house", or "cowboys and indians", or "cops and robbers." A child may pretend he or she is a particular animal and then change roles to another animal quickly and without apparent reason. A child may pretend to be an inanimate object like a car or plane. All a child needs is some space, freedom, and imagination for dramatic play to flourish. Normally, a teacher maintains a "hands off" policy. However, a teacher may be involved if she allows these essential characteristics to prevail. For example, she could say, "Let's pretend we're going to get dressed very warm and go outside and have a snowball fight. Okay?" What shall we put on first? Preschoolers and college students have reacted very well to this kind of opener to help getting started in dramatic techniques. Young children recognize it as play. The authors believe it is good for a teacher to become involved, on occasion, look through the eyes of a child, be childlike, "pretend," have fun, identify with their needs and joys, and not dominate in any way.

Dramatic play is not intended for an audience. In fact, many times a child is so "lost" in himself that he is unaware of anyone observing. Dramatic play is for the sake of self not an audience. However, this does not mean an audience may not exist in reality because teacher and parent alike may learn much by observing dramatic play. If a child suddenly becomes aware of his audience, the listener would do well to compliment or give positive reinforcement to the child or possibly join in. This reaction reduces child inhibition and potential frustration or what a child may consider a loss of privacy.

It should be noted that some authors in the field of creative drama consider dramatic play a prelude to but not a part of creative drama because the latter demonstrates more structure, planning, plot evaluation and formality. Very similar dramatic activities are performed in both however, including action, dialogue and characterization. Both are technically informal types of drama, educationally-oriented not professionally adapted to an audience. Most importantly, play and mime lead directly to creative dramatics and story dramatization.

Sharon Elliott in a recent dissertation, explored the use of dramatic play as a teaching strategy in the nursery school curriculum. The concept of playing "store" was prompted by a field trip and an appropriate play area for the "store." Pictures, books, discussions, and stories added stimulus. It was found the use of dramatic play had a definite effect on children's ability to verbalize their understanding of the topic of store, and indeed strengthen their language and thinking skills.[7] Actually dramatic play by the children, by definition, is spontaneous, however it seems many techniques were used to stimulate that imitation of roles played in a store. Perhaps it could be said the question of structure, stimulus, and adult involvement in dramatic play varies. As a dramatic activity, it may be dependent on environment and experience. Above all, dramatic play is a flexible activity and should be encouraged. Perhaps this explains why dramatists claim the same values for dramatic play as for creative dram even if they separate the two.[8] Beverly Hendricks suggests that the four processes of creative drama should be applied to preschoolers to reach beyond dramatic play—sensitivity, movement, characterization, and dramatization.[9] Mildred Donoghue argues that young children in a creative dramatics program should study dramatic play, and its extension sociodrama, pantomime, puppetry, and story dramatization.[10]

Dramatic Play Activities

In each activity there is a stimulus which motivates the creativity of the participants. The experiences themselves create their own environment of dramatic situations for the child's creative response. These activities are not so much the case of a leader directing a group, as is normally thought of in creative drama but rather an exploration of drama and creativity by both the child and any staff who may be a novice in drama.

1. Dramatic play stimulated by costumes. Material required includes a box containing old dress-up clothes and props. The objective is to stimulate the child by the use of costumes to create a character. The children put on the clothes. Think about a certain character or animal they would like to be. Find a good spot to play and pretend it is a place they like to be. Then they change clothes and become a new person. Questions asked may include: "Where are you now? What are you doing? How old are you? Tell me about what you are wearing. How do you walk? What do you sound like? Where could you be?"

2. Dramatic play stimulated by color and masks. Material required includes several 3-gallon empty ice cream cartons with an 8" by 10" hole cut out and replaced by sheets of colored acetate...red, blue, and yellow. Small holes should be cut in the tops to provide ventilation. The objective is to use color and masks to become a character in dramatic action. The color adds a dimension of "mood" to the hood. Everything may be seen as beautiful, spooky, funny, strange, but whatever it is—is different. The children should put on a mask. Think about the character which they would like to be and proceed as in the game. If children wish to play together, that is fine.

3. Playing House. The only material required is the housekeeping area which probably already exists in many school rooms. The new addition would be the directions for the children. The objective is to invite the child to the House to play a familiar role. They should think about who you want to be before you enter the house. Questions may be asked: "What do you look like? What do you do? Would you like to find some friends and do something together?" Children should be reminded that many people enter a household such as doctors, mailmen, pets, newspaper boys or girls, milkmen, etc. The "men" may in fact be women.

4. Creating an environment. Materials necessary include a sheet of butcher paper with magazine pictures of different locations, felt pens or crayons, and building blocks. The object is to stimulate the child to build an environment in which they can engage in playmaking. Have children paste pictures in one half of the butcher paper. Discuss the places shown in the pictures. Then in the second portion of the paper, encourage the children to draw a picture where they would like to be right now. Finally, if they want to build that place, or another with the blocks, encourage that. Ask them, "What would you be doing in this place you have built? Let's act it out."

(Above activities contributed by Janice E. Steadman, unpublished thesis titled "Drama Environments in Day Care," University of Washington, July, 1975.)[11]

ROLE PLAYING

Role taking, role playing or sociodrama is a natural extension of dramatic play and focuses on a social problem in human relations such as sharing, conflict with siblings, or parental authority. It is more structured than dramatic play.

Role playing is the spontaneous, unrehearsed acting out of a problem situation which involves human relations. In the latter respect it differs from some forms of creative dramatics which cast children into "playing" trees, rocks, gates, bridges, etc. In role taking, the children's only cues to action are their knowledge of a situation which has been described by the teacher. The importance of spontaneity in this activity should be underlined. In real life, children do not have time for studied responses to situations which arise. If they are permitted to study a problem at great length before role taking, they might be prone to react as they think their teacher or parent want them to react rather than responding frankly and honestly. Sociodrama should not be confused with psychodrama which is therapeutically oriented. The classroom is not a clinic.

Role taking may give classrooms a new sense of relevancy by introducing real problems that are frequently confronted in the school and on the playground, in the home and in the community generally.

Participants receive experience and training in problem solving in a very practical sense. Not only does the child have a chance to discuss a problem and "act out" its solution, but he is given an opportunity to evaluate his solution in the light of others that may be presented.

Participants are prone to develop tolerance for other person's feelings and they also discover that there are at least two sides to every problem.

Participants may be assisted to develop personalities that will not require scape goats for the venting of hostility.

Participants will learn, as they explore pertinent dilemma situations, that they are not alone with their problems.

A teacher or group leader begins by reading or extemporaneously relating a story which has a conflict situation typical to the age of the children. If sociodrama is to be a successful experience, the problem presented must seem important to the group. The narrator terminates the story when its dilemma is reached and says to her listeners, "What would you do in a situation like this, boys and girls?" If the story is well told, if the children become emotionally involved with the characters in the story, the teacher will receive an avalanche of suggestions and answers to her question. After briefly discussing the problem the teacher will ask for volunteers to act the various parts. The same dilemma may be role played two or three times. Situations may involve from two to five or six players.

Before the acting begins, the teacher requests the listeners to avoid overt responses such as clapping, laughing or jeering because it may destroy the player's illusion. Ideally, the actors would be unaware of the audience. If the teacher casts other groups to play the same scene before the first group acts, listening on the part of the class may be more intent. Before acting begins, the players must be reassured that anything they may do in the course of characterization will not be held against them. If a child believes his character demands mean, nasty action, then so be it. They must not be criticized for errors, mispronunciations or other deviations from generally accepted classroom behavior. The teacher should tactfully avoid type-casting. A child should not play his own life's role. The acting should revolve around a problem—not an individual.

The scene is enacted without props, staging, lighting or any effort to costume. This is informal drama and the emphasis in on *content* and not the acting. The presentation may be short or extended depending upon the actors' reaction. They might reach a solution or conclude at a point where they feel more information is needed. When role taking, there is no applause for finding a solution or penalty for failure to do so.

Following the presentation, the group should evaluate the results. Portions may be replayed, not to improve acting, but to clarify the ideas expressed. The teacher could guide the evaluation with questions such as the following: Will the solution presented eliminate or modify the causes of the problem. Will the solution eliminate or minimize the bad effects created by the problem? If the solution will solve one problem, will it cause others that are equally undesirable? Simply stated, was the problem solved? How? Is there another way?

Children may be led to find a composite solution if a single suggestion is not satisfactory. After the evaluation, another cast could role play the same problem or the original group could perform again in an effort to eliminate problem solving errors revealed during the evaluation. Sociodrama should be temporarily discontinued if children lose their enthusiasm. If creativity diminishes, pleasure will wane too. Only if motivation is kept high, will role playing lend enchantment to education.

Role playing may have a strong emotional impact on participants and listeners alike. Ministers, youth leaders and classroom teachers have been criticized for conducting role taking activity on the grounds that they may do more harm than good. Those who make this charge must understand that teachers, for example, are compelled to face emotional problems daily, with or without the aid of role playing. Critical handling of a miscreant by an unsympathetic principal or teacher does not offer the opportunity for tension reduction, for replacement of guilt feelings by assurance that may come from role taking however imperfectly handled. Teachers may find comfort too in the realization that role playing has built-in safeguards; if a group's discussion becomes too threatening, if it upsets the "nerves" the group will withdraw and the session comes to an end. It is the responsibility of all who work with youth to acquire sufficient training in speech and psychology to detect a child who needs special assistance and refer him to an appropriate staff specialist.

Situations for Exploration

Ages 5–8: Learning to share toys
The problem: Most of the children line up to use the slide. Sally, the biggest girl in the group, pushes the others aside and takes another turn ahead of her friends. What can be done to help Sally?

Ages 9–11: Learning to be honest
The problem: Johnny's Sunday school teacher urged her children to do good things for people during the week. On Sunday she asked her pupils to stand, one by one, and share the good things they had done for their friends and neighbors and pets during the past week. Johnny listened to all of the reports of his friends. When his turn came, he too stood and recited a list of good deeds . . .none of which he had done. The more he thought of his dishonest act, the more troubled he became. Should he tell his teacher? His father would punish him. His friends would dislike him for lying. What should Johnny do?

Ages 12–14: Choosing desirable friends
The problem: Paul's family owned a fast ski boat that he became adept at operating. Paul was new in his school and had few friends. Dick, Jim and Jack, all members of the football team and popular on campus, were happy to go skiing with Paul but they never volunteered to defray gasoline costs or help clean up the boat after a day's outing. Tim, a quiet boy in the neighborhood and one who did not make friends easily, also enjoyed boating with Paul and he was willing to pay his share of the expenses. He also remained at the dock at the end of the day until everything was "Bristol fashion." One day Paul told his friends that he had to pull the boat from the water and clean off the barnacles. The clean-up party was set for Saturday. Only Tim showed up to help. The other boys claimed they had forgotten. Should Paul invite them again?

Ages 15–18: Learning the rules of acceptable conduct
The problem: Mary was alone in the girls' restroom combing her hair. Her purse was on a table in back of her. A group of girls came into the room and formed a tight circle near the table. Mary glanced at the girls as they entered and recognized some who had questionable reputations. When she turned to replace her comb in her purse, the latter was gone. Mary was both angered and frightened. The week before another girl had been attacked and slashed with razor blades by this group. Should she accuse them of stealing her purse? Should she tell the school coun-

selor and risk being attacked? Should she tell her parents, realizing that they would worry about her? Should she just forget the whole thing? What would you do?

Additional Problem Situations for Role Playing and Discussion

1. Jeff returns from a Boy Scout hike to discover that his father has been hospitalized following an accident. Lacking funds to hire a special nurse, his mother must stay with his father at the hospital. Jeff doesn't mind being alone on their fruit ranch, but he is worried about a bumper apple crop that must be harvested within the next seven days. His neighbors are sympathetic, but they are faced with harvesting too. What would you do if you were Jeff? His neighbors? The members of his scout troup? His mother?
2. Sue finds a purse containing money and identification on her way to school.
3. You have been denied membership in an organization in which all the ''in'' students belong.
4. You have difficulty getting dates at school functions because you are new in town.
5. Bill ''borrows'' money from the family food fund and does not return it. His parents miss the money but blame it on Bill's younger brother.
6. Your history class is studying World War II. How does it feel to be a Japanese-American sent to an internment camp?
7. Jack catches a winning touchdown pass out of bounds but is not detected by the referee. He knew he was out of bounds but went on to score.
8. Your school is having trouble with older boys who run in the halls when classes are changing. Last week a girl was knocked down and injured.
9. Tom's mother died and his father married a lady who had a son Tom's age. Tom is expected to do the yard work and even scrub the kitchen floor, but the other boy does very little. Tom's father doesn't seem to care about this injustice.
10. Jane was taking tickets at the school play and was told by the principal to admit only ticket holders as the function was a sell out. Two couples, friends of Jane, bustled in, thrust three tickets and cash for another in her hand and kept on walking in spite of her protests. Jane was afraid to tell the principal for fear he would think she was weak. A seating problem did not develop, but Jane did not want the money. What should she do?
11. Luke, a Jewish first grader, is abused by his classmates. Sand is thrown at him and he is called names. Third graders have chased him and beaten him on the way home after school. His mother has started to meet him after school, but she must leave work to do so. Luke does not have a father.

It should be mentioned that recent research by Lia Wright[12] suggests that role taking is best utilized by older children, ten and above, because they reflect greater identification with characters and less egocentricity than younger children. She also found that boys gain more from role taking than girls.

PANTOMIME

One of the easiest ways to introduce story acting is through pantomime. This is the art of communication without words. This approach is popular with all ages and it is practiced with varying degrees of complexity from nursery school to college. One form is to have a participant respond to a relatively simple direction. A teacher may ask, "How many of you have eaten watermelon?" The entire group usually becomes involved by raising hands and the teacher then says, "Who would like to show me how to do it?" Another method of handling pantomime is to have the teacher read a story the children understand and have each react to a part in the story. This approach is especially satisfactory for children with very short attention spans even though it does not lend wings to their imagination as much as story acting which is dependent upon the child's ability to recall. Following are exercises that will help children learn to concentrate and also stimulate their imaginations:

Exercises

1. Sink to earth like a snowflake.
2. Fan yourself on a hot day.
3. Pick a rose and "stick" yourself on a thorn as you do so.
4. Feed your dog, cat, bird, etc.
5. Mail a letter.
6. Read a letter containing good news, bad news, frightening news.
7. Eat a sour pickle, candy, spaghetti.
8. Plant a row of seeds.
9. Hide a treasure.
10. Mistaken identity: you speak to a student you do not know.
11. Speak on the telephone during a poor connection.
12. Speak to a long-winded friend on the telephone, and your father wants you to hang up the receiver.
13. Seek and find a seashell on the seashore.
14. Bite into an apple and see a worm hole.
15. Vacuum the rug.
16. Adjust pictures on the wall.
17. Read a love note.
18. Wash dishes.
19. Measure, fry and flip pancakes.
20. Dribble and shoot a basket.
21. Hook a fish, play it and then lose it.
22. Build a house of cards and have it collapse prematurely.
23. Spade a flower bed.
24. Select fruit at a market.
25. Thread a needle and sew fine cloth; then heavy, coarse cloth.
26. Carefully arrange flowers and then angrily shove them off the table.
27. Peel an onion; then a banana.
28. Indicate by your actions that you are confined in a small cell.
29. Kiss your mother; then a boyfriend.
30. Tune in a TV program you loathe...then change channels and show pleasure.
31. Follow directions on a cereal box fold-up.

32. Swing a golf club.
33. Put a worm on a fish hook.
34. Photograph a baby.
35. Put on false eyelashes, contact lens.
36. Walk barefooted on a gravelly stream bottom.
37. Walk as an old man, an inebriate, a flirt.
38. Answer the doorbell as your second boyfriend arrives and your first is waiting in the living room.
39. Mow heavy, wet grass; then mow a light, thin growth.
40. Shave with a straight-edge razor.
41. Walk alone, without light, on a dark, wooded path.
42. Direct traffic.
43. Comb unruly, snarled hair.
44. Hear a noise and then see a doorknob turn while alone at home at night.
45. Attempt to reason with an assailant; then seize a club and drive the person away.
46. Trudge through a foot of thick mud.
47. Act like marionettes.
48. Pitch a baseball.
49. Blow up a balloon, sit on it, and pop it.
50. Pantomime a television commercial.

These exercises may be used as brief assignments for particular individuals or the entire class may pantomime some of these events at the same time in order to introduce the subject. Since all are participants, there is no threat of audience reprisal. Animal pantomime could be used such as a cat stalking, a rabbit hopping, a monkey swinging through the trees, a horse galloping, a chicken scratching and a bird flying. Later topics may be used for extended individual presentations, then pantomime with pairs or groups of children. A story may be read and several persons may act it out with pantomime. Stories such as *The Three Bears, The Three Billy Goats Gruff,* or *The Emperor's New Clothes* are appropriate beginners. The strict rule of not speaking must be enforced. When children's physical movements are easily interpreted, they have succeeded in the use of pantomime. Body awareness and control is steadily improved.

Games

Several games are well known that involve pantomime. 1. Charades is played most often; emphasis should be placed on a clear presentation for easy comprehension. 2. "Who Am I" is a game where children choose someone from history, literature or television and pantomime until the audience guesses correctly. 3. "What Am I" is a similar game. 4. The "Mirror" pantomime is also a well known game. The teacher or one child is the leader and another or the class imitates that person's actions like a mirror. This may be an effective first expeience with pantomime. 5. "Let's Take a Trip" is another idea for pantomime where the children act they are going somewhere using various modes of travel. 6. In brainstorming, the children will develop their own pantomime games which will enhance the use of their bodies for further dramatic endeavors.

Music and Mime

Music is one of the best stimulants for movement. The following have varied and exciting rhythms which are strong and easy to follow. The object is to stimulate the child to move expressively to the music. 1. "Snowflakes are Dancing," Side A 'Electronic Music of Debussy' arranged by Tomita; 2. "Buckarro Holiday" from Side I, 'Copeland: Rodea & Appalachian Spring', Robert Irving conducting the Concert Arts Orchestra; 3. "Suite in A Major" from Side II, 'Johann Sebastian Bach: Lute Music', Walter Gerwig, Lute; 4. "The Brave Hunter" from Dance-a-story series with Anne Lief Barlin. Music side only. The latter may be used with the music and narration when the children are ready. They do not have to worry about creating their own story so they are free to listen, learn, and use their delightful instinct for imagery. They create with their own interpretation what they hear. Through music and narration, children are led to express in pantomime their own ideas, awaken their senses, concentrate on details, learn to characterize, improvise and act out the story. In addition to "The Brave Hunter," other Dance-a-story records include:

1. "The Little Duck"—who swims out to sea and is rescued by a seagull.
2. "Noah's Ark"—and all the animals who came two by two.
3. "The Magic Mountain"—a land of fantasy and enchantment. Excellent for mime.
4. "Balloons"—for free expression and simple technique.
5. "Flappy and Floppy"—the lighthearted rag-doll puppet whose strings break.
6. "The Toy Tree"—Hurry! Hurry! Come and see what's growing on the Toy Tree.
7. "At the Beach"—where the magic of surf and sand lets us be everything we see.

In these selections, the heart of storytelling is clearly linked to the art of pantomime.

CHORAL SPEAKING

Choral speaking is group communication of literature. The interpretation of poetry or rhythmic prose is usually under the direction of a leader. Choral speaking is sometimes referred to as choral reading, choric interpretation, unison speaking, or verse choirs. Suitable for children of any age, choral reading provides a valuable linguistic experience in reading, interpreting, speaking, listening and remembering. It gives the opportunity to improve children's speaking habits through better articulation and enunciation, pronunciation, vocal quality, and vocabulary. Choral speaking also helps the child who is shy or inhibited by providing a group experience in expression. Actually it is a socializing activity for all including the shy and the forward.

Speaking in verse choirs was used by the ancient Greeks during their rites and storytelling. In early Biblical times choral response was also well known. Throughout the middle ages and Renaissance, minstrels and churchmen used choral speaking. In other words like storytelling, this is an ancient art.

In choral reading "casting" refers to the division of parts assigned to different individuals or groups within the chorus. Several types of arrangements are well known:

1. Refrain

Perhaps this is the easiest arrangement for beginners. One student or the teacher recites most of the narrative while the chorus repeats the refrain. The following is a typical example:

GARY GRUNION
By Nancy Briggs and Duane Nishimoto

REFRAIN:
  I'm Gary Grunion.
  I live in the sea.
  I have lots of fun
  Just being me!

I swim very fast
With a dart and a dash
With a flip of my tail,
I make a small splash.

-1- I'm only five inches
  My brother is eight.
  We're fine silver fish,
  Too good for mere bait.

Late in February
Til early fall,
The beaches of
California call.

Spring and summer,
My life is no bore,
For this is the time
I swim to the shore.

(REFRAIN)

-2- On moonlit nights
  The highest tide
  Signals the start
  Of the grunion ride.

Preparing myself
With a shake of my fin,
I catch a big wave
And ride it way in.

I sparkle like a diamond
In the bright moonlight,
With a blue-green stripe
On a body silver-white.

(REFRAIN)

-3- My wife lays her eggs
  While I fertilize them.
  The next wave comes and
  We're back in the swim.

Newspapers announce
"Grunion Run Tonight."
People rush to the shores
To see if it's right.

If we swim too slow,
We'll be left on the sand.
Or worse than that,
We'll be grabbed by a hand.

(REFRAIN)

-4- When someone grabs me,
  It's not for a pet.
  So I make sure that
  I'm slippery and wet!

I twist and I wiggle.
I never will stop.
I move very quickly,
With a flip and a flop.

Safe and secure,
Away from the land,
That is, until spring,
When I do it again!

(REFRAIN)

-5- But what of the eggs
Buried in the sand
After all that trouble
To spawn them on the land?

Waves wash the eggs
Off the beach
Far out to sea
Beyond man's reach.

Two weeks later
Like the sound of a horn,
The fish burst out
Like fresh popcorn.

(REFRAIN with this
change:)

I'm Gary, *Jr.*
I live in the sea.
I have lots of fun
Just being me!

I swim very fast
With a dart and a dash.
With a flip of my tail,
I make a small splash.

2. Antiphonal.

Two part casting or dialogue is the emphasis in this casting arrangement. The two groups may be divided according to the mood of the poem, boys and girls, high voices and low voices, questions and answers in the poem, or dialogue in the poem. Selections that contain contrasts or parallels in mood, or different characterization are well suited for antiphonal casting. An excellent example is Harold Munro's "Overheard on a Saltmarsh."

3. Line-a-choir

More than two small groups within the choir are cast for separate parts. Some lines may be spoken in unison. For example, in this short selection, three rows might be formed in the choir, and appropriately cast as Groups A, B and C.

Two Fat Cats
by Nancy Briggs
All: Three black cats wait for their dinner.
Groups A & B: Two were fat.
Group C: One was thinner.
Groups A & B: Two cried loudly,
Group A: Mee-----Ow
Group B: Mee-----Ow
Group C: One said politely, "I'll eat somehow."
Group A: A small bowl of milk
Group B: Was placed at their feet.
Group A & B: Two cats complained
Group C: While one did eat!

4. Line-a-child

In this casting several children speak separate parts as solos. This arrangement is always popular because tempo and variety are enhanced. The following adaptation is an interesting poem for older children. Speaker 1 and 2 should stand in the middle of the front row. After a few choruses, Sam (Speaker 2) should sit on a chair (sleigh) in front of Speaker 1. An introduction to this poem may be helpful. An explanation of the meaning of cremation could be given by an instructor or a student. This is part of vocabulary building, too.

THE CREMATION OF SAM McGEE
by Robert Service

Chorus: There are *strange* things done in the midnight sun
            By the men who toil for gold;
            The Arctic trails have their ''secret'' tales
            That would make your blood run cold;
            The Northern Lights have seen ''queer'' sights,

Speaker 1: But the queerest they ever did see
            Was that night on the marge of Lake Lebarge
            I cremated Sam McGee.

Chorus: Now Sam McGee was from Tennessee, where
            the cotton blooms and blows.
            Why he left his home in the South to roam
            'round the Pole, God only knows.
            He was always *cold,* but the land of gold seemed
            to hold him like a spell; (hold up clenched fist)
            Though he'd often say in his homely way

Speaker 2: ''I'd sooner live in hell.''

Speaker 1: On a Christmas Day we were mushing our way
            over the Dawson trail.
            It wasn't much fun, but the only one
            to whimper was Sam McGee. *(Sam whimpers)*
            He turned to me, and

Speaker 2: ''Cap''

Speaker 1: Says he.

Speaker 2: ''I'll cash in this trip, I guess;
            And if I do,
            I'm asking that you won't refuse my
            last request.''

Speaker 1: Well, he seemed so low that I couldn't say no;
            then he says with a sort of moan;

Speaker 2: ''It's the cursed cold, and it's got right hold till
            I'm chilled clean through to the bone.
            Yet 'tain't being dead—it's my awful dread of
            the icy grave that pains;

So I want you to swear that, foul or fair, you'll
    cremate my last remains.''

Speaker 1: And we started on the streak of dawn; but
    Gosh! he looked ghastly pale.

Chorus: He crouched on the sleigh, and he raved all day
    of his home in Tennessee; *(rave) (Sam moves to chair)*
    And before nightfall a corpse was all that was
    left of Sam McGee

Speaker 1: There wasn't a breath in that land of death, and
    I hurried, horror-driven,
    With a corpse half hid that I couldn't get rid,
    because of a promise given;
    It was lashed to the sleigh, and it seemed to say:

Speaker 2: ''You may tax your brawn and brains,
    But you promised true, and it's up to you
    To cremate my last remains.''

Chorus: In the long, long night, by the lone firelight,
    while the huskies, round a ring, *(Howl)*
    Howled out their woes to the homeless snows

Speaker 1: O Gosh! how I loathed the thing.

Chorus: And every day that quiet clay
    seemed to heavy and heavier grow:

Speaker 1: And on I went, though the dogs were spent
    and the grub was getting low;
    Till I came to the marge of Lake Lebarge,
    and a derelict there lay;
    It was jammed in the ice, but I saw on it twice
    it was called the ''Alice May.''
    And I looked at it, and I thought a bit,
    and I looked at my frozen chum;
    Then ''Here,'' said I, with a sudden cry,
    ''is my cre-ma-tor-eum.''
    Some planks I tore from the cabin floor,
    and I lit the boiler fire; *(action)*
    Some coal I found that was lying around,
    and I heaped the fuel higher;

Chorus: The flames just *soared,* and the furnace *roared*
    —such a blaze you seldom see;

Speaker 1: And I burrowed a hole in the glowing coal,
    and I stuffed in Sam McGee. *(Sssst!)*
    Then I made a hike, for I didn't like
    to hear him sizzle so;

Chorus: And the heavens scowled, and the huskies howled,
    and the wind began to blow. (Howl)

Speaker 1: It was icy cold, but the hot sweat rolled
    down my cheeks, and I don't know why;

Chorus: But the stars came out and they danced about
            (chorus moves in to cover up Sam)

Speaker 1: Ere again I ventured near;
            I was sick with dread, but I bravely said:
            "I'll just take a peep inside.
            I guess he's cooked, and it's time I looked" . . .
            then the door I opened wide. (Ah!)

Speaker 1: (Pushes chorus back as though he were opening a furnace door)

Chorus: And there sat Sam, looking cool and calm,
                in the heart of the furnace roar;
            And he wore a smile you could see a mile,
                and he said:

Speaker 2: "Please close that door.
                It's fine in here, but I greatly fear
            You'll let in the cold and storm—
                Since I left Plumtree, down in Tennessee,
            It's the first time I've been warm."
            (Stand, move forward)

Chorus: There are *strange* things done in the midnight sun
                By the men who toil for gold;
            The Arctic trails have their "secret" tales
                That would make your blood run cold;
            The Northern Lights have seen "queer" sights,

Speaker 1: But the queerest they ever did see
                Was that night on the marge of Lake Lebarge
            I cremated Sam McGee.

Line-a-child or Line-a-choir may be labeled sequential or cumulative. In the latter, there is a building effect, which adds to the variety of the reading.

5. Unison

In this casting, all voices speak all lines as one. Dependent on the demand of the selection, this may be the most difficult or the easiest casting. To begin, a teacher should use nursery rhymes which the children know. A few gestures may enhance the interpretation without overdramatizing. Reading itself is not a problem since the children will probably speak from memory so that the teacher may focus on expressive techniques. Singsong monotony should be avoided. This is a common difficulty in choral reading. The director should focus attention on meaning and semantics, the plot or idea of the story, and more natural expression should follow. If the children slowly increase their volume throughout the selection, the director should be more aware of the tone color and quality of the children and provide a second of silence to return to normalcy.

Practice improves choral reading. A variety of selections also increases experience and motivation in expressive reading. The use of a tape recorder may improve speaking techniques. Many teachers claim that an audience, small or large, immediately improves the performance of the group. Many narrative poems are available for choral reading. The list found in Chapter 3, Selection of Stories, is a good beginning for reading narrative poetry which interests children.

STORY DRAMATIZATION

In this integral part of creative dramatics, there is a planned execution of roles. Generally, the procedures are as follows: 1. The instructor selects a story. 2. The group is familiarized with that tale. 3. Interrogation in order to build concepts of character, scene and dialogue occurs. 4. The actual re-enactment of the story takes place by the children with a minimum of props. 5. An evaluation occurs. 6. A re-enactment of the story-play takes place. This approach may take several sessions to accomplish. The emphasis is not upon the script or the audience other than the remainder of the class that listens. The players or children are supreme. Dramatization in the middle and upper grades includes those stories with scripts and those without scripts.

Interrogation

The adult's role as leader is to begin dramatization by simply acting out well-known stories withour formal scripts. The leader's role is primarily one of guiding and organizing the enactment of roles in the story. The leader should select good material as discussed earlier in the chapter, and visualize the possibilities for dramatization. The leader should be flexible so that the element of surprise, creativity, and imagination are not ruled out. A good leader will also aid in planning the dramatization by knowing friendly and effective interrogation techniques. These techniques will aid the re-creation of the story by emphasizing the who (characters), where (sequence of scenes) of the story, what (verbal dialogue and non-verbal action), and why. A sensitive and perceptive teacher will focus on ''why'' (motives, feelings, thoughts) particular characters are involved in certain events. A simple chart on the blackboard might help:

WHO
WHERE
WHAT
WHY

The question when and how may be added to this list if the teacher or students desire.

In the story of the Three Bears, the chart may be completed on one board.

After a basic review of each character, further interrogation may follow, and then the dramatization. Once a class is acclimated to this approach, it proceeds smoothly and quickly.

Story dramatization is *for the children who do the acting,* not an audience. Children act out a story, improvising as their creative spirit moves them. *The*

WHO	Goldilocks		
WHERE	Forest	Bear's House	Forest
WHAT	Wandering	Enters Tests porridge, chairs, beds Falls asleep Startled by Bears Screams	Runs Away
WHY	Lost	Curious Hungry Tired Surprised	Afraid

child's willingness to try to develop his artistic potential creatively, not his accuracy as to content, is the important consideration. This premise was illustrated when one group of children, acting out the story of the three bears, happened upon a delightful and startling conclusion. The mother bear spontaneously invited the intruder, Goldilocks, to stay for dinner. Goldilocks accepted and they became friends!

Most story dramatizing is done in a classroom with imaginary or few props. Once again, the teacher will motivate and indirectly guide the children by asking questions:

"What can we use to show where the three bears' house is?"
"What can we use for the three bowls that hold the bears' porridge?"
"Is there anything here that we can use for the bears' beds?"

Suddenly a corner of the classroom may become the bears' house with two chairs serving as the doorway. Books become bowls of porridge. One bench, which mysteriously causes a different response every time a child rests on it, serves as three beds. As long as a teacher-asking, children-telling relationship is maintained, the story-acting situation will remain creative.

Dramatization of stories can be introduced more smoothly if the material acted is not too comprehensive in scope. The children could start with a short scene or only part of one. A beginning effort could be the hot porridge action followed by the decision to go for a walk. This first presentation would terminate at the point where the bears return to their home. Although a story may be well-known to children, the idea of acting it is usually new. Portraying a small portion that may be completed in one session gives the actors and the observers as well a feeling of fulfillment. Their familiarity with a story helps a group pick up the plot easily in the future, thereby offsetting the loss in continuity which results when the clock terminates dramatization.

It may not be advisable to introduce a complete story and act it in the same session. Several sessions normally are required to prepare children for the moment when they volunteer to participate in the presentation of an entire scene or story. During the periods of preparation and acting, the children should be encouraged to forget themselves and try to feel as if they are a bear, tree, rock, or whatever the scenes require. A child actor should not be interrupted as long as he stays in character. A child cannot become creative by being criticized. However, if he winks or makes faces at classmates in the audience, exaggerates his role beyond reason, or otherwise destroys illusion for other actors and observers, he should be quietly replaced without reprimand. He will undoubtedly know why corrective action was necessary and his next attempt will probably be characterized by better judgment.

Importance of Interrogation

A student teacher reported that she had told her class the story of "Goldilocks and the Three Bears" and, after casting it, the children "just sat." These young thespians were new to story dramatization and needed encouragement and guidance. Story-related interrogation of the children would have assisted this teacher.

Children should be asked questions regarding their story that demand action or creative answers. Questions such as "Was the little bear happy?" should be avoided. A nod, a shake of the head, an indifferent shrug, a grunt, or a chorus answer might be the response to this question. Instead, the group might be asked, "What did the little bear say when he discovered that his chair had been broken?" or "What expression could the little bear have had on his face when he discovered his chair had been broken?" Children will feed back casting requirements if the following type questions are asked:

"How many children were there in the story?"
"What kind of animals were there in this story?"
"How many animals do we need to act out this story?"
"Why do we need trees, rocks, or a gate for acting this story?"

Interrogation should also bring out the main points or the key situations of a story. In the case of Goldilocks, the teacher might have asked:

"Why did the three bears decide to take a walk?"
"How did Goldilocks get into the house?"
"What did she do first?"
"After tasting the porridge, what did she do?"
"After eating the porridge and sitting on the chairs, where did Goldilocks go?"
"Where did the bears find Goldilocks?"
"What did Goldilocks do upon awakening?"

When the group is thoroughly familiar with the story and its characters, it is time to prepare for casting. In the foregoing instance of the children who "just sat" after they had been cast into various roles, there was a need for a "warm up." The group must be given opportunities to identify with actions of the characters. Before attempting to cast any of the roles, the teacher should encourage group members to imitate mannerisms of the characters. As the first step toward overcoming inhibitions and orienting youngsters, she might ask: "How do you think the father bear walked?" Two, three, or ten children might go before the class to demonstrate the lumbering gait of the big bear. By similar means, the walk of the mother and the little bear might be shared. Next the group might be asked, "How do you think the little bear would eat?" After this activity is explored, the teacher might ask the following questions:

"What do you think the mother bear said to the father bear when they took their walk?"
"What do you think the baby bear said?"

These questions should be discussed. Then teams of three children could stroll before the group acting and talking in the manner they imagined the three bears did when they walked through the woods. Through this gradual introduction, the children get the "feel" of the plot and its characters. Most important of all, they begin to lose their fear of trying. A timid child who otherwise would have declined to play-act the part of the father bear might volunteer to do so because demonstrating the animal's walk had given him the confidence to try to play the larger part.

It is important for the teacher to prepare and relax a child for creative drama. Although the teacher does not show a child how to act, a teacher must paint a vivid picture and supply plenty of ideas for acting before a child will understand the story and produce meaningful action. The scene from Goldilocks could be acted out by using a unison or mass method where each child chooses a role to play and all the children pantomime simultaneously. This avoids the feeling of actor and audience. After the mass action, a teacher can help children understand that there are many ways to act one role by allowing different children to demonstrate their ideas. Since there is no "right or wrong" in the acting, the teacher can work to improve the existing performance. The starting point is where the child is today and the teacher can work in a positive manner towards clarity of communication. This mass action is a good way to warm-up for acting and will not be chaos with a good teacher. Individual parts and verbal expression may be added the following day.

Volunteers should also be sought to act the parts of trees, bushes, and large rocks found along the path travelled by the bears. Before casting, children could demonstrate actions such as the following:

"How would a Christmas tree stand?"
"How would an oak tree stand?"
"How would a weeping willow stand?"

A pine tree might be simulated by joining hands over head with elbows bent; oak trees might be represented with outstretched arms in a more horizontal position. Weeping willows might be suggested by limp hands with fingers pointed toward the ground, and the child's chin resting on his chest. The group might also be asked, "What kind of weather did the three bears have on their walk?" If the children respond, "Windy," the teacher could ask, "How do trees act in the wind?" Various class members could come into the acting area and demonstrate the swaying and bending that they believe a certain type tree might do.

When preparing older children for story-acting, questions may be more abstract, For example, fourth graders, orienting to "Cinderella" might be asked:

"How did Cinderella feel when she learned that she could not go to the ball?"
"If you had been there as her friend, what might she have said to you?"
"What might you have said to her?"
"What do you think Cinderella said to the prince as she danced with him?"
"What do you think the prince said to her?"
"How did Cinderella carry her dress?"

If children were being prepared to story act "Androcles and the Lion" they could be asked:

"What did the king say when the lion refused to attack Androcles?"
"If the lion had been able to talk, what would he have said when he recognized Androcles?"
"What did Androcles say to the king when he was given his freedom?"
"If the king had not mentioned freedom for the lion, what do you think Androcles might have said to win freedom for the beast?"

Storyacting

After sufficient experience with improvised dialogue and dramatization, some children may want to develop their own theme and plot in a pupil-planned play. Such an endeavor may or may not involve a script. Careful preparation must take place. Upper primary and intermediate grades have used this technique successfully.

Another approach utilized by the authors and other teachers consists of presenting a scripted story immediately to the children. Acting out the story on the first read through is the key to this approach to dramatization. Learning by doing or "draosophics" operates from the initial contact with the story. The teacher as director guides the students through basic blocking toward the presentation of the story-play. As director, again she must be thoroughly familiar with the material. She must allow freedom of expression and creativity yet smoothly guide the progression of events in the story. She must be positive and remember that the players are still supreme in this process of creative drama. Time and attention are saved by not reading the story first, interrogating the listeners and charting the story. Instead comprehension and action proceed simultaneously. After using the script once or twice, then the script may be returned to the teacher and again improvisation of dialogue and action takes place. However structure of the play has been verbally and nonverbally presented by the players the first time through the story. The improvisation of the dialogue and action of the script allows for creativity and individualization. Above all, the student cannot fail. The actual dramatization occurs more quickly than the route of telling, interrogation, and charting in most cases. The process is very much the same, but more of an "instant" technique in keeping with our instant media age.

After selection of an appropriate story, the teacher adapts or "scripts" the story to fit her classroom situation. Just like a storyteller of old, the teacher may take the liberty of adding, deleting, or changing a text of a story in order to make it most appropriate for her particular environment. This approach is not for the purist.

The following "focus" questions make adaptation easier:

1. Are the leading parts appropriate for characterization? For example, in *That's What Friends Are For,* there is a part for an opossum. Since the behavior of such an animal may be difficult for a child to portray, the author changed the part to a rabbit which is much easier to imitate in action and costume.
2. Is the language archaic?
3. Are the transitions in the plot smooth?
4. Is the story too long? Can the narrator summarize several actions?
5. Is there too much narration and not enough action?

In the story, *That's What Friends Are For,* we have simple blocking (enter stage left and exit stage right), a repetitive plot, various animal characters who should speak and act differently, simple props, audience involvement and participation, easy lines, and a moral. Children should "act" the story on the first reading. Words and actions have a simultaneous first impression. With most older students, this story may be practiced twice. Then use of scripts may be discontinued and students should recreate the language and actions to the best of their abilities. Only the teacher and the narrator need the script for appropriate cues. Immediately, facial expression, vocal expression, and gestures will improve. This elimination of script is not always possible with more difficult stories, but adapt accordingly. Do not forewarn children about eliminating scripts because that only makes them more nervous. After experiencing success in story acting, they will not be reticent to use this technique. The teacher must feel free to give constructive advice such as the following: "Please step forward. I would like to hear the elephant a little more. Let us see your shining face." If necessary, the teacher may give a line in order to allow the child to better conceptualize the potential expression. Imitation by the child is a natural learning device. The imitation is still a personal re-creation by the child and is to be considered artistic.

Also as a follow-up or reinforcement at the end of the story, the class may be divided into two groups, lined up and facing each other. The teacher should ask focus questions such as: How does a monkey walk or sound? The teacher then announces each animal in this story twice. For example, she says, "Along comes the bird." Half of the children walk to the other side of the room imitating that animal verbally and non-verbally, and then the other half of the children do the same thing after she repeats the "entrance" line. This approach works skillfully with adults and children. Everyone participates, many inhibitions are squelched instantly. Characterization improves. Above all, a teacher should praise her students. This imitation exercise helps the later presentation of each animal in the story, particularly the entrances and exits. If the story is reproduced later, all children have acted like all of the animals. This activity may also be used to introduce the story.

If children become experienced in these arts, soon they, too, will want to edit and direct their own stories. Even second graders are capable of this creative flurry.

The format preferred for this type of storyacting is delineated with the use of the story title, *The Ripe Bananas*. This particular story interests many different age levels and the popular theme of self reliance. The teacher may remind students that audience right and left are not the same as stage right and left. With this difference in mind it is easy to determine where students should stand. Upstage and downstage were termed accurately. If one placed a piece of chalk at the very back of the stage that was literally higher than the front of the stage by the audience. The chalk would roll from the higher part of the stage to the lower, or from upstage to downstage. This is an easy way to teach children the basic positions on stage. It is logical and children remember it easily. At least a teacher may say, ''Enter stage left and exit stage right.'' And a child has acquired valuable information and some theatrical expertise which may be used the rest of his or her life.

Format for Storyacting

1. Title: The Ripe Bananas

2. Source: Nancy E. Briggs
                    Music Editor: Dell Van Leuven

3. Participants: Ages 7-11.

4. Audience: Remainder of the class, another class, parents or no audience necessary.

5. Characters: (9) Narrator, Monica the Monkey, Rabbit, Lion, Bird, Crab, Spider, Elephant, Giraffe

6. Time: 7-10 minutes.

7. Props: A table, a podium, a shawl for the bird's wings, bananas for the monkey, a crown for the lion, two closed umbrellas for the spider, a scroll with the song printed on it in large letters.

8. Scene: The Jungle.

9. Blocking:

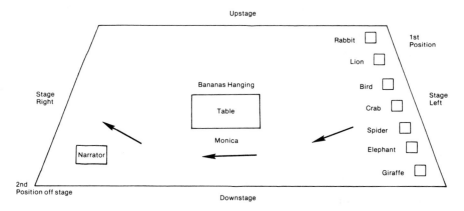

(Animals enter stage right, talk to monkey and exit stage left.)

10. Introduction by Teacher or another Student	Have you ever really wanted something and felt you couldn't get it? I know a monkey who felt like that. This story is titled *The Ripe Bananas.*

Narrator: Deep in the jungle Monica the monkey stared at a bunch of ripe bananas hanging high up a tree.

Monica: Those bananas look so delicious. If only I could reach them, but they are too high for me.

Narrator: Monica walked around and around the tree. She waited for the wind to blow so that they might fall. She waited for them to get so ripe they would fall off the tree. But that did not happen. Monica the monkey became very discouraged.

Monica: I wish I could eat those bananas. I would pick the ripest one. (Pantomime this) I would peel it very carefully. I would eat every bite. Mmm...Mmmm.

Narrator: Monica pretended to eat a ripe banana. Soon her dream was over.

Monica: Oh, I wish I could taste one of those yellow bananas.

Narrator: As Monica stared at the bananas, along came the rabbit.

Rabbit: Hi, Monica. How are you today?

Monica: Oh, I am sad. Do you see those bananas hanging up in the tree?

Rabbit: Yes.

Monica: I wish I had one of those to eat. I am so hungry.

Rabbit: That is a wonderful idea. Eee—Eee—Eee.

Narrator: Monica made lots of happy monkey sounds. The rabbit tried to jump and reach the banana. But the rabbit could not jump high enough. He waved good-bye and left Monica by the tree.

Monica: Good-bye. Thank you for trying to help me.

Narrator: As Monica waited patiently, she heard the mighty roar of the lion.

Lion: Roar. Good day, monkey. Roar.

Monica: Good day, sir.

Lion: What are you doing?

Monica: I am waiting for a fine yellow banana to drop from the top of the tree.

Lion: Well, I could command that banana to drop off the tree.

Monica: Oh, would you? Eee-Eee-Eee.

Lion: Yes...ROAR!

Narrator: The lion's voice filled the jungle, but no bananas dropped off the tree.

Lion: I am King of the Jungle, but those bananas must not know it.

Narrator: Shaking his head, the lion walked away. As Monica looked at the bananas again, she saw a bird flying in the sky.

Bird: Chirp, chirp, chirp. (whistle)

Monica: Hello, friend bird. What a lovely song you're singing.

Bird: Thank you. Why are you standing by this tree?

Monica: I am waiting for a banana to fall.

Bird: Why don't I fly up there and try to cut the stem with my sharp beak?

Monica: Eee-Eee-Eee. That's a great idea. Go ahead.

Narrator: So the bird flew high up in the tree and tried to cut the stem, but she could not.

Bird: Sorry, Monica. Good-bye now. Chirp, chirp.

Monica: I am so hungry for a banana. What can I do?

Narrator: Just then Monica looked down at her feet and she saw a crab and a spider.

Monica: Hello.

Crab and
Spider: Hello. (Said in unison with crab using a high-pitched voice and the spider, a low-pitched voice). How are you today?

Monica: I am so hungry. I want a banana to eat.

Crab: I could cut the stem for you with my sharp pincers, but I cannot climb the tall tree.

Spider: I could climb the tall tree for you with my eight legs, but I cannot cut the stem for you.

Monica: Oh dear, that is the good and the bad of it. Well, good-bye.

Crab and
Spider: Good-bye.

Narrator: Monica was so tired she lay down by the tree and started to cry. Boo, hoo, hoo. Soon the ground shook. She looked up and saw her friend, the elephant.

Elephant: Why are you crying, Monica?

Monica: I want a banana.

Elephant: I will try to reach one for you with my long trunk.

Narrator: The elephant lifted his trunk as high as he could, but it was not high enough.

Elephant: Sorry, Monica.

Monica: Boo, Hoo, Hoo, I am sorry, too.

Narrator: Then along came the giraffe.

Giraffe: What is all the noise about?

Monica: I want a banana from the top of the tree. The rabbit tried to jump and get it for me. The lion tried to command the banana to drop. The bird tried to cut the stem with its beak. The crab and spider could not help me. The elephant tried to reach it with his trunk. And they all failed. They could not get a banana for me. Boo, Hoo, Hoo.

Giraffe: I am sure I could reach the banana for you, Monica. I am the tallest animal in the jungle.

Monica: Oh, goody! EEE-EEE-EEE.

Giraffe: But I am NOT going to get the banana for you.

Narrator: Monica looked puzzled.

Monica: Why not?

Giraffe: You have told me how many animals have tried to help you. But why haven't you tried to help yourself?

Monica: Oh, that banana is too high for me. I cannot climb that high. I am afraid. I might fall.

Giraffe: Your friends were not afraid to try. If you really want that banana, then you must be brave enough to climb the tree and get it for yourself.

Narrator: Monica thought. She looked at the ripe bananas. She could almost taste them as she licked her lips.

Monica: Oh, yes, I want those bananas.

Giraffe: Then you start climbing slowly and carefully. Hold on tightly. I will give you a little nudge with my nose.

Narrator: Monica began to climb. She was afraid at first. But as she climbed she felt brave. She wanted that banana and she was proud of herself for trying. Finally she got up to the bananas and she picked one ripe banana and ate it right there on the branch.

Monica: It is delicious! It was worth it, Giraffe.

Giraffe: Good. Then take the other bananas and slide down my neck.

Narrator: Monica did just that. She was very happy. She made happy monkey sounds all the way down.

Monica: Eee . . .Eee . . .Eee.

Giraffe: The bananas are tasty, but more important Monica, you learned to depend on yourself.

Monica: Right! Thank you so much, friend Giraffe.

Narrator: Monica was very happy. She sat on the ground eating her ripe bananas. And the Giraffe sang this fine tune to her:

Help Yourself

Words and Music by
Dell Van Leuven

Narrator:	
and All	
Animals:	Let's all sing along with the Giraffe.
(back on	
stage)	(Repeat song)

The elements of evaluation in storyacting include: (1) Consideration of the material. (2) The element of creativity and originality on behalf of the students should be apparent. (3) An attention-getting introduction is essential to the presentation of storyacting. (4) The desirability of strong leadership and firm direction, but flexible, should come from the teacher. (5) The evaluation must consider whether the rate of expression is too fast or too slow. The presentation should *not* be choppy because this destroys rate. (6) Stories which are flexible in number of characters are excellent because they adapt to a changing classroom environment. (7) A legible script is essential. (8) A few noteworthy props are advisable in storyacting. If they are made by the children, the effort is to be applauded. (9) An evaluation must consider clear articulation and correct pronunciation. Such language skills are important to any communication. (10) The future teacher should be able to grow in the ability to motivate expression from the characters in storyacting. Without making them feel inhibited or criticized, she must encourage them on to greater feeling and expression. Nothing works as well as praise after a student has accomplished a difficult task. (11) Clarity of directions saves time in rehearsal and increases the credibility of an instructor. (12) Above all, an instructor should make storyacting a positive and rewarding experience for her children because this is primary to the process of dramatization. Her attitude and comments are important in this regard. If reinforcement by praise is used, usually the ability to motivate expression is equally strong. (13) An instructor must be prepared to make quick decisions for unexpected events. This extemporaneous critical thinking ability aids immensely in various directing problems.

Storyacting has been particularly successful with a clear story line like Heide and Van Clief's *That's What Friends Are For*, folktales and Aesop's fables. Virginia Tashjian's *Once There Was and Was Not*, P. D. Eastman's *Are You My Mother?* Harve Zemach's *The Judge: An Untrue Tale*, Pollack's *The Clown Family's Good Manners*, Claire Boiko's *Small Crimson Parasol* have proved successful for this style of dramatization.

Impromptu Dramatization

There is little planning or interrogation in this type of dramatizing of stories. After the story has been told or read, the teacher may ask, "Shall we act out the story?" A few moments must be spent on character assignment and identifying each scene.

That's What Friends Are For may be successfully used with very young children who cannot read in an impromptu dramatization. Before telling the story, the teacher assigns three children to each character. This way each one in a class of 27 would be involved and the story would be acted out several times. Then the teacher proceeds to tell the story by means of a flannel board to reinforce the characters in the story. At the end of the story, the first group of nine young Thespians immediately start to recreate the story. The teacher recaps the narrator's part again. The story may be creatively reproduced three times. The children feel successful and indeed they are!

Using a flannel board.

There are several schools of thought on the subject of rehearsals in creative dramatics. One school says that the group needs only a few minutes to design their production. Another says planning the play slowly and carefully is important to the process of drama. Still another group feels scripts are useful to the creative reproduction of a story; more planning and preparation is done by the teacher but more time is spent on the process of dramatization by the pupils. All schools maintain that drama should be free, creative, spontaneous and child-centered even if the process results in a special program for parents or another classroom. It is important to experience different approaches to creative drama.

Flannel board objects adhere to clothing while story acting.

STORY IMPROVISATION

Story dramatization is the center of many creative dramatics programs. Story improvisation follows story dramatization. Improvisation means the creation of characters and scenes based on a particular story, however their development is not confined to what occurred in the story. The story is the departure point for improvisation. The children should move "beyond" the original story and create their own story. They may extend the story forward or backward. The change in time element is important.

For example, in *Little Red Riding Hood,* the group might be asked, "How did Little Red Riding Hood discover that her grandmother was sick? How did she decide what she would take to her Grandmother's? Why wasn't Little Red Riding Hood in school that day?" First, second, and third graders are able to respond well to these questions and to create scenes leading to the point at which the story opens. The teacher may also ask, "What did the hunter, the grandmother, and Little Red Riding Hood do after the wolf was killed?" Again the possibilities for improvisation are innumerable. The addition of characters is possible. One child suggested that Little Red Riding Hood's father came and took her home so she would be safe and sound. The addition of characters or the expansion of those in the story is another valuable means of improvisation. Minor characters like the hunter may suddenly take on a new dimension. One child suggested that the hunter and the grandmother fell in love, got married, and the Grandmother never was lonely anymore. Such imagination in dramatization is very creative. Almost every story has minor characters who could affect the plot more than they do if their roles were maximized.

SUMMARY

Creative drama consists of many types of activities most of which are characterized by the influence of storytelling: dramatic play, role playing, pantomime, puppetry, choral reading, story dramatization including storyacting and impromptu dramatization, and story improvisation. The values, selection of material, casting the play, and evaluation of the activity were also discussed. It is good for the teacher, librarian, camp counselor, or parent to be familiar with a variety of techniques to teach creative drama. Storytelling naturally leads to creative drama and story dramatization. The child is central to the activity. The process of communication is stressed more than the product. An audience may be used, but the players remain the supreme concern of educators.

NOTES

1. Sister Dorothy Prokes, *Exploring the Relationship Between Participation in Creative Dramatics and Development of the Imaginative Capacities of Gifted Junior High School Students,* (New York University, 1971), *Dissertation Abstracts,* Vol. 32, No. 5 (November, 1971): 2555A-2556A.
   Marilyn Eisenstadt Gootman, *The Relationship Between Dramatic Play and Self Concept in Middle Class Kindergarten Children,* University of Georgia, 1976, *Dissertation Abstracts,* Vol. 37, No. 7 (January, 1977): 4203-A.
   Sharon Elliott, *The Use of Dramatic Play as a Teaching Strategy in the Nursery School Curriculum,* Wayne State University. *Dissertation Abstracts,* Vol. 37, No. 5, (November, 1976): 2559A-2600A.
2. Winifred Ward, *Playmaking with Children,* (New York, Appleton, Century Crafts, Inc.), p. 264.
3. Billy Tyas, *Child Drama in Action: A Practical Manual for Teachers,* (New York, Drama Book Specialists/Publishers, 1971), p. 101.
4. Patricia E. Grasty, "Creative Dramatics: No Age Limit", *Elementary English,* Informal and Ed Drama, Vol. 51, No. 1 (January, 1974): p. 72.
5. Dorothy Heathcote, "How Does Drama Serve Thinking, Talking, and Writing?" *Elementary English,* Vol. 47, No. 8 (December, 1970): p. 1077.
6. Peter Slade, *Child Drama* (London: University of London Press, Ltd., 1967).
7. Elliott, *The Use of Dramatic Play.*
8. Martha Dallman, *Teaching the Language Arts in the Elementary school,* 2nd Ed. (Dubuque, Iowa, Wm. C. Brown, Co., 1971), p. 303.
9. Beverly Lusty Hendricks, "Beyond Dramatic Play," *Communication Education,* Vol. 20, No. 3, (Sept., 1977): p. 198.
10. Mildred Donoghue. *The Child and English Arts,* (Dubuque, Iowa, Wm. C. Brown, 1971), p. 82.
11. Janice Erickson Steadman, "Drama Environments in Day Care," Children's Drama Master's Thesis, (University of Washington, unpublished material, July 31, 1975).
12. Lia Wright, "Creative Dramatics and the Development of Role-Taking in the Elementary Classroom," *Elementary English,* Vol. 51, No. 1, (January, 1974): p. 89.

6   The Child as Storyteller

The objective of this chapter is to assist playground directors and teachers in their efforts to convince children that the fun of storytelling is for everyone. This activity usually begins with "Show and Tell." A preschooler's "story" may consist of a two-liner: "This is my new doll, Susie. My birthday was yesterday." Lower elementary grade youngsters may be encouraged to express themselves by describing vacation trips or games they like to play. The objective is to involve the child as storyteller. A child develops rapport with a story character

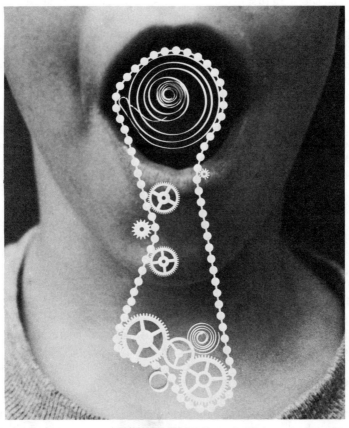

The child as storyteller.

when the discovery is made that they have parallel interests or experiences. A child will identify vicariously with situations not encountered personally. As children hear a teacher's stories, they will begin to incorporate similar ideas in their creations. Children's television programs also exert an influence in this regard. Stories told by children gradually evolve from a simple listing of events to the form of an introduction, body and climax-conclusion.

THE VALUES OF STORYTELLING BY CHILDREN

Attitudes

During World War II an American destroyer was torpedoed in the Pacific. When the missile struck, personnel began to leap into the water. As the abandoned ship settled into the sea, a lone sailor was observed rushing from one depth charge ''can'' to another defusing them so they would not explode and kill his buddies in the water. When the last charge was disarmed, the destroyer rolled on her side and slid stern first into the ocean taking the unnamed martyr to his death. Martyrdom of another sort can be found in Shel Silverstein's *The Giving Tree*. The apple tree gives a boy her shade, fruit, limbs for climbing, and later, building material for a house and a boat. The boy, now a man, continues to selfishly *take* and the tree selflessly to *give*. Finally, the man, now old and tired, returns to the remains of the tree and the latter permits him to sit and rest on her stump.

Arnold suggests that a storyteller's choice of material is motivated not by the story's theme but by the story's outcome.[1] Themes such as love, hate, indifference and greed are unified by the story's plot but capped or superceded by the outcome. This is another example of the whole being greater than the sum of its parts. A story written by a child or selected by him for telling may provide an outcome that is primarily an expression of his convictions which have developed from his experiences and thoughts. For purposes of analysis, each story told may be condensed into an import that ignores incidental details and focuses on the core of the story. When all the imports are placed side by side, a profile of a storyteller's attitudes and intentions may emerge. The plot sets up a problem and the outcome resolves it in a manner characteristic of the storyteller. One child might tell a story which indicates that breaking school regulations does not pay; another might demonstrate in a story that breaking regulations might pay. The first child would be positively motivated, the second negatively. Research indicates that high achieving students and professional individuals are positively motivated in contrast to the negatively motivated, low achievers who number among school dropouts and ineffective workers.

If on the basis of Arnold's research, it becomes possible to analyze a child's attitudes through the import of the stories he tells, it becomes the province of teacher and parent to attempt to determine what the child is trying to say. Application of the moral to a child's subjective circumstances, if that can be determined, would be the first step in providing assistance. Were a junior high school student to choose to tell the story of the sailor's sacrifice, he might indicate that he would be willing to lay down his life for those he loves. A sixth grader telling *The Giving Tree* conceivably might have guilt feelings about continually taking from his parents and rarely reciprocating. The attitude of the man-boy would vindicate his selfishness. The foregoing suggests that child-told stories could become a teaching aid. Before definitive conclusions are reached by a classroom teacher, however, consultation with special staff members is recommended.

Improved Speech

Storytelling might prove to be a powerful motivating factor when precepts fail. A child who mumbles his words might ignore a teacher's suggestions to open his mouth when he speaks. However, if peers complain that they cannot understand his story, he could be motivated to improve his speech pattern. Children must be understood when they use the telephone, buy a loaf of bread, or participate in classroom discussions. If the activity is marked by encouragement, recording stories for playback by the child during free time may encourage speech improvement. Children will refuse to volunteer stories if such action results in discouraging criticism.

Encourages Sharing

Nothing succeeds like success. One successful storytelling experience will encourage another. Peer approval awaits the child who expresses himself well. A child who is permitted to select his own story or experience for sharing will feel confident with it and have a desire to communicate again.

Increases Exposure to Literature

Children have been known to read prodigious numbers of stories before they find "just the right one" to share with their classmates. In the course of this activity they find themselves looking into the mirror of life that literature represents. A high school student who chose to describe a scene from *The Grapes of Wrath* discovered that literature can be rugged as well as gentle. Also, by choosing a story that will please both himself and his friends, he is learning the first principles of audience adaptation.

Speaking Presence

Finally, if a child is permitted to show her favorite toy in her pre-school group and continue oral sharing through high school, stage-fright will prove to be very manageable. Unfortunately, "show and tell" is discontinued too soon in a child's experience. One second grade teacher explained that she eliminated this activity because "...it takes time and the kids don't have anything important to say." Second graders might not be able to make many earth-shaking pronouncements but an opportunity to tell a story before their class contributes to the development of poise and the ability to develop ideas that could serve them handsomely later in business and community.

MANAGEMENT OF THE CHILD-TOLD STORY

Most of the preceding chapters have dealt with the teacher as the storyteller. Several of the early authors in the storytelling field have been adamant in their pronouncements that stories should be told to children by adults. They reasoned that, since children's literature was written by mature persons, it should be interpreted by mature persons. They also expressed the belief that (a) children are incapable of portraying a wide range of emotions, (b) children fail to comprehend the communicative aspects required of the situation and (c) children are too self-centered to project the meaning the author wished to convey. Perhaps these early authors had in mind an occasional audience of children gathered in an auditorium to hear a storyteller, perhaps a Saturday story hour at a library, or possibly an activity in a municipal recreation program. They could hardly anticipate the dynamic impact that today's classroom teachers are exerting on their pupils' interest in the oral communication of literature. The publishing industry is assisting to stimulate interest in children's literature by its release of folk and fairy tales and other children's classics at nominal prices. Many youngsters come to school today laden with their favorite story books. Education specialists have placed considerable value on group-mindedness and procedures for inculcating the ideals of unselfish behavior. Under the prevailing philosophy, a teacher is hesitant to discourage children from bringing their favorite books to school. However, if she attempted to tell or to read all of the stories brought into her classroom by her pupils, little else would be accomplished in the school day. One solution is to have children tell their favorite stories.

When Children Should Participate

A teacher is the model for storytelling effectiveness and she should tell the majority of the stories. At the beginning of the school year, she should spend several weeks weaving stories into her daily teaching before introducing the role to children. This is necessary in spite of the fact that children are more likely to bring stories to school after summer vacation than at any other time during the school year. The following principles should provide some guidance for the teacher:

1. The child should be allowed to tell a story when he feels he wants to do so, not on a set assignment schedule. Real sharing, in the storytelling sense, grows out of a desire to communicate, not out of the compulsion that of necessity must characterize most classroom assignments.
2. No child or group should be permitted to dominate a story-sharing period. Every pupil should have an opportunity to tell a story before any member of the group is allowed to tell a second time.
3. If it appears that many children are reluctant to enter into storytelling activity, the teacher should defer child-told stories for several weeks. When story-sharing is resumed, children who did not participate in earlier sessions should be encouraged to be among the first to share.

Children are usually eager to tell stories in advance of Halloween, Thanksgiving and Christmas. These three occasions seem to have more immediate meaning to children than most other holidays of the school year. Perhaps this is due in part to the presence of stories in increasing numbers which are available in home, school and public libraries. Commercial advertising and home observances of these holidays also enhance their importance. Rapport between a student audience and a student storyteller is more likely to be evidenced for a story told just prior to one of these days. This is a result of group anticipation of the approaching occasion. In order to realize maximum participation in story sharing during these holidays, a teacher may find it advisable to discuss all three dates early in October. During this discussion she should ask which students would like to share a Halloween story, which would prefer to tell a story about Thanksgiving, and which would like to tell a Christmas story. Logically, she will explain that, because time is limited, no child will be permitted to tell a story for more than one occasion.

Children in some fifth and sixth grade classes have been trained to tell stories in kindergarten-primary age groups.[1] Students who volunteered for training for this activity were given an opportunity to tell their stories during lunch periods. The result of this endeavor was improved speaking ability, a sharpened interest in literature and reading and finally, more children were exposed to good stories in spite of an overtaxed library facility. Many other opportunities for child-storytelling may be made available. Children should be encouraged to recount tales before campfires sponsored by both organization and family groups. When fires blaze in hearths on cold winter evenings, both parents and children may share stories. Halloween parties may be enlivened by child-told stories. The latter are being employed with increasing frequency in church school lessons. One church group has organized some of its youngsters into a story telling club which visits shut-ins and bedridden children. Classroom teachers may make units on Mexico, Japan, the American Indian and other social studies more interesting by encouraging students to prepare and share stories about these people and their lands. Permitting children to tell stories will enable them to participate more intimately in church, school, home and organization activities.

THE CHILD AND THE STORY

Because storytelling by a child has educational value for him in the various facets of the communicative process, a teacher should point out the elements which contribute to effective oral expression. An involved explanation is neither necessary nor desirable, but the following general principles should be discussed with the children (a) *Story Selection*. Everyone in the class should enjoy the story selected by the storyteller. It should appeal to both boys and girls. It should deal with persons other than the storyteller himself, his family, or his pets. It should be a story which the storyteller has heard or read, one he likes, and one which he has rehearsed many times. (b) *Time Limits*. Most children are willing to become storytellers. Too often their train of thought is sidetracked midway through the story. Digressions from the theme creep in, and the child ends up monopolizing the entire period. As one teacher so aptly put it, "Getting children started with storytelling is no problem; what I want to know is how to stop them." A five minute time limit is ample for nearly every child-told story. This will enable more children to participate and, if enforced, will produce better story preparation. A member of the class may be designated as timekeeper and this duty rotated among the group from day to day. The timekeeper should raise his hand at the end of five minutes, and stand at the end of six minutes. The five minute signal would indicate that a one minute "grace period" remains in which the story must be concluded. The time limit should be clearly stated by the teacher before beginning any child-told stories. She might demonstrate this by designating a student timekeeper and then proceeding with a story of her own. (c) *Posture*. This will depend upon where the story is being told. If the group is small and seated in a circle a child may remain in his place; if a child is shy, it would be preferable to have the story told from the desk rather than have the child frightened out of participating at all; ideally, in a classroom, the child-storyteller will stand where the teacher tells her story ...from the front of the room. This facilitates delivery and insures easy viewing of the narrator by members of the class. (d) *Expression*. Usually, children are less inhibited than adults. Subconsciously, they enjoy identification with all of the characters in a story. Gestures should be encouraged, vocal variety praised, and mood-conveying changes in facial expression complimented. (e) *Audibility*. In defiance of an old axiom, in a child-told story, children should be both seen and heard. A teacher may wish to sit in the rear of the room and signal the storyteller if he is inaudible. The usual sign is simply a raised hand. A child should be informed in advance of the signal to be used. (f) *Rate*. The rapid rate at which many children speak can prove a serious obstacle to effective storytelling. The child must be assisted to realize that his story is new to the class and that it must be delivered slowly enough for everyone to follow the plot. Children should be encouraged to let the action in the story determine their rate of utterance. Identification with the characters and the details of the story is necessary to effect this. If the child has difficulty with the latter, it might be necessary to have him volitionally reduce his speed. This may be accomplished by having the teacher sit at the rear of the room and hand signal. The radio-television director's signal is a taffy-pulling gesture with both hands. This action intrigues most children. (g) *Visual Aids*. When child-told stories are first initiated, it is entirely in order for children to use illustrated stories, and to show pictures simultaneously with the action of the tale. They should be advised, however, to bring stories with pictures which are large enough to be seen by the entire class. Examples of appropriate sized pictures should be exhibited. When using a story with pictures, the illustrations should be held high enough for all to see, and they should be shown long enough to provide an adequate impression of a scene or character. As the children become accustomed to their role as storytellers, it is advisable for the teacher to ask them to tell a story without using visual aids. This should not be an actual requirement, for some youngsters may never be able to present a story without the support of a picture. Young storytellers may be motivated in this direction by challenging them to use such vivid descriptions and such vital expression in their voice and gestures that everyone can be made to see the scene or character. (h) *Teacher Assistance.* Frequently some children will forget the plot at some point or perhaps omit an important character. The teacher may assist the child if she knows in advance which stories are going to be told. She may wish to encourage her students to give her the book just prior to the child's presentation in order that she may act as prompter. If a child should forget, become exceedingly nervous, or fail to respond to prompting the teacher may help him "save face" by saying, "Tommy, you have certainly aroused our interest in your story. Would you read the rest of it?" The teacher might offer further help by asking members of the class how they thought the story concluded. If this does not stimulate the memory of the storyteller, she could ask him to tell the story again on the following day. When possible, the child should be assisted to finish the story on his first attempt.

CRITICISM OF THE CHILD-TOLD STORY

While lasting benefits in oral communication skills may result from the child-told story, it is usually not a curricular subject and never a discipline. Criticism of student presentations needs to be handled diplomatically. A shy child should be guided gently toward the development of confidence before his classmates. The exhibitionist needs kindly advice to show him how to fit his expressive nature into a structured situation in which sharing is the goal. Assuming that only two or three children can present their stories in a given day, the teacher may easily jot down her observations on each presentation. As soon after the story hour as possible, she may speak with each child participant individually. He should be praised for that which was commendable about his performance and then given a tactful suggestion or two which will help him tell his next story. Sharing is one of the major goals in elementary education and it is recommended that entire class join in evaluation. The teacher must structure the evaluation to conform with the goals the group is currently striving to attain. For example, prior to the story the children might be told, "The tale Jack is about to tell has interesting characters. Let us see if we would want them for friends." Following the story, the group may discuss the level of characterization reached by Jack. In a like manner, children may be prepared to discuss the description of scenes, the sequence of action, plot development, word choice and other aspects of story development.

PARTICIPATION STORIES

Stories of this type may be told by either teacher or child. They depend on the active participation of all class members for their effectiveness. Student participation follows an established cue line in the story and may take the form of bodily activity, words or nonsense syllables. Participation stories are strictly for fun. Indeed, teenagers and adults seem to enjoy them as much as children. In general, participation stories should be short and uncomplicated. Usually a maximum of eight different cues can be remembered by the middle and upper grade children, and eight different participation responses appear to be the limit of memory for this age group. A good participation story can be told (played) many times before the same group during the school year. The initial success of a participation story depends upon the clarity of the cues and the action called for. Both of these are the responsibility of the storyteller and they must be thoroughly explained before beginning the story. It is advisable to rehearse the audience before beginning the actual story. The action desired for each cue must be clearly explained. For example, a storyteller might say, "When you hear the word 'tiger,' make a *grrr* sound. Let us all make the *grrr* sound now for practice." After all cues for action have been explained, the teacher may double back and ask, "When I say the word 'tiger,' what is the sound you are to make?" Rehearsal of this kind will make the participation story more pleasurable for all concerned.

Participation stories.

CHOOSING PARTICIPATION STORIES

Many teachers have found it expedient and effective to adapt familiar folk tales to participation story form. If a teacher elects to do this (with "The Three Billy Goats Gruff," "The Three Bears," "The Gingerbread Boy" or any other well-known story), she should try to put the action on vocal participation at the ends of sentences. Otherwise, the story becomes almost unrecognizable because of imposed interjections. Following are versions of three stories which have met with enthusiastic response in the classroom, around the campfire and on playgrounds. A host of similar stories abound, many of which are familiar to a reader.

One Winter Night
Cues

Wind	—Ho-o-o-o	Grandfather's Clock—Click Tongue	
Cat	—Meow-ooo	Horse	—Neigh
Dog	—Arf-arf-arf	Cow	—Moo-oo
Baby	—Cry	Loud Noise	—Yell
Asleep	—Snore	Rain	—Hands
			Slapping on Knees

It was a stormy winter night. The *wind* whistled down the chimney of the little farm house, and the *rain* beat against the windows. Inside, the family sat around the fireplace. The *cat* and the *dog* played on the hearth, mother held the *baby* in her lap, and above the sound of the *wind* and *rain* could be heard the ticking of the old *grandfather's clock.*

Out in the barn the *horse* and the *cow* grew restless as the *wind* blew *harder,* and *harder* and *harder.* Hearing a *loud noise,* the man and his *dog,* leaving the warm fireside to the *cat* and the *baby,* hurried outside to the barn to see what the *loud noise* could be. The wind had only blown the barn door open and the *horse* and the *cow* were safe, so the man and his *dog* returned to the warm fire, where the *baby* and the *cat* were sound *asleep.*

The *rain* and the *wind* grew *softer,* and *softer* and *softer,* and above all could be heard the ticking of the old *grandfather's clock.*

Brave Little Indian
Cues

Brave Little Indian — Put one hand to the back of your head with fingers showing above the head.
Indian walks on the road — Slap one knee, then the other.
Indian walks on the bridge — Slap chest with fists.
Indian swims — Rub hands together, being careful not to slap them.
(On return trip, speed up the tempo)

Once upon a time there was a "Brave Little Indian Boy" (sign) who lived in a village with many other "Brave Little Indian Boys" (sign). One day the "Brave Little Indian Boy" said to the others, "I'm going out to find a big brown bear." And all the other "Brave Little Indian Boys" said, "UGH."

So the "Brave Little Indian Boy" started to walk, walk, walk, walk, (sign) until he came to a bridge. Then he began to walk, walk, walk, walk, walk, walk, (sign) until he got to the other side. Then he began to walk, walk, walk, walk, walk, walk, walk, (sign) until he came to a river. Then he began to swim, swim,

swim, swim, swim, swim, swim, swim, (sign) until he got to the other side. Suddenly, he stopped. The "Brave Little Indian Boy" (sign) saw a big, brown bear. He turned around and started to run, run, run, run, run, run, run, run. (sign) When he came to the river, he began to swim, swim, swim, swim, swim, swim, swim, swim. (sign) When he reached the other side, he began to run, run, run, run, run, run, run, run (sign) until he came right up to the village. And he said to all the other "Brave Little Indian Boys" (sign), "I saw a BIG BROWN BEAR." And all the other "Brave Little Indian Boys" (sign) said, "UGH."

Here We Go On A Lion Hunt

(This version of "The Lion Hunt" is the basic story. Use your own words. The plan is, that one person sits before the group, tells the story, and leads out the action.)

Once upon a time, in an African village, there was a brave Chief whose name was O-o-o-o-o-o! (Speak the Chief's name in a low tone, BEATING CHEST AT THE SAME TIME.) He had a devoted wife whose name was Ah-h-h-h-h-h! (Speak the wife's name in a high tone, BEATING CHEST AT THE SAME TIME WITH BOTH FISTS.)

Now it happened that a lion had been stealing the sheep, belonging to the people of the village. Somebody had to be chosen to hunt the lion. Who do you think it was? Well, it was O-o-o-o-o-o.

The villagers gathered outside the hut, and when their chief came out, there arose a great hubbub. (FOR HUBBUB, ALL FEMALE VOICES CHANT "SODDA WATTA BOTTL," OVER AND OVER AGAIN IN A HIGH VOICE WHILE MALES SAY SLOWLY AND RHYTHMICALLY IN LOW VOICE, "RHUBARB RHUBARB.") After the people had said fond good-byes to their chief, they opened the gate (PUT HANDS TOGETHER, THEN STRETCH THEM WIDELY) and closed it behind him. (CLAP HANDS BACK TOGETHER.)

It was a beautiful day. O-o-o-o-o-o walked along (TO REPRESENT WALKING, SLAP LEFT THIGH WITH LEFT HAND, THEN RIGHT THIGH WITH RIGHT HAND, ETC., IN SLOW WALKING RHYTHM.) He looked to the right of him (DO SO) and looked to the left of him (DO SO) and sniffed the spring air (SNIFF) but there was no lion around.

So he continued to walk along with ease. (WALK) Before long he came to a covered bridge, but he didn't stop. (FOR COVERED BRIDGE SOUND: THUMP CHEST WITH RIGHT FIST THEN LEFT FIST, ALTER-NATELY, IN SAME RHYTHM AS WALKING.) He walked right on and still no lion.

Before long he came to a wide creek. He stopped. (STOP) (POINT) Crocodiles! (PUT BASE OF PALMS TOGETHER, SNAP FINGERS TO-GETHER SEVERAL TIMES TO IMITATE CROCODILES.) He walked backwards to get a good running start (DO SO) and ran (FASTER MOTIONS THAN WALKING) right up to the bank. (STOP) He couldn't make it. So he backed up again. (BACK UP AGAIN) Then he ran just as fast as he could to the bank. (RUN UP AGAIN) He stopped. He couldn't make it. He backed up the third time. "This time I'm going to make it if I have to swim," he said. So he ran up to the creek, dived in and swam (DO IT WILDLY) to the other side. There he shook himself off (DO SO) and started to look out for the ferocious lion. He looked to the right of him (DO SO) and to the left of him (DO SO) and sniffed the sweet spring air, (DO SO) but he saw no lion.

He even climbed a tree (DO SO) and looked out (DO SO) but saw no lion. So he came down. Now he walked up the side of a tall hill (WALK SLOWER, PANT) and then through the tall grass to the mouth of a cave. (SWISH HANDS TOGETHER FOR TALL GRASS) He looked in cautiously, first to the left of him (DO SO). No lion! Then to the right of him (DO SO). No lion! Then he looked straight ahead. G-R-R-R-R-R-R-! LION!

O-o-o-o-o-o started back to the village as fast as he could go . . .through the tall grass, down the hill, around the tree, across the creek through the covered bridge. The tribesmen made a terrific hubbub when they saw he was coming back. Quickly they opened the gate, let him in, closed it, and the lion was running so fast that he hit his neck on the gate, broke it, and died. Everybody, little and big, lived happily ever after.

(ON THIS LAST PARAGRAPH REPEAT ALL THE ACTIONS OF THE STORY)

Word Scramble

Another variation of the participation story is the word scramble. This delightful means of stimulating thinking consists of taking the following list of words (or a list of a teacher's own choosing, or a list of words volunteered by a group of children), dividing the class into groups of six or eight children, and instructing each group to prepare a story incorporating the words on the list:

sword	boy	mountain	moonlight	box
ransom	TV	space ship	shoes	chair
witch	care	lungs	shipwreck	pail
path	pirate	snow	girl	tree
beautiful	pen	sniff	candle	haystack
cheese	kiss	tongue	spinach	toe

Picture Stories

Another means of encouraging children to tell stories creatively is through the use of pictures that stimulate young imaginations. The following books by Mercer Mayer provide illustrations and basic plot but the children must take it from that point. Each child may develop his own tale with language, and dialogue appropriate to his level of experience.

Bears New Clothes (Bear acquires dilapidated clothing)
Birds New Hat   (Two birds quarrel over ownership of a top hat)
Bubble Bubble   (Fantastic animals from magic bubble maker)

Nearly all of Maurice Sendak's illustrations as well as those found in the Caldecott Medal Books may be used to play the happy and exciting picture story game.

Creative Participation Stories

Another approach to participation stories involves listeners to an even greater extent because they contribute the sound they choose for certain words. For example, in the selection titled "Mr. Peepers" by Celeste Anlauf, the storyteller first relates the tale to the children. Second, the teller and the children decide the important words that are often heard in the story. The teller writes the words on the chalkboard. Together the teller and the children decide upon a sound, word, or phrase that seems appropriate for the word. For example, these are popular words and sounds chosen from the story: Mr. Peepers: eeee (monkey sound), "Orvy": oh, boy, "circus": oom-pa-pa; "ringmaster": ladies and gentlemen; "popcorn": pop-pop. Finally, the story is retold by the teller with the help of the children. The teller begins the story and pauses appropriately for the children to make the accompanying sound after the teller says each of the selected words. The addition of the children's contributions to the telling of the story makes Mr. Peepers come to life.

Mr. Peepers

Once upon a time, in a town much like yours and mine, there lived a small boy named *Orvy*. *Orvy* was a hard worker. He helped his mother with the chores and made his bed everyday. One day, while he was on his way home from market, he noticed a big sign. Do you know what was coming to his town? The *circus!* *Orvy* was so excited! He loved the *circus;* especially the animals. So he went right over to the place where they were putting up the big tent and asked to speak to the *ringmaster*. He asked the *ringmaster* for a job in the *circus*. The *ringmaster* said that he thought *Orvy* was young, but that he would give *Orvy* a chance to take care of the most mischievous animal in the whole *circus*. His name was *Mr. Peepers*. *Mr. Peepers* was a monkey who was always getting into trouble. He would wander away from his cage and scare people because he was so big. *Orvy's* job was to keep his eyes on *Mr. Peepers*. So *Orvy* and *Mr. Peepers* quickly became friends. They did everything together. But one day *Orvy* was watching the lion tamer practice taming the lion and forgot all about *Mr. Peepers*. Orvy looked high and low and couldn't find *Mr. Peepers* anywhere. Finally, he came to the popcorn stand and there was *Mr. Peepers*. He had just eaten his sixteenth bag of popcorn. *Mr. Peepers* developed a terrible stomach ache so *Orvy* took him home, put him to bed and gave him some medicine for his stomach. *Mr. Peepers* and *Orvy* grew to be best friends and as *Orvy* grew older he became master of all the animals in the circus.

Participation stories have also been referred to as sound stories in the literature of storytelling. They are a popular form of involvement of children in creative drama. Sounds and motions from children help create the sounds and moods within a story. Body sounds include stamping, patting, clapping, scratching, snapping fingers, brushing hands together or on thighs, smacking lips or tongue, making a clicking sound with the mouth, whistling and so on. Crumpling paper or cellophane or tin foil, moving a large piece of cardboard, or shaking a coffee can with objects inside make a variety of sounds. Percussion instruments may also be added to the repertory of potential sounds for a story. In addition, sounds may be soft or loud, fast or slow, repetitive or changing. If musical instruments are used, the storyteller and children should consider the possibilities for sound such as tempo or speed, dynamics or force, pitch or location on the keyboard, tonality or major and minor notes, and touch or staccato or legato. Each story should use the appropriate sounds to relate the mood and message intended by the author and teller. Above all, sound offers new and different techniques of telling a story and involving children.

SUMMARY

This chapter hopes to encourage storytelling by children. A child-told story may provide both parent and teacher with some insights into a child's underlying attitudes, it can result in improved speech, a willingness to share with others, a youngster's deeper appreciation of good literature and finally, a greater poise and confidence when speaking to a group. Children usually begin to tell stories to their classmates in the early grades and hopefully, continue for the rest of their lives. This activity should always be fun and not a mandatory assignment. Sharing should grow out of a desire to communicate. Stories told by children should have a time limitation and be interesting not only to the narrator but to his classmates as well. Teachers should assist children who forget their stories and criticism should be tactful, constructive and occasionally conducted privately. Every effort should be made to give children feelings of adequacy after they have told a story.

NOTES

1. Magna Arnold, *Story Sequence Analysis* (Columbia University Press, New York, 1962), pp. 9-14.

Listening

7

A DEFINITION

Most individuals would agree that seeing is not the same as reading. However, many persons have been prone to equate hearing with listening. The latter is actually what the mind does with what the mechanism of the ear presents to it. The term "auding" has been coined to describe the process of hearing, listening and cognition. Cognizing would include such things as imagining, recall, linking one idea or object to another, and reasoning. To neglect or deny a child an opportunity to develop cognitive abilities would place the youngster at a severe disadvantage. Children should be trained to listen.

Listening.

ITS IMPORTANCE

Research indicates that of all the waking hours of the day, seventy-five percent are spent in verbal communication and of these, forty-five percent are consumed in listening and thirty percent in speaking. The average listener retains
only twenty-five to fifty percent of the main ideas he hears and it is estimated that
we operate at a twenty-five percent degree of our potential when we listen. The
foregoing observations place a heavy emphasis on the need to teach listening.
When a young person enters the adult world, to avoid penalty, he must be
equipped to listen and respond intelligently to a variety of situations.

LISTENING HABITS

The American people, generally, have been called poor listeners. Many persons turn on the radio and simultaneously read a book. All too often, college
students find a lecture period the ideal time to prepare an assignment for the next
class. The advertising men fill their radio and television copy with exaggerated
claims in a frantic attempt to capture the attention of consumers. Indeed, this
generation has grown accustomed to a noisome existence. This existence is made
tolerable, however, by ignoring a certain amount of speech, music, advertising
claims and the irritating cacophony of thousands of automobiles seemingly
headed in the same direction at the same time.

Added to the problem of noise are the tensions, the pressures and the dead-
lines which go hand-in-hand with a highly competitive urban culture. Small
wonder that, as audiences, people are easily distracted; that they are impatient for
the speaker to ''get to his point''; that to many of them, creative and constructive
listening is a time-consuming luxury they can no longer afford.

What are the implications of these poor listening habits for children? *Basically, the child is a mediocre listener.* He is self-centered and his attention span
is brief. This has been true through centuries and in all cultures which possess
recorded histories. Until the last generation or two in this country, however,
adults have been models of listening behavior for their children. Young and old
alike trooped into the Chatauqua grounds, sat on hard benches in the heat of
summer, and listened to the artists and lecturers of yesteryear. Of course Robert
G. Ingersoll and William Jennings Bryan were beyond the comprehension of
pre-adolescents, and the social implications of *Uncle Tom's Cabin* were lost to
children. Notwithstanding, under the adult listening code of sixty years ago, the
youngsters were silent. Watching the reaction of parents and older brothers and
sisters, these children became aware that adults found satisfaction in paying attention.

Sixty years ago, churchgoers sat as a family. Children sat through Sunday
school *and* through church. It would be ridiculous to claim that the behavior of
all children was exemplary. Some infants cried, some toddlers wiggled and some
juniors became fidgety. In spite of these obstacles to a reverent mood, every
child could observe about him the respect and response of adults to the sermon.

Chautauqua has been replaced by the ubiquitous, uncritical and half-listened to television set. A child now observes his adult models talking to each other as they watch *their* programs and leaving him alone in the room during *his* programs. Few children under the age of twelve can be seen these days sitting in the pews of urban churches. Shuttled off to their peer groups while the regular worship service is being held in the sanctuary, they can no longer learn first-hand the meaning of reverential listening. Thus it is that the listening habits of late twentieth-century American children are primarily conditioned by the adult community. The pressures and tensions which afflict grownups are reflected in their children.

WHY CHILDREN DO NOT LISTEN

A child who is a poor listener frequently has this habit well-established before he enters a classroom. If parents greet their child's efforts to speak with, "Not now, Junior, can't you see I'm busy," or "Come back after this program is over," or "Please be quiet...can't you do anything but ask questions?" etc., the rejected juvenile communicator may learn to look upon negativism as a normal response as he attempts to communicate orally. Parents who lack the patience or stamina to work sympathetically with their child as he struggles for the skill to express his feelings may find themselves rewarded with inattention. They will hear themselves saying, "Can't you get anything right?" "I've told you six times to close the door!" "Is there something wrong with your ears?" In the last instance the parent might have inadvertently asked an intelligent question. A child's auditory perception must be normal if he is expected to develop adequate listening behavior. Assuming that a child's hearing is normal, the fact remains that he, not his parents or later his teacher, is the controller of the learning process. He possesses the power to "turn off his ears" when he becomes exhausted or loses interest. It has been indicated that listening is a reciprocal process between a sender and a receiver. In order to learn to listen, a child must have an attentive listener who is genuinely interested. Kindergarten teachers report that their good listeners usually have a mother or someone else who cares for them, who will listen sympathetically and carefully when they wish to speak.[1] The climate for learning established by a classroom teacher has a significant effect on the learning process. Even though a teacher is not formally trained in listening techniques, if she develops a warm, friendly atmosphere with her pupils, she will find that learning through attentive listening will take place. Children cannot be made to listen, they must *want* to do so. Children may develop poor listening habits in a hostile classroom environment because they feel threatened either by the teacher, the group, or both of these.

It would appear that educational attitudes and processes have also contributed materially to the development of poor listeners. For years it was believed that listening depended upon the ability to hear and the child's intelligence, and that schools could do little about either of these. This would be equivalent to saying

that reading ability depended only upon eyesight and intelligence. Equally erro-
neous was the point of view that practice and intelligence were the only significant components of efficient listening.[2] Although most of a child's day is devoted to activities that require listening skill, there has been inadequate training
in this area. Teachers and curriculum builders have assumed that because a child
could *hear*, that he could automatically listen and comprehend. Obviously, it is
an error to assume that listening, especially on complex levels, is something that
a child does naturally. Training must go beyond teachers' well-meaning admonitions, "Now children, please pay attention," or "Please listen carefully." There
must be an appreciation of some of the problems encountered in listening. For
example, Wiksel[3] wrote that in reading, a child is able to adjust his speed to the
degree of difficulty of the material; however, when listening, such an adjustment
is not possible because the speaker sets the pace and the listener must try to
follow. A spoken word is gone on the wings of sound and there is no time to
retrace one's steps and reflect. Another cause of poor listening behavior may
grow out of instructional procedure. Children are not challenged and stimulated
by a dull rehash of textbook assignments which frequently terminate in a "ping-
pong" type question and answer period. If a teacher can perform the difficult
task of personalizing instruction, i.e. showing children why subject matter is important to them as individuals, then the teaching of listening is simplified. Although they comprise only a fraction of the school day, periods devoted to
storytelling, role playing and creative dramatics can contribute much toward the
growth of good listening habits among children. The attention and response of
the class in the story situation should assist an instructor to understand what
contributes to good listening for the group as well as for individuals within the
class.

TELLING AND LISTENING

Because so much attention is currently devoted to promoting group-
mindedness among school children, it will prove helpful to examine the contribution of storytelling to acceptable group listening behavior. Those who have
worked with children know that they are easily distracted by miscreants in a
group. On the other hand, story interest can be so high that the group can exert
considerable pressure for conformity upon a mischievous youngster. When listening is the thing to do, more children will listen! It has been found that stories
which have outgrown their effectiveness for a child in the home situation because
of repeated telling, have been received enthusiastically by the same child in the
classroom. Group sharing of responses is indeed an important attribute in
storytelling. A child may be fascinated by the reactions of others to a story which
is very familiar to him.

Many factors enter into the degree of empathetic response a class registers for
a story. Among these are the several items involved in choosing the right story
for a particular age group, the preparation of a story, the mode of presentation

and the use of visual aids. Good listening results from an interrelation of each of these factors. The following additional suggestions will assist to make telling and listening close companions. A storyteller must be sensitive to signs of poor listening as she tells her story. The shuffling of feet, whispering and yawning are overt indications that attention has strayed. More subtle signs of inattention, however, are of equal importance to a teller. The vacant stare, while not distracting to other members of a class, indicates a lack of interest. The day-dreaming child will fail to react immediately to a humorous turn in a story, although he will respond to gesticulation or radical changes in voice by the storyteller. Exaggerated laughter or surprise likewise indicates that a child is not following the story. A teacher who is constantly alert to these and other covert signs of inattention, will be a better communicator. She will want to determine why a child is not listening, and will make a special effort to accommodate this individual in her next story. For example, after school she might ask the child if he enjoyed the story. Regardless of the answer, (which would probably be in the defensive-affirmative), she might then ask him to help her choose a story for the next session.

An objective teacher will also analyze her own presentation for possible causes of inattention. It has already been stated that the proper technique for storytelling is interpretation, rather than acting. The story is chosen for its intrinsic merit and not for its potential value as an acting piece for a raconteur. Thus, throughout a presentation, the emphasis is on the story and the reaction of those who hear it. Fortunately, unlike an actress who plays before a darkened house, a storyteller interprets in a well-lighted classroom where she can see the responses of her listeners. If she adapts to the needs of her group, if she is expressive with her face and voice, the larger, overt physical gyrations of an actress are not necessary for maximum listening.

IMPROVING LISTENING EFFECTIVENESS

Wherever groups of children gather to hear a story, adults discover considerable variations in youngsters' abilities to think as they listen, separate key ideas as the story progresses, and relate the appropriate ones to their own lives. In Lundsteen's experiment in critical listening, it was found that there appears to be an independent ability (or abilities) to listen critically. Encouragement is found in the conclusion that the ability to listen can be improved by practice.[4] The following exercises, separated by general grade categories, are designed to assist this process.

Lower Elementary Grades

1. Assuming that there are twenty-four children in a group, have them form three groups by counting off, 1, 2, 3, 1, 2, 3. Arrange each group of eight one behind the other facing the front of the room. Whisper a short message to the head child in each line. Ask him to relay the material, in a whisper, to the child in back of him. Continue this procedure until the message has been passed to every child in

the line. Ask the last child to repeat aloud what he heard and then compare it with the original statement whispered to the first child. Listening drill begins in this exercise with the count-off. After playing this game several times, children call out their number more accurately and quickly and the accuracy of the whispered message improves.

2. Play "Simon Says," "Blindfold Man" or similar games that demand auditory discrimination and coordination.
3. Play "Find My Drawing" (or toy) placed on the chalkboard ledge. One child describes his object and the teacher permits a volunteer to bring it to its owner.
4. Tell a story and encourage children to draw a picture of a character, scene, etc.
5. After hearing a song, ask for a volunteer to describe the story behind the song.
6. Read a short paragraph containing an idea that "doesn't belong".
7. In all group activities, make a policy of not repeating instructions. If repetition is necessary, call on the children to repeat what has been stated.
8. Give a series of instructions to the group, increasing the difficulty of the action, i.e. "Kristi, take the book from my desk and place it on the table." To the next participant, "Jack, take the book from the table, turn to page 20 and show the picture to Shannon." etc. The game continues until someone fails to follow instructions properly. Make the instructions simple enough that feelings of adequacy are realized. The teacher should "tailor" the instructions to fit the intelligence level of the child she plans to call. In the illustration above, Jack might have listened but lacked the ability to recognize "20". If the game is played during a mathematics lesson, the instruction might be appropriate.
9. Tell a story and ask the children to suggest a title for it.
10. Play a tape containing familiar sounds i.e. boat whistle, church bell, traffic, ocean waves striking beach, bird call, siren, etc. More sophisticated sounds may be played to older children.
11. If a story being told contains a repetitive rhyme, encourage children to join in the refrain.
12. Sensitize children to daily sounds about them, i.e. bird sounds, laughter, sound of a jump rope striking the ground, sound of a skate board, etc.
13. The teacher may tell a story that includes words from the day's spelling lesson. She may preface her story by saying, "Today I am going to use some words in the story which you have just learned to spell. Let us see how many you recognize."
14. A story may include familiar items, i.e. "Today our story is going to have some animal friends in it which we saw at the zoo. Let us see if we can recognize them."
15. A story may have some special characteristic, i.e. "How many of you enjoy happy surprises? Good! Today's story has a special ending . . . let us watch for it."

Upper Elementary Grades

1. Have older children listen for the demagogue's tricks such as expressions and emotional appeals which are used to disguise false claims. Some television commercials might be used for this exercise.
2. Have a portion of a group do a choral reading and strive for clarity and accuracy of pronunciation. The balance of the class may serve as constructive critics.
3. After a story has been told, have the children discuss the action and pick out what appears to be the most important situations. This and other listening exercises should be enjoyable and devoid of serious penalty. Improper administration of listening exercises may instill a dislike for both listening and stories!

4. Tape record a child's story. Let him hear it alone or with the teacher as he prefers.
5. Have children listen for initial, medial, and final sounds, i.e. initially, "rip", "run", "ride"; medially, "moon", "soon", "boot"; finally, "going", "coming", "walking". This exercise is especially helpful for children seeking to improve English as their second language.
6. Have a volunteer compress the gist of a story in one sentence, i.e. "The boy climbed the mountain, saved his friend, and was given a medal."
7. Play the game "Twenty Questions." Several weeks after telling a story about Jane Addams, a teacher may reinforce the biography by asking the question, "Who loved nature, had pity for the poor and devoted most of her life to helping them?"
8. Play, "When I Grow Up I Want To Be...." Pair up the group and let them interview each other for ten minutes. Each child must then answer the questions, "What?" "Why?" and "How?" i.e. "Mary wants to be a doctor so she can help sick people. She wants to go to college to learn how to do this."
9. Have the children prepare, in a discussion situation, their own standards for courteous, critical listening.
10. The teacher tells a story and stops short of the climax; the children complete the story as they think it should be.
11. With older children, have a student read a statement which is illogical. Let the class listen for the fallacy, identify it, and then discuss it.
12. Have a student present the steps in artificial respiration. Encourage the children to take notes and then call for volunteers to describe this lifesaving process without recourse to written material.

TESTING LISTENING EFFECTIVENESS

Storytellers frequently ask themselves, "How am I doing?" "Do my children respond because they love the story period or are they really absorbing ideas?" If the interest with which a group listened can be determined, improved story selection and presentation may result. Some of the means of measuring listening are as follows: Stories may be told back by the children. By asking two or three children to tell the story as they heard it, their degree of attention can be determined. For example, one child could be asked to start a story, another to tell a sequential part of it and a third child could be asked to provide the conclusion. Usually volunteers are asked to start tell-back. A child who had not volunteered may be asked to pick up the thread of the story from the first student. Another variation of tell-back consists of such questions as "Who can tell us the names of all the characters in the story?" or "What character did you like best, Steven?" or "What was the most exciting part of the story for you, Susan?" A third form of recall is that of showing pictures from a well illustrated book and asking members of the group to reconstruct the story from the drawings. Children who fail to respond adequately during tell-back should not be reprimanded. This period following a story is merely a measure of listening. It has served as a technique to motivate a better response for the next story.

SUMMARY

This chapter has indicated the inadequacy of listening habits of today's school children and has suggested means of improving attention during storytelling sessions. Setting the stage for good listening requires the elimination of distractions and the creation of comfortable conditions for the listeners. Storytellers must view their efforts objectively and avoid mannerisms that detract from the story's content. Good listening is mandatory if storytelling is to promote feelings of group-relatedness, idea sharing, interest in problem solving and an appreciation of good literature. No means of measuring listening is foolproof. An inattentive child may have heard the story before, may understand a story but possess little artistic ability, or he may be fearful of self-expression. As far as listening is concerned, a storyteller's goal may be two-fold: (1) the discovery of factors of motivation which best influence her class to listen, and (2) the constant improvement of her techniques as a storyteller.

NOTES

1. Gloria L. Horrwith, "Listening, A Facet of Oral Language," *Elementary English,* 43, (December, 1966), pp. 858-859.
2. Ralph G. Nichols, "Teaching of Listening," *The Educational Digest,* (Nov. 1949), p. 34.
3. Wesley Wiksell, "The Problem of Listening," *Quarterly Journal of Speech,* 32, (December, 1946), p. 506.
4. S. W. Lundsteen, "Critical Listening: An Experiment," *Elementary School Journal,* 66: 311-315, 1966.

Visual Aids

8

PURPOSE

The purpose of employing visual aids when storytelling is to enhance the material being presented and thereby assist in the realization of a story's objective. The use of pictures, chalkboards, artifacts, flannel board objects, color forms and puppets are justifiable to the extent that they clarify a story's content, and do not detract from it.

Visual Aids.

DETERMINANTS IN CHOOSING VISUAL AIDS

A visual aid must be appropriate to be effective. A narrator should ask, "Is this visual aid suitable for the mental age of my class?" Assuming that the item is appropriate in this regard, the next question might be, "Does this aid clarify the point to be stressed in my story?'' *An aid must stress the point a storyteller is trying to make*. When conducting an Indian unit, one teacher ran into difficulty by displaying a totem pole made by the Haida of British Columbia when telling a story about Navaho culture. A child in the class, who had lived in Alaska, pointed out this obvious error, much to the teacher's embarrassment. Visual aids must belong to the story and not be introduced simply because of their novelty. Choosing a visual aid may be limited to the equipment that is available. The lack of opaque and slide projectors may eliminate some stories. If a story with a flannel board is planned, the board and easel should be available at the appointed hour. If a story is to be told in a school or library other than the one normally used, the program chairman should be apprised of the storyteller's needs in advance. Similar arrangements should be made for staging and properties required for puppetry. Those who tell stories soon learn that visual aids are usually time consumers. Ample time must be provided to use them effectively.

To summarize, the various functions of visual aids are to (1) increase understanding, (2) clarify the message, (3) gain attention of the listener, (4) improve imagery, (5) dramatize the story, (6) add color and variety to the story, (7) employ another medium to enhance the communication, (8) prove the point of the story, (9) improve the mental picture or visualization of the story, and (10) give examples which may be needed in the story.

GENERAL RULES FOR THE USE OF VISUAL AIDS

1. They should be large enough to be seen by all of the class.
2. Show everyone who is in the room listening.
3. Do not stand in front of the visual aid while using it.
4. Keep talking while showing visual aids.
5. Use the visual aid at the appropriate time in the story—when it is relevant—otherwise it may distract from your storytelling. When it is no longer necessary put it away, and erase your blackboard material when it is not relevant.
6. Do not have too many visual aids.
7. Show them long enough for each person to see and enjoy.
8. Do not turn your back to the audience as you show your visual aid.
9. The aid should enhance the story line, not be an appendage.
10. Observe the feedback of your audience in order to tell you how to react and adjust your use of visual aids. Adapt to age level and sophistication of the audience.

TYPES OF VISUAL AIDS

A storyteller is the most popular and effective visual aid! In addition to the narrator, there are several forms of visual aids frequently used in storytelling. They consist of pictures and chalkboards, objects mentioned in a story, flannel boards and color forms, and puppets.

Pictures and Chalkboards

Often times more pictures than necessary are used to tell a story especially if there is a picture on every page. If a story is told, usually a few pictures will enhance the story line adequately. By simply showing them at the appropriate times, they do not detract from the story. Caldecott award winners have excellent illustrations. Many of Dr. Seuss's stories come to life because of his colorful illustrations. This judgment must be made by the storyteller. Each story may or may not have an appropriate visual aid which enhances and clarifies the story line.

Sometimes the artistic talent of the teacher encourages her to reproduce several pictures from a book, especially to enlarge them so all in the classroom may easily see them. This endeavor makes the story more special to her and to the listeners. Her commitment is apparent and the children usually appreciate it.

Pictures are the most commonly used visual aids, but often they are misused. Some storytellers read each page and then slowly show each picture to every child which doubles the time necessary to tell the story. Many a child becomes bored with this redundant procedure. Too many pauses in a story are distracting. A teacher should keep talking while showing the visual aid. If the pictures are shown too quickly, many children do not grasp the meaning of the picture. Obviously, the teller or reader must watch the audience closely for feedback as to the rate of using the visual aids. These same rules apply to drawings on the chalkboard.

Objects Mentioned in the Story

When using items mentioned in a story such as Indian grinding bowls, clothing, or baskets, it is preferable to show these objects after the story has been told. More creativity on the part of the children is involved if they build a mental picture of a teepee or an animal based on the storyteller's description, *before* seeing the object. If a narrator said, "Bill's favorite sled dog was named 'Wolf'" and simultaneously displayed a picture of the animal, every child would see the same dog, and little thought would be given to the matter. However, if the dog is vividly described, each listener will develop his own mental image of Wolf and thereby participate in the story more intimately and creatively. Another advantage of showing the picture after the story is the unbroken continuity of the presentation. Delay, digressions and loss of interest due to some children's failure to pick up the thread of the story sometimes results from punctuating telling with picture showing. If the visual aids are durable, there are advantages in allowing children to handle the objects after a story has been told. It is not advisable to have the teacher explain an object and then start it on its way around the class while she continues to describe another visual aid. This practice puts one visual aid in competition with another. The preferred method is to place the items, after they have been explained, on a table and permit the youngsters to examine them at their leisure.

The use of visual aids will be more successful if a few simple suggestions are followed. All aids used should be large enough to be seen easily from the back of the room. When displayed, the item should be held high enough for all to see. Do not let lecterns, flag stands or other classroom furnishings obscure the children's sight line. If the students have faith that the storyteller will display an object long enough for all to see, better classroom decorum will result. Whenever visual aids are shown, the teacher should make certain that the audience is reminded of the relationship of the visual aid to the story they have just heard. Attention should also be directed to aspects of an item that might be lost in a casual inspection by a child. Interesting details of a wood carving, for example, should be pinpointed by the teller. By showing objects at a story's end and taking time to discuss them, the teller will learn which items are most effective to the development of a story. Lastly, the visual aid should be so familiar that it can be handled with ease and confidence. If primitive man's tools for making fire by friction are being displayed (such as the bow, spindle, socket and board) they should be assembled into position without fumbling or dropping parts of the assembly.

Flannel Boards and Colorforms

Although a told story followed by illustrations is more conducive to creative thinking by the listener than a flannel board story, the latter (like puppetry) serves an important function in storytelling.

Values

For years educators have appreciated the value of visual aids in the learning process. They agree that some children learn more quickly with visual aids rather than with auditory stimuli. Along with storytelling, the teaching of spelling, arithmetic, science and other subjects can be enriched and stimulated by use of flannel board stories. Like the puppetry activity, flannel board stories may be integrated with art to facilitate the child's artistic development. Once a group has decided upon a story, all members may assist the teacher in preparing the story's pictures for mounting. The children may also derive aesthetic pleasure from drawings they make for flannel board application. Flannel boards have high entertainment value and they rightfully have been referred to as magic boards. Youngsters never seem to tire of seeing pictures cling to their near-vertical surfaces. An introverted child may be encouraged to participate in group activity by placing one of the pictures mentioned in the story on the flannel board. This is certain to be a successful experience and it will encourage him to try again. Nursery and kindergarten children work tirelessly and imaginatively building on a flannel board with ''blocks'' of different sizes, shapes and colors. Flannel boards may be used as a means of follow-up to reinforce a story that has just been told. For example, after telling ''Jack and the Beanstalk'' a teacher may say, ''Children, you have just heard the exciting adventures of Jack. Will you raise your hand if you would like to help us tell the story again?'' There is usually an enthusiastic response at this point and the teacher will then produce the flannel board and pictures for the story which have been previously arranged in numerical order. Then she asks, "Who can tell how this story begins?" Mary volunteers, "Jack was lazy and lived in an old house with his mother." The teacher says, "Mary, you listened carefully. Would you like to put Jack's house on the magic board?" This method is continued until the children have retold the story they have just heard. They are rewarded for volunteering by being permitted to build a story with pictures. Use of a flannel board as "feedback" permits a story to be told initially with maximum imaginative play. In addition, the children are stimulated visually as the story is retold.

Procedure for Use

Flannel boards may be constructed in any shape and size and the latter will determine in part, the procedure for use. Small lap boards are balanced against the body or held as a teacher sits before youngsters who are usually on floor mats before her. If a large, easel-type board is used, care should be taken to see that it is firmly anchored. The professional aspects of a flannel board presentation are lost when flimsy supports waver or the board crashes to the floor. Easel-mounted boards frequently are adjustable which permits kindergartners to reach and see the board with the same ease enjoyed by sixth graders. Regardless of the size board used, it must be easily seen by all members of the audience. With large boards, a teacher should stand to one side as she works, being careful not to obstruct the view for children sitting along the sides of the room. Pictures should be arranged in proper sequence before beginning a story. The order should be double-checked before beginning narration. This procedure is simplified if a number is placed on the back of each picture. The latter should be held or placed facedown, with the numbered side up. If possible, pictures should be kept out of sight before placing them on the board. Each object should be a surprise. Usually, a picture will be placed on the board simultaneously with the pronouncing of the word that identifies it. For example, "At that moment Jerry saw an Indian (teacher places picture of Indian on flannel board) emerge from the forest." This procedure may be varied. If a teacher is telling a participation story involving identification of a described picture, she might say, "It is round, red, grows on a tree and makes delicious cider. What is it?" When the children respond, she places a picture of an apple on the flannel board. Pictures must be involved in the immediate action or they detract from the story. As soon as the action sweeps past the picture of a character, even though the narrative returns to the same picture later, it should be removed from the board. For example, when retelling the story of "The Three Little Pigs," the three pigs might be shown walking down the road together on their way to build their three houses. When the story shifts to the little pig who built his house of straw, the other two pigs should be removed from the board. It is disconcerting to have pictures slide from the board before their removal is desirable.

Procedures for making pictures are as follows: Pictures of people or objects (cut from magazines, coloring books, or old textbooks) should be glued or pasted to construction paper to increase their stability. When the children draw the pictures for a story, they may work directly on construction paper. Then each picture should be carefully cut out. The reverse side of the picture is then prepared for adherence to the flannel board by gluing felt or flannel on it. Some teachers prefer to use small strips of medium-grained sandpaper instead of felt or flannel. Today small pieces of velcro may be attached by glue or rubber cement to the objects for a very secure hold to the flannel board. In some stores they may be purchased in the shape of small circles with adhesive on one side. Velcro insures adhesiveness.

In the construction of flannel boards, for the base of the flannel board you will need a piece of heavy cardboard, Celotex, plywood, Bristol board, ¼" Masonite, or the back board from carpet samples. A 3' x 4' board is recommended because this size provides space for using large pictures that may be viewed easily in the classroom. If the board is to be transported, it will prove advantageous to use either plywood or Masonite because these materials hold hinge screws satisfactorily. Boards of this type should be built of two sections, measuring 3' x 4' each. To cover the base board you will need a piece of long-fibered nap flannel (the color should be appropriate for background of stories) cut approximately 3" larger than the board. This dimension will provide a 1½" overlap on all sides. Pull the flannel tightly over the board and tack it on the reverse side. Fold it neatly at the corners and bind the edges with masking tape. If you are constructing a board in two sections, be sure to cover each section with flannel before attaching the hinges.

Colorforms are a relatively new product on the market. Essentially they consist of a plastic "felt board" and smaller pieces of plastic in the shapes of the objects or pictures for telling or creating stories. Once the plastic has been chosen for the colorform board, any small thin piece of plastic will automatically adhere to that board. Very colorful objects may be used as visual aids in storytelling because of this new creation of colorforms. Colorforms also "stick" to windows, mirrors, refrigerator doors, etc. Therefore, the teacher may have a handy "board" already present in the classroom. All that may be needed are small thin pieces of plastic with appropriate markings or designs. Colorforms are also durable.

Puppetry

Puppetry is considered a form of creative drama as mentioned earlier. The use of puppets has been widespread. They have been found in Egyptian tombs and were used in rituals of ancient Greece and Rome. Early history of China, Japan, and India records the use of puppets. In Japan, the puppet play or Joruri was more extravagant than the Kabuki. During the medieval period, puppets were used in religious drama and as entertainment. Many countries developed their favorites such as Punch and Judy from England and Petruchka from Russia. Today the Shari Show and the Muppets demonstrate children's love of puppets as visual aids.

The term "puppets" has been known to include everything from finger plays to marionettes. Marionettes or string puppets are quite complicated for children in elementary school classes to use. There are numerous kinds of puppets to be made and enjoyed by children. These include finger puppets, fist puppets, glove puppets, stick puppets, rod puppets, shadow puppets, hand puppets, papier mache puppets, box puppets, paper bag puppets, sock puppets, and marionette or string puppets. All are discussed in this unit. Although storytelling with puppets does not take the place of creative drama resulting from story-acting described in Chapter 5, it nevertheless may contribute richly to a child's development.

Values

Puppet play helps a teacher understand her class members more fully. Youngsters identify puppets with real people and actual life situations. A child who acts the part of a father in a story and who is prone to be antagonistic toward his make-believe family, might be revealing inner feelings that explain in part the puppet-operator's cause of nail-biting or other forms of emotional maladjustment. Puppet play may serve as a stepping stone to other forms of creative drama. Some children who are afraid to participate in story-acting, will often volunteer to take part in a puppet play. The puppet serves as an aid, a means of detracting attention from the child to the puppet, and consequently reduces some of the pressure felt by the child when performing before other class members. Because the puppet-actor normally is not visible to the audience, puppet story-acting has proved to be an easy first-step for some youngsters toward the development of poise in oral communication. This activity not only helps a child overcome stage fright but it also encourages the development of an expressive inflectional pattern. Because the child is not usually visible during production, facial expression cannot be seen in the puppet itself. The young actor must be helped to identify fully with the part he is playing and reveal his feeling through his voice . . . through his *inflectional pattern*. Helpful exercises that will assist a child to achieve inflectional flexibility may be found in the Appendix.

Story-acting with puppets also helps children to adjust to and become cooperating members of a group. This process may be assisted by stressing the importance of working as a team and not as individuals. A child who becomes petulant and refuses to let his puppet play in a story, must be made aware that the entire casts' success is dependent upon his cooperation. A child not only experiences speech improvement and emotional and intellectual development through "putting words in a puppet's mouth" but he may also be given an opportunity to improve his artistic ability. After a suitable story has been told, members of the audience who wish to participate may be encouraged to prepare puppets. It has been found that children usually identify themselves more quickly with puppets they have constructed. Lastly, this activity is valuable for the sheer joy it brings children. Puppet-acting of stories encourages children to hurry to school in the morning! Tom Smith knows that before long he will be Leo the Lion. Mary Jones is eager to become a frightened Chicken Little. Time speeds away in this magic land of adventure and fancy.

Other important values of puppetry were discovered in recent dissertation research. George Neff found that the creative imagination of young children was enhanced by the use of puppet performance and construction.[1] Donald Myers discovered that group puppet activities improves adjustment capability of mentally retarded subjects as measured by the California Test of Personality.[2] Edward Bartunek concluded that puppets seem to fill a universal human need for a unique language medium.[3] There may be value to everyone when the use of puppets accompany storytelling.

Characteristics of a Story for Puppet-Acting

Most stories which are suitable for story-acting may be adapted to puppetry. The first requisite is action. The tale must move briskly. "The Three Billy Goats Gruff," "The Little Red Hen" and "The Gingerbread Boy" are but three of many tales suitable for puppetry. Because the preparation of puppets is so time-consuming, stories selected should be those which the children will want to repeat. Generally, stories which are in demand for retelling, as far as interest is concerned, will be safe for puppet-acting. The story should contain characters that present challenging, imaginative subjects for puppet construction that are not impossible to construct. For example, a child might be able to sketch the fierce countenance of the North Wind but be at a loss to draw a gnu. Showing the children a picture of a gnu for reproduction destroys much of the creativity that should attend art work of this nature. Instead, a teacher might create a mental picture for the class by saying, "Today, children, I am going to tell you about a strange-looking animal that lives in far-off Africa. It is the size of a large deer and has an ox-like head and horns. Its tail and mane look like those of a horse. It is brown and stands four and one-half feet high. That is the distance from the floor to this mark on the chalkboard." After the children have had the fun of trying to draw a gnu, they should be shown a picture of one. A final characteristic of a story for puppet-acting concerns its number of characters. The size of a puppet stage usually determines how many characters can be accommodated. Usually six children and their puppets will prove to be the maximum number that can be handled satisfactorily in one scene.

Before the puppets are constructed, a story should be selected. Children love to make puppets and may spend much too much time on the puppet construction and not have a story or script in mind. It is best to start with a story. Select an appropriate story for puppetry and rewrite it in script form. Next, construct the puppets carefully. Several types of puppets may be used in one story. The children may help decide with some guidance from the instructor what kind of puppet should be made for a particular character. After the production, a child may wish to find other stories which use some of the same characters. A story index which lists animal or types of characters used in various stories may be a helpful reference.

For example, children in a fourth grade scripted the story of Potter's *The Tale of Peter Rabbit*. They wanted to use it at Easter time. They decided to make sock puppets into rabbits. They did an excellent job. In practicing the story they discovered that they liked to act out the story almost like story dramatization in creative drama. They used the front of the room as their stage. They walked around and used appropriate nonverbal gestures to reinforce the verbal message that the puppets on their hands delivered. They did not want to be confined to a small puppet theatre. Peter Slade in *Child Drama* suggests that children do not need a puppet theatre in order to use their puppets.[4] Surely a storyteller may use a puppet to tell a story and stand in front of the class and not need a theatre. Freedom of expression and movement is a key to the interpretation of puppet stories. Many other rabbit stories may be discovered for the children: *The Velveteen Rabbit, I Am a Bunny, Runaway Bunny, Brer Rabbit, The Egg Book*, etc.

Puppet Theatre

A puppet theatre is not necessary for a puppet production. However, if it enhances the story line or if the children create one, it is a worthwhile project. Stages may be simple or complex.

1. Turn a table on its side, add butcher paper and have the children paint on color appropriately.

2. Place a broomstick on top of two chairs. Drape a blanket or sheet over the broomstick and you have an instant theatre.

3. Cloth or cardboard may be pinned or taped across a doorway or a window making a simple theatre. The cloth only has to be high enough to conceal puppeteers.

4. A piece of flannel the full length of the door may be used. A hole will be cut in it low enough for the children to reach, yet still be concealed. The felt is attached actually at the top of the doorway with an expandable clothes hanger rod used in some cars and closets.

5. The best boxes for a puppet theatre are probably a refrigerator box or a stove or large appliance box. Dependent on the size of the children, select a box and decorate it appropriately.

6. Smaller wooden or cardboard boxes which set on tables are also used to make puppet theatres.

7. A puppet theatre out of wood is a more permanent fixture. A wooden theatre may be very large like a screen with three sides.

8. One of the most satisfactory blinds for this purpose is a 4' x 8' piece of fibrous wallboard 3/8'' thick. It is relatively light in weight, it allows for scenery to be thumbtacked to it, and it stores easily. The blind may be supported on the

reverse side by two sawhorses. It is advisable to wire the wall board to the sawhorse to prevent the actors from being inadvertently exposed during their production! Regardless of the type stage used, it should be high enough so that the children can sit on small chairs behind it. Add a curtain on a string across the opening.

9. Some individual storytellers prefer a tray with two holes for their hands to come up through the bottom as a kind of puppet theatre. The tray is held up by ribbons or string around the storyteller's neck, much like wearing a necklace. The tray may be colorfully decorated and it is a unique approach to storytelling.

10. In the case of the marionette, the child must stand or sit above the puppet in order to work the strings. This situation requires not only the turned table or the sheet over the bottom part of the door, but the upper part must be hidden behind a sheet or blanket also which may be suspended from the top of the door jam or the ceiling. It should be fastened a foot or two in front of the lower sheet also. Children may stand behind chairs and manipulate their marionettes on the seats of the chairs effectively. They do not need to be completely hidden at all times.

11. The shadow puppet theatre will be explained later in this unit.

Producing a Puppet Story

The requisites for a story for puppetry have already been discussed. However, the children-participants should have some voice in the selection of a story. A teacher might select several stories with desirable characteristics and the students could select from these. Primary grade youngsters could vote for the tale of their choice. Middle and upper grade children should have the same privilege or, being more mature, they should be encouraged to write a story of their own. Character casting is actually preliminary to puppet-making for each actor should construct his own puppet. Actual casting is preceded by orientation to the story explained in Chapter 5. Even though a child will not be visible to the audience when the puppet is manipulated, it is necessary that he go through the procedure of standing before his peers and characterize his puppet in some way. If he is playing the Papa Bear in ''Goldilocks and The Three Bears'' he might share the bear's reaction when it discovered that someone had been sleeping in his bed. This helps him to ''feel'' the part and influences his inflectional pattern as he speaks for his puppet. Every scene in a story should be assigned a different cast, if necessary, to insure a role for each child. In addition to developing a sympathetic identification with the parts they are to play, the actors must be made aware of the mechanics of puppetry. They should hold their puppets at the correct height during the presentation. If the puppet is held too high, the child's arm will be exposed; if the puppet is held too low, the character will appear to be walking on his knees. Either of these conditions will cause undue laughter and destroy artistic illusion. The evaluation of puppet acting will follow essentially the same lines as those set forth in Chapter 5 for story acting. Emphasis should be placed on inflection, projection of the spoken word and its intelligibility. The children should agree, beforehand, on standards for helpful conditions backstage, such as the absence of noise, correct handling of puppets, cooperation with the group and willingness to follow instructions. Praise must not be too lavish or too scant. Puppetry, like story-acting, must leave the participants feeling adequate and encouraged.

Types of Puppets

Finger Puppets

A piece of felt or construction paper should be made into a snug tube for the finger. The felt may be sewn up the back, and the paper may be glued, pasted, or stapled. Decorate the felt or paper in order to make it look like the desired character. Attach another piece of material for the face if desired. One instructor told several stories about mice. Then she gave each student a small piece of gray felt that would fit over their index or "pointer" finger, a box full of buttons, beads, cloth, ribbons, paper, etc. She instructed the students to create their favorite mouse character from one of the stories. Later they acted out the stories with their imaginative finger "mouse" puppets.

A finger puppet may be made by creating the face of the character on paper or felt and leaving a short narrow strip at each side in order to become a band like a ring to fit around the puppeteer's finger. All fingers may be used, but the index finger of each hand probably allows the most flexibility.

As the famous story, "Thumbelina" from Hans Christian Andersen suggests, a finger puppet may be made from a thumb by merely marking a face on the inside of the thumb and adding a piece of yarn for hair or a piece of cloth for a headscarf. Little puppets like this are delightful in some stories, and should not be ruled out because of their simplicity.

Finger puppets may be constructed in many ways from different things such as styrofoam balls, peanut shells, small potatoes, etc. Merely place the object on the finger and construct an appropriate face on it.

Fingers may also be used as the legs on one variety of puppets. In other words, fingers are down not up in this type of finger puppet. The child may draw the face and torso of a character. Where the top of the legs should be, cut out two finger holes. The head and body may be stuffed with soft paper toweling in order to give a fuller effect. Pipe cleaners may be used to give some stiffness. Little paper shoes may be glued on the child's fingernails in order to look like feet. This is a clever finger puppet that can walk across the table.

Another variation on this type of finger puppet can be the puppet whose face is drawn on the upper wrist of the child, whose clothes are attached over the hand with the extended thumb and little finger as arms, whose legs are the first two fingers and whose paper shoes are glued on the fingernails of the first two fingers. Hair or a hat may be attached with sticky tape; in fact, all clothes of paper or material may be applied with sticky tape. The child should remember to hold the ring finger back. This finger is not needed in the operation of the puppet. Consequently, a little older child may utilize this type of puppet.

Another interesting finger puppet is to turn the fingers down toward the table and extend the middle finger or "Mr. Tall Man" on which you may attach the head of an animal like a lion, rhinocerous, or bear. If the head is made out of felt and sewn like a tube with the bent middle finger fitted snugly inside, you have an animal finger puppet that walks on the table.

Fist Puppets

The bare hand is used as the face of the puppet. The hand is held in a loose fist and the mouth becomes the part between the thumb and first finger. The features are applied with water colors or marking pens. Lips, beards, and mustaches may be colorfully added. The eyes of the puppet are drawn closer to the knuckles. The addition of hair or a hat makes the puppet come to life. The interesting feature of this puppet is that the mouth moves as the puppet speaks. A child may wear a glove and decorate it appropriately so that the hand is never marked and the puppet is more permanent. If gloves are used, the features may be applied in many media.

Glove Puppets

One type of glove puppet has already been mentioned. For finger puppets on a glove, each of the finger tips may be decorated on the underside of the glove. The head may also be placed on the two middle fingers, and the first and little

Yarn

Attached Cloth

Ring Finger
Held Back

Paper Shoes

finger may serve as ears. As a very useful puppet, a small piece of velcro may be sewn on the inside tips of each finger of the glove. Then many different faces may be made out of felt and put on the fingers when appropriate. This is a superb visual aid for many kinds of stories. To insure security of attachment, a small piece of velcro may also be sewn to the back of each felt face. This puppet also has permanence.

If a glove is used with fingers down, a small ball of yarn or a styrofoam ball may be attached to the back of the hand and from it several yarn legs may be attached to the fingers creating the illusion of a spider for *Charlotte's Web* or an octopus. Any number of other animals may be created from a glove in this position.

If a mitten is used instead of a glove, the large shape forms the head for the puppet. It may be decorated with cloth, buttons, beads, or paints. This may be easier than gloves for younger children to use.

Stick Puppets

This type of puppet is very popular because it can be made inexpensively, accurately, and simply. The object is usually made of oaktag, heavy construction paper, thin metal or cardboard and then attached to a stick. Every front facing puppet should have a back, and every side-facing puppet should have two sides in order to look either direction. The puppet may be very simple or complex. It may be copied directly from a storybook or imaginatively created by the child. Two paper plates may be glued together with a dowel stick between them. Decorate the plates and the puppet is complete. The object may be given a three-dimensional appearance by stuffing the figure. A paper cone for the nose, face, or body gives the same effect. The stick may be marked at the bottom when the figure faces forward or stage right. This will quickly tell the puppeteer if the puppet is facing the correct direction so that the very thin "side" apearance is not shown the audience. The puppet must face completely forward or backward, or completely to one side or the other if it is a profile puppet. Otherwise the object is not clearly viewed.

Styrofoam balls may be good heads cut to fit on a dowel. They may be round or egg-shaped and colorfully decorated. Other innovative objects such as soap, wooden spoons, clothespins, etc., may be placed on a dowel to make a stick puppet. The stick may be a tongue depressor, doweling rod or any other piece of wood approximately the same size.

Rod Puppets

A rod puppet is basically a stick puppet which has two parts forming the object which are attached to each other by a clasp allowing freedom of movement. A stick is attached to one part and a rod is attached to the other. This animation may be achieved in many different ways, but essentially one hand holds the stick and the other the rod which moves. For example, a stick could hold the cut-out object of an ostrich body while the rod operates the head of the ostrich. As the head moves up and down, it gives the appearance of walking, running, eating, or hiding its head in the sand. This is made possible by attaching the bottom of the neck to the top of the body by a clasp or brad. Thus, an animate animal puppet is produced. This puppet should also be able to be viewed from both sides front and back or right and left sides like the stick puppet.

Shadow Puppets

This type of puppet is an extension of the stick or rod puppet. A special Shadow Theatre must be used for this type of puppet. A strong light must be directed upon a translucent screen out of a lightweight sheet, gauze, muslin, or architect's tracing paper. The latter may be attached to a frame or a device to hold it in an upright position. Scenery may be cut out in black and pinned directly to the screen. When the puppet is placed between the light and the screen a shadow is created. Obviously, the audience should sit on the opposite side of the screen.

The puppeteer should work his stick or rod puppets as close to the screen as possible in order to make clear sharp shadow puppets. There are several means to create color in these shadow puppets. Colored transparent paper like cellophane or stronger material may be used in constructing the puppet. The acetate will give a unique effect to a puppet theatre. A puppet may have colored buttons, eyes, stripes, clothes, etc. Certain features of an animal may be accented like the red flame from a dragon's mouth or the blue water spouting out of the top of a whale's head. The entire puppet show may be more colorful by attaching colored tissue or acetate to the screen. The light bulb may also be changed to different colors to add special effects.

Hand Puppets

Perhaps the best known puppet is one that fits over the hand. The thumb forms one puppet arm. Into the head are fitted either the first, second, or third fingers, or a combination thereof. The remaining fingers operate the other puppet arm or are tucked in fist position. Dependent upon the dexterity and coordination of the child, he or she will learn to insert and use the appropriate fingers. It is good, however, for a teacher to be familiar with several possible ways to hold and operate a hand puppet in order to inform the student. The entire hand is equivalent to the puppet's upper torso. Many hand puppets sold in stores are made to fit adult hands and are too large for children's hands. The best pattern is the size of the hand of the child who intends to use the puppet.

This kind of puppet is quite flexible and animate. It is responsive to verbal cues and dramatic action. Children have little difficulty in making creative and imaginative hand puppets. The head may be decorated with sequins, colored felt, buttons for the eyes, ears, nose, and mouth. If the accessories are sewn on, they will last longer than if glued. The puppet's head may be slightly stuffed. The body or arms may use similar decorative effects. The head may be made out of a styrofoam ball. The ball is cored in order to allow a finger to be inserted. The head may be a tennis ball, a vegetable, a fruit, a block, a light bulb, a box, or any imaginative object. There is almost an endless variety of types of hand puppets.

Infants in particular enjoy washable hand puppets. Early in their development they recognize faces and such an animate toy delights the youngest child.

Puppets have universal appeal.

Instructions For Making A Hand Puppet
For A Young Child

1. The most important element is a face on the puppet. Infants recognize a face as early as six weeks old. So whether you make a clown, a snowman, Santa Claus, boy, girl, or whatever, the puppet should have clear and distinctive features on the face. Second, the arms of the puppet should be flexible enough to hold hands with the child or tickle him/her.

2. The puppet should be sewn from material that is not fuzzy. A polyester, not a felt, is advisable because it is easily washed along with infant clothing and will not become fuzzy if the baby sucks it or puts it in his/her mouth. Bright colors and old clean scraps of material work beautifully. Use of sequins, yarn, and buttons are not advised.

3. All stitching may be done on the outside of the puppet. All work on the face may be done before the two sides are actually sewn together around the edges. This makes decorating the face easier.

4. This puppet may be made before the baby arrives and will be an excellent toy for your child especially for traveling. It is easy to carry, lightweight, and the baby becomes attached to it quickly. Young children like the animation and movement of the puppet as you manipulate it on your hand. You may place the baby on his/her tummy and lay the puppet in front of him/her so the infant can touch and manipulate it. It is undoubtedly an excellent investment in toys and a personalized gift for your own or another's child.

Papier Mache Puppets

Volumes have been written on the use of papier mache. There are many ways to make papier mache. Here are five suggestions:

1. The papier mache pulp or sawdust and plaster of paris mixed with wheat paste or wallpaper paste makes an excellent compound to construct the head of the puppet.
2. Cellu-clay Instant Papier Mache may be used.
3. Newspaper or the familiar brown paper towels cut in strips may be dipped in wheat paste and water, or
4. Flour and water, or
5. White liquid glue and water to make a simple compound for construction.

Crumple the paper and plan the shape of the head. The paper strips should be dipped in the paste and then wrapped around a crumpled newspaper or a balloon firmly attached to a dowel rod. Work the head into the desired shape adding different features like a chin, lips, horns, nose, bill, mouth, ears, etc. Allow drying time, then paint the head and use beads, yarn felt, etc., to add details. Through the opening at the neck of the puppet, the balloon may be popped or the crumpled paper removed so there is room to hold the head on the child's finger. Finally, attach a circle of cloth to form the costume. It may or may not have arms like the hand puppet. In effect, the papier mache puppet may be a papier mache head on a dowel with a body operated like a hand puppet.

Box or Object Puppets

A box makes an excellent base for a puppet. The box may simply be the head of a hand puppet or a larger box like a milk carton may be the body of a puppet with smaller boxes attached to form the head and arms. Match boxes, jello boxes, tissue boxes and others help make interesting box puppets. Egg cartons may be used to form the mouth and teeth of a crocodile puppet by attaching some green material to one end. One young student made a convincing snake puppet from egg cartons.

Paper Bag Puppets.

Paper Bag Puppets

This type of puppet is inexpensive, easily decorated, and may have a workable mouth. This type of puppet is popular with young children. The head is drawn on construction paper and glued on the bottom of the folded bag with the top of the mouth slightly carried over the bottom edge of the bag. The lower lip is attached to the side of the bag and the tongue or inside of the mouth is under the overfold of the bag. The mouth operates rather effectively in a paper bag puppet which accounts for their popularity. If the bag slips in the children's hands, be sure the bag is small enough for their hands and use sticky tape on their fingers to help grasp the bag at the overfold or mouth portion. The side of the sack below the mouth may be decorated like the body of the character.

A paper bag may simply be placed flat on a table and colored like the desired character. For example, young children may easily create the "wild things with yellow eyes" from Maurice Sendak's *Where the Wild Things Are* by this means of puppetry.

Paper bags may also be stuffed to create a full round head, a dowel inserted, and a string or ribbon tied around the neck of the dowel. The head may be simply or elaborately decorated to represent the story character. The body portion may also be decorated and holes may be cut for the arms of the puppet, actually the fingers of the child. The fingers which represent the arms of a person or front limbs of an animal, may show in the front of the bag. With the index finger supporting the head, the thumb and middle finger may appear in the front of the bag as the front feet of a little mouse. However, the holes for arms are usually cut in the sides of the bags and the fingers extended which represent arms of the character. Paper arms may be added and attached by brads. If the paper bag is stuffed and made into the head of a character and tied around a stick, we have a combination paper bag and stick puppet. A paper cup or cone-shaped cup make an excellent nose. Several cups may be used as ears for the puppet.

Suggestions for making paper bag puppets include:

1. Use cotton as hair, beard, mustache, or clothing decoration.
2. Use yarn for hair or decor.
3. Use material glued to paper bag as clothing. Use denim for jeans. Use corduroy to make the bear for Don Freeman's *Corduroy*.
4. Curl construction paper for hair or eyelashes.
5. Make a paper nose that stands up on the bag and is three dimensional. The nose may be normal or pointed. A pig's nose may be made by simply drawing a circle and putting two dots in it.
6. Add a paper tooth or more on the top flap of the bag or top of the mouth.
7. Use cellophane paper, styrofoam shapes, pipe cleaners, sparkle, tissue paper, kleenex, or feathers for variety. For a feathered effect, cut paper in layers or like fringe, or use a simple square of paper, 1'' by 1'', folded corner to corner and placing the fold on top, glue the back side to the paper bag. Several of these folded squares may easily become the breast of an owl.
8. Add paper arms and legs to the body of the sack. Paper arms may fold forward or backward and then forward like the leg and paw of a bear. Arms may be attached with gold fasteners or brads which makes them moveable. Legs especially those of a bird may be added with two strips of paper in an accordian fold, and glued to paper feet at the ends.
9. The mouth may be made with an oval circle, folded in the middle and attached under the flap. The upper part of the circle may extend beyond the flap and be folded up and glued on the bag flap in order to become the top lip. The bottom part of the oval circle may extend down a small bit below the flap and become the lower lip. It is important to decorate the inside of the mouth.
10. When making paper bag puppets with very young children, some parts may be previously cut out and they can glue them on. Rabbits may be made by three-year-olds very easily. Have the paper top of the head, the ears, the black paper whiskers, and some cotton available for the youngsters to glue on the bag. Ask them to color on the eyes, mouths and some markings on the inside of the ears. The children really feel like this is their own creation when some minor parts are added by them.

This suggestion was contributed by Jeannine Arterburn, Preschool Director, Broadacres, Rolling Hills Estates, California.

Sock Puppets

Like paper bags, the toes of stockings may be stuffed to make the head of the puppet. Add a dowel and a string around the neck, and you have a simple puppet. Two slits in the body portion of the sock will provide openings for the fingers which represent arms. Nylons may be stuffed and represent the heads of persons. They really do look like skin. Then decorate appropriately so they look like they have eyes, ears, nose, and mouth.

Sock puppets made with a mouth are very gratifying to children because the mouth usually works so well. If all features are sewn on, the puppet has permanence. For younger children, features would have to be glued on, however. Perhaps the most important feature is the mouth in the sock puppet. The authors have experimented with this type of puppet for many years because from a communication viewpoint, it is perhaps the best form of simple puppetry to stress good speech.

A tube sock is the best type of sock to use when making a sock puppet, but any sock will do. Smaller socks for smaller hands are advisable. The toe of the sock should be pushed as far in as possible so that the thumb operates the bottom jaw and the fingers operate the upper jaw. This will create a large and workable mouth. Once the toe is pushed in sufficiently, the sock should be sewn or "tacked" on both sides of the thumb in order to hold the thumb securely when operating the bottom jaw. In other words, just sew a few stitches to secure the inside bottom of the mouth to the outside neck region. If a tongue is sewn inside the mouth, it should also be attached to the bottom inside of the mouth and be certain that when the mouth is closed the tongue does not protrude. We do not recommend using the heel and toe of a sock to make a mouth because the puppet usually looks like it has a tremendous overbite. This is especially true when a child operates it.

This approach to making sock puppets allows the creation of many types of animals. By adding pieces of felt, pom-poms, earrings, hats, straw, yarn, cotton balls for stuffing the inside of the sock, etc., almost any animal or type of person may come to life. A spectacular lion may be made from a yellow sock trimmed with two or three circles of yellow and brown felt which look like a mane. A giraffe may be made with a long neck, because the sock covers the child's arm like a sleeve. Add brown spots and two tiny horns on the top of the head. The socks may be easily dyed to make them any color.

Animals that may be created out of socks include the walrus, monkey, dog, cat, donkey, pig, wolf, snake, dragon, duck, goose, reindeer, frog, lamb, horse, rabbit, camel, chicken, turkey, owl, and elephant by using a second stuffed sock as the trunk. A turtle may be created by putting a green sock through a round hole cut in a small painted tissue box. Pipe cleaners usually provide enough stiffness

Sock Puppets.

for ears on a rabbit or donkey. An adorable dog named "Rags" may be produced by using rug yarn and hooking it through the sock.

If a stiffer mouth is desired, cut the sock and add cardboard. For example, in a baby chick puppet a pointed mouth is necessary. A small slit for the mouth should be cut in a yellow tube sock. Cut the cardboard shape for the mouth. Cut two pieces of material at least ¼ inch larger than the cardboard and place the cardboard between the two pieces of material (orange felt) and pin in place on the sock which is turned inside out. Then stitch carefully in place. Sew the material and not the cardboard. Turn the sock right side out and add stuffing or cottonballs underneath to give more shape to the head. The knuckles should always be held high when operating a sock puppet. Add black felt eyes, and a "peep" from the child, you have a baby chick. These mouths are remindful of the Muppets especially if they are cut like two half circles. Numerous exciting possibilities await the child who makes sock puppets.

Marionettes or String Puppets

This type of puppet requires more skill to create and operate than other types of puppets. But for older children, it is a challenge. The figure is attached to strings which are operated by a control stick in the form of a cross. The head is moved from side to side by tipping the stick up and down, whereas moving the puppet forward at the same time gives the appearance of walking. The strings attached to the ends of the horizontal stick usually operate the arms. Tipping that

A SIMPLE TWO HAND CONTROL PLAN
FOR A MARIONETTE

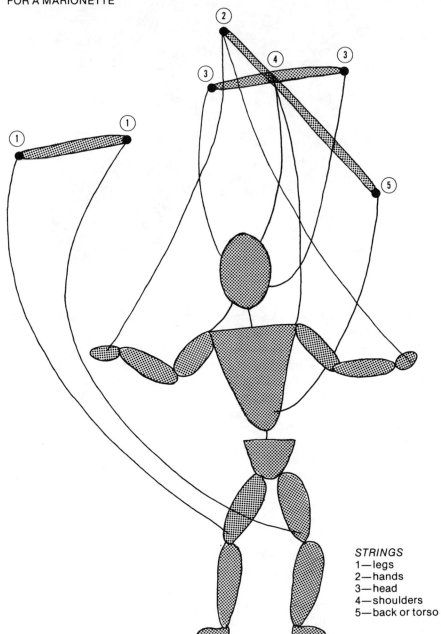

STRINGS
1—legs
2—hands
3—head
4—shoulders
5—back or torso

stick right or left gives animated gestures to the figure. A marionette may be made from wood or other carved material, heavy cutouts, or stuffed animals or dolls. One of the easiest methods of beginning this study of marionettes as a visual aid is to purchase several old used stuffed toys from a Goodwill store. They are easy to manipulate. Attach strings or nylon cord at the appropriate places and staple it to a control stick. Practice. You may be amazed at the results. If a child operates the head and one arm or the other, this is a good beginning. An ostrich is an interesting animal to construct for this type of puppet. Make the feet out of heavy wood, the neck and lout of cord or rope, and the body and head out of styrofoam balls. This type of puppet has interesting and unique movement.

SUMMARY

In this unit, visual aids were defined in terms of type, functions and rules of use. Values and determinants of their usage were considered. Visual aids include pictures and the chalkboard, objects, the feltboard and colorforms, and puppets. The value of puppets in particular was indicated. Types of puppet theatres were introduced. Characteristics of producing a story for puppets were explained. Numerous kinds of puppets were discussed: finger puppets, fist puppets, glove puppets, stick puppets, rod puppets, shadow puppets, hand puppets, papier mache puppets, box puppets, paper bag puppets, sock puppets, marionette or string puppets. Above all, visual aids should enhance the story.

NOTES

1. George William Neff, "The Creative Imagination of Young Children As Revealed in a Puppet Construction and Puppet Performance Test," *Dissertation Abstracts,* (January, 1964), Vol. 24, No. 7, p. 3206.
2. Donald George Myers, "A Comparison of the Effects of Group Children," *Dissertation Abstracts,* (March, 1971), Vol. 31, No. 9, p. 5234-A.
3. Edward Paul Bartunek, "The Use of Puppets for Christian Education," *Dissertation Abstracts,* (July, 1965), Vol. 26, No. 1, p. 205.
4. Peter Slade, Child Drama, (London: University of London Press Ltd.), 1967, p. 318.

Creative Approaches to Storytelling

9

Communication is the key to the art of storytelling. There are numerous ways in which that communication may be improved, stimulated, and utilized for discovering new frontiers of storytelling and the learning of language and literature. The following suggestions given by instructors of storytelling and creative drama are intended to provide innovative approaches to the experiencing of those disciplines. New experiences are vital to learning; therefore, new methods of teaching may mean new vistas in an ancient art. These exercises are for college students and/or children.

ORAL READING AND ARTICULATION

Children, as well as adults, need to learn to speak clearly, for poor articulation habits can develop rapidly.

We want to play ball and have a good time.
Wewantoplayball andhaveagoodtime.

The two forms of the sentence illustrate some of the language differences in English as we write, read or speak it. The first is important for the eye, but the second is equally important for the ear.

We talk in "run ons," not in single words. Words are spoken in breath groups in rhetorical and musical phrases. Often the way we pronounce a word is not the way it is spoken in the stress pattern or cadence of a phrase.

The problem is that some children do not read aloud well. They need fun drills and practice in cadences, articulation, and other idiomatic characteristics of speech.

Start with stop consonants, then present words in phrases. Next work in cadences and stress. Then finish with context, they key to effective oral reading.

An assignment that is fun for the children is to write a script of news events and simulate a TV news report. Rehearsals can be pleasurable as standards are set, and evaluation implemented. Work sessions should be short and frequent rather than lengthy and unduly spaced. Don't forget to make a check list for phrasing, place-keeping, voice quality, pitch, rate, repetition errors, sing-song voice, and even posture and facial expression.

Contributed by Dr. G. Bruce Loganbill, Professor, California State University, Long Beach.

TELLING TWO TALES

This is an assignment I have tried with success in storytelling classes.

a. The student studies the various theories of the origins of stories;
b. The student selects, prepares and presents a story reflecting a particular theory (cosmology seems most popular) from the past;
c. As a contrast or comparison, the student then presents a modern "cosmology" story.

The same exercise may be done with various types of stories, such as fairy tales, legends, etc., instead of various theories of the origins of stories. Many students tend to create their own stories rather than to present other writers' modern version. This alternative may or may not be allowed by the instructor.

Contributed by Gloria Hassan, M.A., Speech Communication, Instructor at California State University, Long Beach.

CREATING A STORY

Instructions to the class are to finish one of the following stories. Students should recall principles of good storytelling when completing these selections.

1. In Slippery Rock, Alabama, a fine yellow house with a red door stood in the middle of town. The yellow house had many rooms and a high stone fence surrounding the yard. No one in the town was allowed near the house except the mailcarrier and the delivery boy from Magero's Market. His name was

_____.

2. Sammy the Sucker was the biggest and sweetest sucker in the Candy Shop on Main Street. Sammy loved to be placed on display in the big Candy Shop window and smile at all the people walking by . . .

3. Raindrops trickled down the window like snakes crawling down winding paths. Rain pounded on the roof, and washed all the sidewalks outside the window. "Mom, what can I do when it's raining outside?" asked _____.

An excellent response has been given to these introductions. Every story may be completed if so desired. Even the very young can finish the story expertly. The following story was given by a 5 1/2 year old, Roxanne Smith. The story was tape recorded so that every phrase was accurately restated. She chose to finish the second story in the assignment.

Sammy the Sucker

He always looked out the window and smiled and smiled at people.

One day Sammy the sucker wanted to be a person. He didn't know how to become one so he waited and waited for his friend to come and see him in the window. Then he saw his friend whose name was Joey. Joey came into the store. Joey said to the man, as Sammy smiled at him. "I would like this sucker right here."

The man said, "He will cost two dollars."

The boy said, "Oh goody." And Sammy smiled more.

After he paid for him, the man said, "Thank you. I'll go get it." Sammy laughed, but so quietly the man could not hear him. Sammy wanted Joey to have him very much.

Joey removed Sammy's paper and threw it in the trash. Sammy said, "Joey, I want to be a person. Can you turn me into one? I've heard of a Joey who was a magician. Are you that Joey?"

"Yes, I am," said Joey, which explained why he wasn't surprised that Sammy could talk.

"Goody." said Sammy. "Where's your house?"

"Right here," said Joey. They went to the house. "I have to turn out the lights first." Then he went to work in the dark. They had to wait ten hours in the dark. Then, after they waited, Sammy went out into the light.

And he said, "Oh, goody! It worked!" And Sammy got a job as a salesman in the candy store and lived happily ever after. THE END.

Contributed by Dr. Nancy E. Briggs, Associate Professor of Speech Communication, California State University, Long Beach.

STIMULATING IMAGINATION

By tasting different foods, a child has an opportunity to concentrate on the texture, the flavor, and the process of eating. Through imagination, the child can recreate the process of eating that food or what happens to the food in the process of digestion.

The procedures of this creative drama project seek to stimulate the imagination through the sense of taste. Use lemons, grapes, sugar cubes and peanut butter. Taste the first food. What does it feel like? How does it taste? When it is gone, pretend you are eating it again. Then do the same with the other foods. Pretend you are the food. What happens to you when you are eaten?

This exercise in sensory awareness needs a minimum of adult guidance so that the child does not move too quickly. The child needs to concentrate and experience each step carefully. If the child is blindfolded, it becomes a game to discover and use imagination to figure out what the food is. More leading questions may be needed to complete the exercise such as: What do you look like if you are a particular food? What do you feel like? Do you make any noise when you are eaten?

Contributed by Jan Steadman, M.A. Children's Theatre, Stage Manager, Los Angeles Shakespeare Festival Young People's Tour.

CREATIVE DRAMA EXERCISE: THE HIJACKING

This exercise is an experience in creative drama. It is intended to develop students' ability to create meaningful, consistent characters who are being subjected to a rather unusual and extreme emotional situation, and to improvise a sequence of events from beginning, through the middle, to the end. An indefinite number of students may take part at one time, though probably no more than 20.

The setting is an airport terminal in one part of the room, with the airliner in another part. The airliner is simply suggested with chairs arranged in rows of double seats, with an aisle between. Seats for pilot and co-pilot are in front. A table to represent the ticket counter is all that is needed in the terminal area, though stations should be established for the main entrance, the security check point, and the airliner entrance passage.

Students are asked to volunteer to be two stewardesses, the ticket agent, the security guard, the pilot and the co-pilot. If the group is large enough, other airport personnel may be designated. The rest of the group is told to imagine themselves to be specific passengers who might be going on the airliner to a predetermined destination.

The entire group is instructed to close their eyes while the instructor secretly designates one of the passenger-players to be the hijacker. Only the hijacker thus knows who s/he is on the plane.

At the call of "Places," everyone takes his or her position in the playing area, with passengers arriving randomly, checking in, getting acquainted with other passengers; and the playing progresses as the group creates the scene. At some point, the hijacker will take over the plane and the other passengers will react in character.

The only specific suggestion from the instructor will be that the group should arrive at some kind of resolution within a designated time period.

Contributed by Dr. Jed H. Davis, Professor of Theatre Arts, University of Kansas.

OUTLINE OF STORYTELLING PROJECT

1. Select a *real* audience (neither this storytelling class nor a hypothetical audience) for whom you will prepare a program.
2. In essay form describe the audience in detail and then *analyze* it in detail.
3. Select a theme appropriate for that audience and explain your reasons for that choice.
4. Find appropriate stories and activities on that theme and prepare a program 30-45 minutes in length. Estimate the amount of time needed for each story, activity, transitions, etc.

5. Although you may include feedback activities in your program, be sure the *emphasis* is upon *storytelling*. (A rule of thumb you can follow is at least 50% of the total program on storytelling and a minimum of two stories.)
6. Items 1, 2 and 3 should be in essay form. Use the following format for 4 and 5.

TITLE OF PROGRAM

                                                          Time
Introduction: Write a brief introduction to your program   _____ min.
1st Selection: Name, Author, Source, and brief summary   _____ min.
Feedback and/or Transition: Describe either or both if you have
    both   _____ min.
2nd Selection: Name, author, source, and brief summary (and
    so on)   _____ min.

Contribution from Dr. Dorothy Skriletz, Professor of Speech Communication, California State University, Long Beach.

POETRY

Poetry is fun for children and there are so many creative ways to interest children in experiences with poetry. Children learning counting while composing poetry proves effective.

ONE IS FUN

**One is fun if you run
    with your dog
Watch TV, or order a hamburger and bun.**

**Two is great for merry-go-round rides
Telling a story, and slippery slides.**

Etc....

Activities:

1. Read aloud; always refer to speech standards.
2. Take turns, placing large numbers in sequence on bulletin board.
3. Incorporate a group of 3-5 students reading from scripts (Readers Theatre). Some phrases are read individually, others read as a group.
4. Develop a collage for the poem.

Contributed by Dr. G. Bruce Loganbill, Professor of Speech Communication, California State University, Long Beach.

CREATING A BIOGRAPHICAL STORY

The purpose of this exercise is to teach story composition through a biographical assignment. Students choose a modern living (or dead) person with whom at least some of us are familiar. Their own family is banned unless famous. Students are then to tell one incident in the life of this person that has some inspirational point. The success of this varies, usually they do not do as well in this assignment as in others, but it teaches them the anatomy of a story and what *is* and *isn't* interesting.

Contributed by Dr. Steve Buck, Professor of Speech Communication, California State University, Long Beach.

FOLLOW-UP STORY ACTIVITY

After the telling of a story, the teacher may ask the students to participate in this creative linguistic and cognitive game. Write the name of a prominent character in the story on the chalkboard. For example, the instructor writes on the chalkboard, "D A N I E L" from a cutting of Daniel Boone's biography. Then to the right of the word, lists three or four categories vertically. Select from the following possibilities: COUNTRY, ANIMAL, FLOWER, CITY, FOOD, STATE, NAMES OF PEOPLE, PLANTS, MADE-UP WORDS. Then have the students fill in the blanks either individually, collectively, or in teams. For example, the name of a country that starts with the letter D is the Dominican Republic and with the letter A is Afghanistan. This game has a variety of approaches. It requires concentration and knowledge of various kinds. The instructor may discount an answer if it is spelled incorrectly. This adds another dimension to the study of language arts.

Contributed by Dr. Nancy E. Briggs, Associate Professor of Speech Communication, California State University, Long Beach.

READERS THEATRE FOR CHILDREN

Readers Theatre can be incorporated as a method for children to present story literature. Readers Theatre is a stylization of reading performance whereby two or more interpreters read literature to an audience causing them to experience the literary ideas and emotions.

Readers Theatre also refers to the various preparations leading to a performance, including selection or creation of script, adaptation of material, analyzing and interpreting the author's idea and attitudes, staging, casting, and rehearsal. The child becomes involved in the activity which allows the techniques to become the powerful instructional and aesthetic tool it can be.

Stories and poetry can be combined around an idea or theme, or a single story can be edited and presented. Children become involved in the interpretation of the plot and characters as performed, sharing the literature through the group process.

Readers Theatre is related to speech, theatre, and oral interpretation, yet it has distinct techniques.

1. A physical script usually is held by each reader.
2. Off-stage focus presents stylized presentation.
3. A close reader-audience rapport is developed and maintained.
4. Scenery, props, costumes, and makeup are not used.
5. A narrator, speaking directly to the audience, usually introduces the key idea and situation and ties the story segments together.

Children find Readers Theatre pleasurable, and they learn wide reading habits, discrimination in reading, social leadership skills, oral fluency, idea and characterization relationships, listening skills, appreciation of literature, and visualization and imagination. It has been said that Readers Theatre can be a comprehensive learning situation within which objectives can be experienced.

Contributed by Dr. G. Bruce Loganbill, Professor of Speech Communication, California State University, Long Beach.

BUILDING A REPERTORY OF STORIES

For my last assignment in storytelling, students are given five minutes to prepare a story that I have picked out of their 30 story cards. They may use their card for notes. The anticipation (anxiety) is great but by this time they are pretty good storytellers and they are amazed at how well they do under that pressure. It usually is their best job, if not best at least most animated performance they give.

Contributed by Dr. Steve Buck, Professor of Speech Communication, California State University, Long Beach.

STIMULUS FOR CHILDREN TELLING STORIES

Probably the most helpful device for encouraging children to tell stories is to provide them with visual aids, in particular several pictures simply drawn by the instructor or the students themselves. These pictures help the child keep the sequence of events in the story clearly in mind. Inhibitions are diminished when visual aids are used by children in storytelling.

Contributed by Dr. Nancy E. Briggs, Associate Professor of Speech Communication, California State University, Long Beach.

TELLING A "YARN"

The only equipment needed to ''tell a yarn'' is a 4 oz. skein of four ply yarn throughout which simple overhand knots have been tied at intervals varying from twelve to thirty inches. Roll the yarn into a ball. A short piece of chalk may be tied to each end of the skein to facilitate rerolling the ball. One child will begin an original story slowly unwinding the ball of yarn as he does so. Another child will begin to reroll the yarn as the ball unwinds. When the storyteller encounters a knot he passes the ball to the child who was doing the winding and the latter continues the story; another child will roll the yarn for her, etc.

Contributed by Charlotte Wagner, M.A., Cerritos Community College, Norwalk, California.

STORYTELLING OUTSIDE THE CLASSROOM

Students may be assigned to tell three or more stories per semester outside the classroom to audiences of their choice. Sunday school classes, orthopedic hospital wards, day camps, nurseries or the public schools may provide listeners for this assignment. Students should be forewarned of the importance of selecting appropriate material for the mental age of the group to be addressed. Storytellers give a two-minute report of their experience to classmates.

Contributed by Dr. Joseph Wagner, Professor of Speech Communication, California State University, Long Beach.

ADJECTIVE NOUN DRILL

This drill will assist students who suffer from a paucity of descriptive adjectives; it also provides excellent opportunity to develop use of appropriate synonyms. A professor may begin the exercise by saying, "Wee child". In selected order students may respond, "small girl", "tiny waif", "little orphan", "minute sibling", etc. A variation of this drill consists of simply requesting that an appropriate adjective precede a noun, i.e. "dog" may become "yellow dog", "lazy dog", "unconscious dog", or "sleepy dog". In addition to an adjective, a synonym may be required for the noun, i.e. "flea-ridden canine", "noble mastiff", etc. The same procedure could be followed for verbs and adverbs.

Contributed by Charlotte Wagner, M.A., Cerritos Community College, Norwalk, California.

VISUAL IMAGERY

Stories may be enlivened by colorful, imaginative descriptions. Students may be asked to describe something seen on their way to class or comment on a scene enjoyed or abhorred on their last vacation. One storyteller might say, "I walked past an old house." Another might observe, "I walked past a house that once thrilled to a new coat of paint and sparkling glass. Now it stood alone, abandoned, looking darkly through cracked panes at a weed-choked yard where happy children once played." Instructors may encourage descriptions such as the latter by conducting adjective-noun, verb-adverb and general vocabulary drills.

Contributed by Dr. Joseph Wagner, Professor of Speech Communication, California State University, Long Beach.

MASKS FOR CREATIVE DRAMA

This assignment works extremely well for children, especially educable mentally retarded or educationally handicapped children because inhibitions and speech problems are significantly reduced with the use of masks or puppets. Construct masks out of paper bags. Use tempera paints for painting bags the appropriate colors. Cut out holes for the eyes and a hole for the mouth to aid breathing and projection of the voice. Add trimming such as construction paper beaks which protrude, white construction paper teeth (where appropriate), ears, paper circles around the eye holes, paper eyelids with fringed eyelashes, etc. A story like *Chicken Licken* may be easily presented with the use of these masks. The teacher or the children may make the masks dependent on the time available for the activity. Most important, the children act out the story with spontaneous and creative dialogue. Masks may be preserved when not in use by storing them in a large plastic clothes bag.

Paper Bag Masks for "Chicken Little".

Contributed by Dell Van Leuven, B.A. Liberal Studies, Elementary Education Volunteer Assistant with Educable Mentally Retarded, Perry School, Huntington Beach School District.

STORIES AND MUSIC

The elementary school teacher is in a unique position of being able to introduce children to many and varied activities for educational purposes. It should be pointed out that one does not only tell stories in a traditional way, but stories can be told showing the relationships between oral communication, drama, art, and music. This is a wonderful way to have the teacher tell stories using visual aids. Use slides in a slide projector and pictures cut out and mounted so that they can become a part of the story. Most of all, how alive the story would become when the storyteller wants to use a musical background. This is a good way to introduce the children in the elementary classroom to good music. How alive would the story of ''The Nutcracker'' be if the teacher could tell the story to the beautiful music composed especially for this well-known story by Tschaikovsky. Playing the music while telling the story would enable the children to gain an insight into the beautiful music of the world's greatest composers as in the story of ''Peter and the Wolf'' with music by Prokofiev or with older children ''A Midsummer Night Dream'', with Mendelssohn's music. Of course, this is the type of project that an instructor could not put together on the spur of the moment, but it would entail planning, editing, and compilation of the story and the music. However, the results of such an endeavor would be rewarding to both the children and the teacher.

For a variation of this type of project, the teacher, if he/she plays the piano or some other type of musical instrument, particularly musical instruments of the portable type such as a guitar or a violin, could play while the story is being related. This would give the children in the classroom an understanding and appreciation for the methods of the minnesingers, the meistersingers, and the balladeers of the Middle Ages, as well as storytellers of today. How educational it would be to have someone playing the guitar and have the children sing with them, telling a story, of ''Micky Banjo'' or ''Le Scarpine per ballare,'' etc. Once children have the story and the music set in their minds, they may work out some choreographic routines to supplement the meaning of the story. The teacher could introduce the project to the children; once it has been introduced to the children, the teacher could then allow the creative minds of the children participating to continue working with the materials and add more decor to the narrative. How about viewing Walt Disney's *Fantasia* for ideas? Participating in such a project would challenge the children in the classroom, particularly the more mentally advanced ones. Once they have worked out the narrative with the music and some choreographic embellishments, then they could add visuals to it, coordinating a number of media to present an effective narrative.

Contributed by Professor Jim Dighera, Department of Speech, Cerritos Community College, Norwalk, California.

THE ORIGINAL STORY

Tell an original story the plot and characters of which are suggested to you from one of the following: (1) a picture (2) a newspaper article (3) an object, or (4) a locality. The item suggesting the story does not have to be presented or described, but it may be if it will assist in telling the story. However, be able to tell afterwards how the idea for the story developed from the item selected. In the case of the news article, do not be bound by the details of the news story, but on the other hand, do not present the story as fact.

Contributed by Dr. John Wills, Professor of Speech Communication, California State University, Long Beach.

STORIES FROM OTHER LANDS OR CULTURES

Tell a story that originates from another country or culture. (Authentic ethnic cultures of the United States, such as the American Indian, will be acceptable.) Although the story is not to be primarily used as instruction in the culture, it should have some flavor of the culture of origin if possible. Be prepared to explain obscure terms or unique cultural assumptions contained in the story in ways that small children will understand. While folktales are excellent, stories with definite authorship are also acceptable as long as the author is from the land or culture chosen.

Contributed by Dr. John Wills, Professor of Speech Communication, California State University, Long Beach.

SEMESTER STORYTELLING PROJECT

Each student will turn in a file of 35 synopsis cards on stories appropriate to indicated levels. Follow the form on card files in the text. Use only one card per story. Submit in large envelope or appropriate container. Cards should be classified as follows:

5 stories for holidays (only one story per holiday)
5 stories illustrating moral, ethical values, or to improve understanding of handicapped persons
5 stories for which visual aids may be used to best advantage
5 biographical stories (primary grades may substitute some animal stories)
5 stories which lend themselves to dramatization
5 stories which give instruction in some academic field
5 stories originating in some other land or culture

This project is an essential requirement of the course.

Contributed by Dr. John Wills, Professor of Speech Communication, California State University, Long Beach.

A COMMUNICATION STRESS PROFILE OF A STORYTELLER

Background

Stress has existed as long as the human race. Relatively recent research has led to increased clarification and appreciation of its role in communication, including story-telling and related forms of communication. Approaches and definitions vary. However, communication stress may be defined as a demand-centered combination of behaviors which either promotes or interferes with communication. The behaviors include perception and evaluation of the demand in the communication situation, basic physical mobilization of the body in response to the demand, and expression of stress. The evaluation may be charted on a scale from desirable to undesirable. The mobilization is in terms of the intensity of internal activity on a unidirectional scale; the expression may be considered from desirable to undesirable with regard to listeners' reaction to teller.

Communication Stress Profile

My own review of the literature, research, and application of findings on stress support the advisability of giving students some scientifically based feedback with regard to their own Communication Stress. The Communication Stress Profile serves this purpose.

Using the term ''profile'' in the sense of the representation of the highlights of a process, the Communication Stress Profile can give the student feedback regarding the communication stress components of his storytelling and related activities. Three instruments, (two written examinations and one piece of equipment) have satisfactory validity and provide information relevant to each of the three dimensions of Evaluation, Mobilization and Expression.

The Lamb Speech Anxiety inventory yields information regarding the degree of anxiety the storyteller experienced during the presentation.[1] It is a written self report which is filled out immediately after the presentation by the storyteller. This report gives a measurement of the storyteller's evaluation of the situation. The Mullac and Sherman Behavioral Assessment of Speech Anxiety is the second written examination instrument.[2] It is filled out by the listeners during the presentation. It provides a measurement of the degree of expressed stress. Both of these instruments are easily completed and scored. The third instrument involves a piece of equipment called the Psychological Stress Evaluator and gives us data regarding intensity of internal mobilization activities of muscles and glands affecting speech.[3]

A satisfactory and useful profile can be obtained without the Psychological Stress Evaluator which is not widely available. However, when one uses Lamb and Mullac, the Psychological Stress Evaluator may validate the conclusions.

Procedures

The first procedure is to explain Communication Stress, its operation and dimensions. Second, have the student, or students, do a storytelling presentation, with concommitant tape recording for eventual stress analysis with the Psychological Stress Evaluator, and listeners filling out the Mullac form. Third, the storyteller completes the Lamb self report.

These three steps lead to the composition of the communication stress profile of the storyteller. The evaluation and expression components illustrate the intensity and direction (desirable-undesirable) of the stress; while the mobilization dimension reflects intensity only. From the profile components of direction and intensity we can determine, or at least infer, whether the stress promoted or interfered with the story telling.

Evaluation

Having completed the profile, the instructor can tell the storyteller "like it was." Feedback continues when the student is given information on his stress utilizing the profile, the instructor, and fellow students in a discussion to interpret, clarify and satisfy. Discussion of possible sources of stress and individual management methods in order to utilize stress consistent with its basic function as an auxiliary power during communication, are suggested topics.

Contributed by Dr. John Healy, Associate Professor of Speech Communication, California State University, Long Beach.

NOTES

1. Douglas H. Lamb, "Speech Anxiety: Towards a Theoretical Conceptualization and Preliminary Scale Development," *Speech Monographs,* 39, 1972, 62-67.
2. Anthony Mullac and A. Robert Sherman, "Behavioral Assessment of Speech Anxiety," *Quarterly Journal of Speech* 60, (1974) 134-143.
3. Dektor Counter Intelligence and Security Inc., Psychological Stress Evaluator.

Appendix
Voice Improvement Exercises

EXERCISES FOR FREE SPEECH TONES

Conditions which are conducive to free speech tones are necessary before beginning voice exercises. Bodily relaxation and control of breathing must be achieved. Two fifteen minute drill periods daily, consistently observed, should appreciably contribute to a storyteller's mastery of delivery.

Relaxation

1. Sit comfortably and let the head move downward relaxing neck muscles. Move the head slowly from left to right until neck muscles feel relaxed.
2. Lie down and consciously relax the entire body beginning with eye closure, feel the brow, lips, lower jaw, arms, hands, fingers, legs, feet and toes relax. This drill may be conducted partially when standing or seated. Watch for opportunities to relax when waiting for traffic lights, restaurant orders, etc. . . .The more relaxation is practiced, the more instantly it may be achieved.
3. From a standing position, let the head move downward, bend at the waist, let the shoulders droop and the arms hang limply. When a sensation of full relaxation is achieved, move the torso upward, return the shoulders to an attitude of easy erectness, and finally raise the head.
4. Same as in (3) to the point where the body is bent at the waist. From this position sway from left to right as an elephant might sway its trunk. This is an excellent drill for children.
5. Counting to six in each position, move the head forward, backward, left and then to the right.
6. Let the jaw drop to an open mouth position. With the jaw down and relaxed, pull down gently on the chin and move the jaw in a circular manner to relieve muscle tension.
7. Relax and whisper "oh-ah." Now vocalize the same sounds keeping your throat and mouth as relaxed as possible.
8. Whisper "oh" and increase the whisper to vocalization. Maintain the feeling of relaxation.

Control of Breathing

1. Exhale then inhale deeply. As you expel the air, count as long as you can comfortably do so. Repeat two or three times and attempt to increase the count without losing the sensation of comfortable exhalation.
2. Inhale just enough air to count to ten comfortably. There should not be a volume of air to exhale at the termination of the count. Repeat this exercise with counts of 5, 15, 20, 25 and 30.
3. Inhale deeply and exhale counting aloud as follows: 1,2,3,4; hold, 5,6,7,8; hold, 9,10,11,12, etc. as long as exhalation is not forced.
4. Walking at a normal stride, inhale for six paces, hold for two, and then exhale for six paces. Vary the number of paces to develop facility in estimating the amount of inhalation and exhalation required.
5. Lie down, breathe normally and note that breathing is "centralized" toward the base of the rib cage where the lungs are larger than they are at the apex and the ribs are more flexible. Place your hands at the base of the rib cage and feel the expanding and contracting action.
6. Lie down, place a small book on the "V" to be felt between the ribs of the lower rib cage, and breathe normally. This will assist to "feel" where breathing activity should be centered.
7. Stand and speak to an imaginary person at 5, 10 and 15 foot distances; call to a person 25, 50 and 100 feet away. Let the pressure for projection come from the centralized breathing area . . . "push" up from there.
8. Inhale just enough air to read the following lines:
    a. Halt!
    b. Halt! Who goes there?
    c. When love and skill work together, expect a masterpiece.
    d. I envy the beasts two things—their ignorance of evil to come, and their ignorance of what is said about them.
    e. Originality is simply a pair of fresh eyes.
    f. I served with General Washington in the Legislature of Virginia, before the Revolution, and, during it, with Doctor Franklin in Congress. I never heard either of them speak ten minutes at a time, nor to any but the main point, which was to decide the question.

Quality

In the simplest terms, quality is a characteristic of tone, it is a personal subjective opinion which depends upon an individual's judgment of what sounds "good" or "bad" in vocalized tone. More specifically, changes in the strength and relationship of secondary vibrations of the vocal tones account for what is considered desirable or undesirable tone quality. The latter is also affected by such physical factors as a weak or cleft palate, adenoidal growths, inflamed vocal folds, weak breathing, etc. A normal, responsive physical organism is necessary if good quality is to be achieved. If we respond physically to mental reactions of fear, love, joy, etc. the character and strength of secondary vibrations of our vocal folds will assist to modulate the tone into desirable quality. This is a more complex restatement of the point made earlier to the effect that "impression precedes and determines expression." The following exercises should aid the development of conditions that are generally considered to be desirable:

1. All words containing sounds "m," "ng," are characterized by nasal resonance. Words without these sounds should not be nasalized. Strengthening muscles of the soft palate will assist in eliminating excessive nasality.
   a. Pronounce gah-ah, gah-ah, gah-ah several times. Develop an awareness of the soft palate as it raises to close the entrance to the nasal cavity on the "gah" sound.
   b. Same as exercise "a" with the substitution of "kuh-guh" for "gah-ah."
   c. Check for the presence of a weak soft palate closure of the entrance to the nasal cavity by placing a small purse mirror under the nostrils and saying, "This is the house that Jack built." The latter statement contains no nasal sounds and ideally, there would be no indication of warm air from the nostrils on the mirror.
2. Flatness and hardness may be caused by tensions in the throat and they may also result from a hard, cold, indifferent personality.
   a. Repeat exercises suggested for relaxation of the neck and facial area.
   b. Read the following lines and identify as fully with the thought as possible:

> Never borrow
> Idle sorrow;
> Drop it!
> Cover it up!
> Hold your cup!
> Joy will fill it,
> Don't spill it,
> Steady, be ready,
> Good luck!
> Henry Van Dyke

> I want to be a Highbrow,
> With air of perfect poise,
> Who lifts a scornful eyebrow
> At all the rough world's noise;
> Oh, I could fill with glee so
> Desirable a shelf,
> A Highbrow seems to be so
> Delighted with himself.
> Berton Braley

> Tiger, tiger, burning bright
> In the forests of the night,
> What immortal hand or eye
> Could frame thy fearful symmetry?
> William Blake

Out of the night that covers me,
Black as the Pit from pole to pole,
I thank whatever gods may be
For my unconquerable soul.
In the fell clutch of circumstance
I have not winced nor cried aloud
Under the bludgeonings of chance
My head is bloody, but unbowed.

Beyond this place of wrath and tears
Looms but the Horror of the shade,
And yet the menace of the years
Finds and shall find me unafraid.

It matters not how strait the gate,
How charged with punishments the scroll,
I am the master of my fate:
I am the captain of my soul.
William Ernest Henley

3. Throatiness or gravelly voice quality is frequently caused by a faulty breathing habit which fails to support tone throughout a sentence, especially on the final words or syllables. The improper use of chewing and swallowing muscles in voice production may also cause this abnormal condition. Persons who must speak frequently during their working day may develop voice fatigue due to misuse of these muscles. Instead of projecting tone from the abdominal, central breathing area, these individuals increase muscular activity in the throat which builds up tension.
   a. Review exercises suggested for centralized breathing.
   b. When reading, compel yourself to inhale at the completion of each sentence. Inhaling more breath than a sentence requires may find a reader beginning the next sentence with an inadequate breath supply. This may result in forcing air from the lungs and the development of throaty quality.
   c. Review exercises for breathing according to sentence length.
   d. Prepare adequately for all speaking engagements in order that fright induced feelings of inadequacy will not tense breathing muscles which in turn may deny a speaker proper breath support.
4. Breathiness is frequently caused by a speaker's failure to bring his vocal fold together tightly enough to prevent loss of air or by failure to adjust the folds quickly enough during sound production. Additional causes may be ill health that robs one of the energy needed to vocalize or fear that may literally leave one speechless.
   a. Voiceless consonants such as "f," "s" and also "sh," are the most wasteful of the exhaled breath stream. Practice an immediate initiation of vowel sound following the "h," for example, to guard against loss of breath. If tone production lags, breathiness will develop on the "h."
   b. Listen carefully to be certain that vocalization begins immediately following the initial consonant in the following combinations:

oh	ho	at	fat
heat	sheet	you	shoe
arm	farm	aye	fie
aim	shame	aim	hame

c. As a means of developing self-confidence and breath control simultaneously, practice the following lines after visualizing a situation which would justify such a reaction:

> Hold that line!
> Shoot the shortest sailor!
> Faith! Father has found his fiddle!
>
> Home is the sailor, home from the sea,
> And the hunter home from the hill.

d. Whisper each of the following vowels, a, e, i, o, u, and then vocalize them to develop an appreciation of the amount of breath wasted on whispering in contrast to vocalization.

e. Pronounce the following words being careful to expend as little breath as possible on voiceless consonants:

> fortune, ship, failure, sister, success, sing,
> summon, silent, full, fear, excel, theater,
> feign, sooth, freshen, hand, fire, session,
> hallow, hollow.

Strength

Varying degrees of strength or volume are required in daily oral communicative efforts. A telephone conversation calls for minimal expenditure of energy whereas hailing a taxicab may be a test of one's projective powers. Good projection depends upon controlled breathing, normal functioning of the vocal folds in order that a pure tone may be produced, proper modulation of the fundamental tone by secondary vibrations, and finally, the coordination of these several systems. More specifically, in order to project effortlessly in the classroom or on the playground, a teacher with a good voice must learn to pronounce vowels fully and with proper duration, must develop a pleasing rhythm as opposed to staccato speech and must articulate clearly in order that her message will be understood. Variation in pitch is also necessary for effective projection.

1. Pronounce the following words and exaggerate, in fully relaxed manner, the vowel sounds. *Think* of the word's meaning before producing it.

crash	happy	pain	bitter
privation	embrace	fear	fool
sniff	howl	growl	snarl
fluffy	slide	whimper	snap
implore	urge	free	enslaved
roll	low	rest	lullaby

2. Recite the alphabet stressing vowel sounds.
3. Count from one to ten stressing vowel sound. "Push up" from the central breathing area to improve projection.
4. Read the following commands to an imaginary person fifty feet distant. Project, do not simply increase loudness and tense throat and facial muscles.
   a. Close the gate!
   b. Call the police!
   c. Open in the name of the law!
   d. Your car's door is open!
5. Speak the following words and imagine that each time you do so, a listener calls, "I can't understand you!" Speak each word four times increasing the projection each time.

go	row	float
ahoy there	ah	oh
goat	goad	goal

6. Stand about thirty feet from a friend and begin to converse. Walk slowly toward each other as you do so. Now reverse the procedure and back away from each other as you converse. Increase or decrease projection as circumstances demand; avoid loudness and the development of laryngeal strain.
7. Strengthen weak tones by speaking the following words with enthusiasm. Think of a situation which would justify the word before speaking.

excellent	marvellous	safe	victory
ours	free	treasure	keys
voices	heat	food	serum

8. Interpret the following lines with freshness, with attention to vowel production, and with care to do centralized breathing:

> Ring out, wild bells, to the wild sky,
>   The flying cloud, the frosty light;
>   The year is dying in the night;
> Ring out, wild bells, and let him die.
> Ring out the old, ring in the new,—
>   Ring, happy bells, across the snow;
>   The year is going, let him go;
> Ring out the false, ring in the true.
>
>   Alfred Tennyson

9. Projection is impaired by articulation that is hasty, indifferent and characterized by laziness of the lips, tongue and jaw. Use of a tape recorder in recognition of articulation problems and in drill work will prove helpful.

a. Exaggerate the "t," "d" and "ing" in the following words:

world	first	coming	trying	discordant
white	ground	unstained	going	evade
mist	just	get	cawing	lightning

b. Avoid contracting the following combinations:

| don't you | won't you | didn't you | going to |
| would you | could you | can't you | thought you |

c. Read the following passage clearly with special thought to "t" and "d" sounds:

> Night's candles are burnt out, and jocund day
> Stands tiptoe on the misty mountain tops:
> I must be gone and live, or stay and die.
> Shakespeare, *Romeo and Juliet*

Pitch

Pitch in speech is of two types, i.e. *interval* or *step* which takes place between words and syllables and *inflection* which takes place during tone production. These two types of pitch in combination determine what is referred to as *speech melody*. Storytellers seek to develop a conversational style which requires a flexible, responsive vocal mechanism, a discriminating mind and a friendly, positive outlook on life. Monotonous speech may be of two types, i.e. *plateau* and *monotony of variety*. A speaker with plateau monotony drones along without pitch change in a dull uninspired manner; monotony of variety is manifest in the "bishop's tone" or "sing-song" manner of presentation that finds the same inflectional pattern being repeated by the speaker without regard for the content of the words spoken. Changes in pitch reveal a speaker's intellectual and discriminatory abilities and attitudes. If a child is asked to count to ten, he will probably rattle off the count without inflectional change. However, if this child is asked what he received for Christmas, his face would probably brighten and through inflectional change a hearer would know which gift was most cherished. This is pitch change in action!

1. Inflection is a continuous pitch change whereas interval is a definite step, a break in the utterance of sound. The following exercises provide opportunity to differentiate between these two types of pitch change and they will offer opportunity to sharpen one's use of them.

a. Using a piano or a musical instrument, strike notes randomly and attempt to duplicate them with your own voice.

b. Read the following lines with pronounced use of the interval:

> Was heard the old clock on the stair,
> "Forever—never!
>   Never—forever."
>   Longfellow

c. Speak the following lines haughtily; eagerly; compassionately; angrily; sadly; happily:

> Farewell!
> It was the housemother!
> The window is open!
> Are you the custodian?
> Is my bath ready?

d. Read the following lines and accent a different word in each sentence each time you read it.

> I love you.
> Call my parents.
> The boat is sinking.
> This is my sister.

e. Have a friend read the following lines and as he does so, keep "score" on the number of intervals and inflectional changes:

> I must go down to the seas again, to the
>   vagrant gypsy life,
> To the gull's way and the whale's way
>   where the wind's like a whetted knife,
> And all I ask is a merry yarn from a
>   laughing fellow-rover,
> And quiet sleep and a sweet dream when
>   the long trick's over.
>   "Sea-Fever," John Masefield

f. Speak the pitch changes in an octave beginning on a low pitch and ending high; reverse the procedure and return to the low pitch.

g. Speak the words, "Answer the doorbell," indicating positive conviction, indifference, doubt, fear.

Appendix

Critique Form Suitable for Use in College-University Storytelling Classes

Critique Form Suitable for Use in College-University Storytelling Classes

STORYTELLING CRITIQUE

Name: _____   Date: _____

Story: _____

	Excellent	Good	Fair	Poor
Introduction				
Was the introduction brief?				
Did the opening command attention?				
Was the conflict situation established?				
Was the transition to the body of the speech smooth?				
Body				
Were digressions avoided?				
Were key situations clear?				
Was emotional appeal used?				
Was suspense employed?				
Did the climax have emotional power:				
Did the characters seem lifelike?				
Conclusion				
Was the transition to the conclusion smooth?				
Did the conclusion draw the story together satisfactorily?				
Was the conclusion brief?				
Delivery				
Appearance: Neatly, inconspicuously dressed? Good posture?				
Gesture: Unobtrusive? Avoidance of nervous mannerisms? Appropriate?				
Language: Accurate? Colorful? Fluent? Appropriate?				
Speech: Conversational? Articulate? Easily Heard?				
Eye Contact: Furtive? Indirect? Direct? Audience adaptation during story?				
Overall Impression				

Remarks:

STORYTELLING CRITIQUE

Student's Name _____

Story _____

	Excellent	Good	Fair	Poor
Selection of material, meet the assignment?				
Introduction				
Characterization				
Dialogue				
Grammar, pronunciation				
Colorful, descriptive language				
Transitions				
Gestures				
Posture, stance				
Eye contact				
Vocal inflection				
Rate				
Easily heard				
Suspense				
Emotional appeal used				
Plot clear				
Digressions avoided				
Conclusion				
Special effects: sounds, visual aids, other creativities				
General appearance				
OVER ALL EFFECT				
ADDITIONAL REMARKS				

STORYTELLING EVALUATION

	EXCELLENT	GOOD	NEEDS IMPROVEMENT	OTHER COMMENTS
The Story				
Appropriate for audience intended				
Introduction and mood establishment				
Use of aids to fit story				
Literary value of story				
Follow-up to story				
Other comments				
Storyteller				
Use of Voice:				
volume				
pitch variety				
rate				
articulation				
pronunciation				
overall effectiveness				
Use of Body:				
posture				
eye contact				
use of notes				
gestures, movements				
responsiveness to audience				
Overall Preparation and Effectiveness				

OTHER COMMENTS:

Critique Form Suitable
For College Student Directors
of Story Dramatization

STORYACTING OR CHORAL READING CRITIQUE

	Excellent	Good	Fair	Needs Improvement
1. Selection of Material				
2. Creativity/Originality				
3. Introduction to Selection				
4. Firm Director, Leadership Demonstrated				
5. Rate of Telling				
6. Use of Children (# and character assignment)				
7. Script for Everyone Promptly				
8. Visual Aids, Props				
9. Provision for Chorus				
10. Ability to Motivate Expression				
11. Clarity of Directions				
12. Encouraging, Positive Reinforcement				
13. Decision-maker				
14. Editing of Script				
15. Blocking				
16. Adherence of Script to Suggested Format				
17. Action or Participation in Other Selections				
a.				
b.				
c.				
d.				
18. Overall Effectiveness				

COMMENTS:

STORYTELLING EVALUATION

The Story	EXCELLENT	GOOD	NEEDS IMPROVEMENT	OTHER COMMENTS
Appropriate for audience intended				
Introduction and mood establishment				
Use of aids to fit story				
Literary value of story				
Follow-up to story				
Other comments				
Storyteller *Use of Voice:*				
volume				
pitch variety				
rate				
articulation				
pronunciation				
overall effectiveness				
Use of Body:				
posture				
eye contact				
use of notes				
gestures, movements				
responsiveness to audience				
Overall Preparation and Effectiveness				

OTHER COMMENTS:

PRE-SCHOOL

Author	Title	Publisher	Year
Anderson, Lonzo	Two Hundred Rabbits	Viking	1968
Blaine, M.	The Terrible Thing That Happened at Our House.	Parents	1975
Brooke, Leslie	Johnny Crow's Garden	Warne	1903
Brown, Margaret Wise	Country Noise Book	Scott, W. R.	1940
Brown, Margaret W.	Important Book	Har-Row	1949
Brown, Margaret W.	Runaway Rabbit	Har-Row	1972
DeRegmer, Beatrice	Red Riding Hood	Antheneum	1972
DuBois, Wm. Pene	Bear Circus	Viking	1971
Eastman, P. D.	Are You My Mother?	Beginner	1960
Ets, Marie H.	In The Forest	Viking	1944
Fisher, Aileen Lucia	In The Middle of the Night	Crowell	1965
Flack, Marjorie	Story About Ping	Viking	1933
Foolen, Elizabeth	The Three Little Kittens	Hale	1966
Freeman, Don	Corduroy	Viking	1968
Fulton, Mary	My Friend	Western	1973
Gag, Wanda	Millions of Cats	Coward	1928
Goodall, John S.	Adventures of Paddy Pork	Harcourt	1968
Hader, Beraa & Elmer	Big Snow	Macmillan	1962
Hazen, Barbara	Why Couldn't I be an Only Kid Like You, Wigger?	Atheneum	1975
Hoban, Russel	Best Friends For Frances	Har-Row	1969
Hogrogian, Nonny	One Fine Day	Macmillan	1971
Hurd, Edith (Thacher)	Last One Home Is A Green Pig	Harper	1959
Keats, Ezra Jack	Snowy Day	Viking	1962
Krinsley, Jeanette	The Cow Went Over The Mountain	Western	1963
Langstaff, John M.	Frog Went A-Courtin'	Harcourt	1955
Leaf, Munro	Story of Ferdinand	Viking	1936
Lenski, Lois	Papa Small	Walck	1951
Le Sieg, Theodore	Ten Apples Up On Top	Beginner	1961
Lionni, Leo	Frederick	Pantheon	1967
Lipkind, William	Finders Keepers	Harcourt	1951
Lobel, Arnold	Frogs & Toads Are Friends	Harper	1970
Lopshire, Robert	Put Me in the Zoo	Beginner	1960
Manhood, K.	Why Are There More Questions Than Answers Grandad?	Bradbury Press	1974
McCloskey, Robert	Make Way For Ducklings	Viking	1941
Merrill and Solbert	The Elephant Who Liked To Smash Cars	Pantheon	1967

Mithchell, Lucy S.	The Here and Now Storybook		1941
Munari, Bruno	Circus In The Mist	World	1969
Nass, E.	Sam, Bangs and Moonshine	H.R.&W.	1966
Palmer, Helen	A Fish Out of Water	Beginner	1961
Potter, Beatrix	Tale of Peter Rabbit	Grosset & Dunlap	1968
Rand, Ann	Sparkle and Spin	Harcourt	1957
Rey, Hans A.	Curious George	Houghton	1951
Ringi, Kjell	The Stranger	Random	1968
Stone, Jon	The Monster at the End of This Book	Golden	1977
Walters, Jerry	Dumbo	Random	1972

GRADES K-3

Adelson, Leone	All Ready for Summer	David McKay Co.	1956
Adler, D.	A Little At a Time	Random	1976
Afanaser, Alexel	Salt	Follett	1965
Allen, Jeffery	Mary Alice, Operator #9	Little	1975
Anguland, Joan W.	Love is a Special Way of Feeling	Har Brace J.	1960
Annett, Cora	The Dog Who Thought He Was a Boy	Houghton	1965
Ardema, Verna	Why Mosquitoes Buzz in People's Ears	Dial	1975
Asbjornsen, Peter Moe, Jorgen	Norwegian Folktales	Putnam	1967
Atwater, Righard	Mr. Popper's Penguins	Little	1938
Barclay, Isabel	O Canada!	Doubleday	1964
Balian, L.	Humbug Rabbit	Abingdom	1974
Barrie, James	Peter Pan	G.&D.	1970
Barry, Robert	Mr. Willowby's Christmas Tree	McGraw Hill	1963
Basile, Giovanni Bold Neapolitan Fairy Tales			
Belloc, Hilaire	The Bad Child's Book of Beasts	Knopf	1965
Belmelmans, Ludwig	Madeline	Penguin	1977
Belmelmans, Ludwig	Madeline's Rescue	Penguin	1977
Better Homes and Gardens	Better Homes and Gardens Storybook	B. H. & G.	1970
Bloch, Marie Halun	Ukrainian Folk Tales	Coward-McCann	1964
Bolliger, Max	The Giants Feast	A-W Childrens	1976
Boston, L. M.	The Sea Egg	Harcourt	1967
Bridwell, Norma	Clifford the Big Red Dog	School Bk. Service	1969
Briggs, R.	Mother Goose Treasury	Coward	1966
Brown, Marcia	Cinderella	Scribner	1954
Brown, Margaret W.	Little Lost Lamb	Doubleday	1945
Backley, Peter	Okolo of Nigeria	Simon and Schuster	1962
Buehr, Walter	Rubber: Natural and Synthetic	Morrow	1964
Charlip, R.	Fortunately	Parents	1964
Colum, Padraic	The Stone of Victory and Other Tales	McGraw-Hill	1967
Corbett, Scott	The Case of the Gone Goose	Atlantic-Little	1968
Daniels, Guy	The Tsar's Riddles	McGraw-Hill	1967
De Angeli, Marguerite (lofft)	A Pocketful of Posies: A Merry Mother Goose	Doubleday	1961
DiNoto, Andrea	The Star Thief	Macmillan	1967
DuBois, Williams P.	The Little Pigs	Viking	1970

Duvoisin, Roger	Petunia	Knopf	1950
Enright, Elizabeth	Zeee	Harcourt	1965
Estes, Elenor	The Hundred Dresses	H Beace J.	1974
Evans, Katherine	One Good Deed Deserves Another	Whitman	1964
Flack, Marjorie	The Snow Party	Pantheon	1959
Floethe, Louise Lee	The Story of Lumber	Scribner	1962
Follett, Robert J. R.	Your Wonderful Body	Follett	1961
Ford, Anne	Davy Crockett	Putnam	1961
Gantos, Jack	Rotten Ralph	H.M.	1976
Garland, Rosemary	To Two-Minute Stories	Grosset & Dunlap	1977
Gay, Zhenya	Who Is It?	The Viking Press	1957
Greene, Carla	Soldiers and Sailors, What They Do?	Harper	1963
Grimm Brothers	Grimm's Fairy Tales	Grosse & Dunlap	1968
Grimm Brothers	Rumplestilkin	School Bk. Service	1974
Grimm's Brothers	Snow White	Laroosse	1975
Gruelle, Johnny	Raggedy Ann Stories	Gruelle Co.	1947
Gwynne, F.	The King Who Rained	Dutton	1970
Haley, Gail E.	A Story, A Story	Anthenum	1970
Harris, Joel C.	Uncle Remus Stories	Schocken	1965
Haviland, Virginia	Favorite Fairy Tales Told in Ireland	Little	1961
Heide, F. R.	That's What Friends Are For	School Bk. Service	1971
Hermanns, Ralph	River Boy	Harcourt	1965
Hewitt, Anita	The Bull Beneath the Walnut Tree and Other Stories	McGraw-Hill	1967
Hoban, Russell	A Baby Sister for Francis	Harper	1964
Hughes, R.	Gertrude's Child	Quist	1975
Hume, Lotta Carswell	Favorite Children's Stories from China and Tibet	Tuttle	1962
Ickis, Marguerite	The Book of Patriotic Holidays	Dodd	1962
Joslin; Sesyle	What Do You Say Dear?	School Bk. Service	1977
Keats, Ezra Jack	John Henry	Pantheon	1965
Kraus, R.	Leo the Late Bloomer	Dutton	1973
Krauss, Ruth	Wait for William	Random	1961
Lauber, Patricia	The Story of Numbers		
Lenski, Lois	The Little Farm	Walck	1943
Lenski, Lois	The Little Train	Walck	1940
Lent, Blair	Why the Sun and the Moon Live in the Sky	Houghton & Mifflin	1968
Lionni, Leo	The Biggest House in the World	Patheon	1968
Lionni, K. Leo	The Alphabet Tree	Patheon	1968
Lobel, A.	A Birthday For the Princess	Har-Row	1973
Marshall, James	George and Martha	H.M.	1974
McCloskey, Robert	Make Way For Ducklings	Viking Press	1941
McClung, Robert	Buzztail	William Morrow and Co.	1958
McKee, David	Lord Rex, The Lion Who Wished	Abeland	1973
McPhail, David	The Train	Little, Brown	1977
Milne, A.	Winnie the Pooh	Dell	1974
Mosel, Arlene	Tikki Tikki Tembo	School Bk. Service	1974
Mosel, Arlene	The Funny Little Woman	Dutton	1972
Munch, Theodore	What is Light?	Benefic	1960
Mess, Evaline	Sam, Bangs, and Moonshine	Holt	1966

Mure, Eleanor	The Three Bears	Walck	1970
Paterson, Diane	Smile For Auntie	Dial	1976
Piper, Watty	The Little Engine That Could, Aesop's Fables	Platt	1976
Raskin, Ellen	Nothing Ever Happens on my Block	School Bk. Service	1973
Ransome, Arthur	The Fool of the World and the Flying Ship	F. S. & G.	1968
Rey, Hans A.	Curious George	Houghton Mifflin	1941
Russell, Franklin	The Honeybees	Portal	1967
Sandburg, Carl	The Wedding Procession of the Rag Doll and the Broom Handle Who Was In It	Harcourt	1967
Sechrist, Elizabeth (Hough) and Woodsey, J.	It's Time for Easter	Macrae	1967
Seeger, Ruth	American Folk Songs For Children In Home, School and Nursery	Doubleday	1948
Sendak, Maurice	Higglety Pigglety Pop! Or There Must Be More to Life	Harper	1967
Seuss, Dr.	Cat in the Hat Comes Back	Beginner	1958
Seuss, Dr.	The Larax	Random	1957
Seuss, Dr.	How the Grinch Stole Christmas	Random	1957
Seuss, Dr.	The Cat in the Hat	Beginner	1957
Schulz, Charles	He's Your Dog Charlie Brown	New Am. Library	1974
Schulz, Charles	Happiness is a Warm Puppy	Determined	1962
Silverstein, S.	The Giving Tree	Har-Row	1964
Simons, Norma	All Kinds of Families	A. Whitman	1975
Slobodkina, Esphyr	Caps for Sale	Addison Wesley	1947
Smith, Dottie	101 Dalmatians	Avon	1969
Smith, Emma	Emily's Voyage	Harcourt	1966
Steadman, R.	Bridge	Collins-World	1975
Steig, William	Sylvester and the Magic Pebble	Simon & Schuster	1969
Sugita, Y.	Helena the Unhappy Hippopotamus	McGraw	1974
Surany, Anico	A Jungle Jumble	Putnam	1968
Tabor, John	John Tabor's Ride	Atlantic: Little	1966
Taylor, Mark	The Bold Fisherman	Golden Gate	1967
Turin, Adela, Bosina Nella	The Real Story of Bonanos Who Wore Spectacles	Two Continents	1977
Turin, Adela, Bosina Nella	A Fortunate Catastrophe	Two Continents	1977
Travers, Pamela L.	Mary Poppins	Harcan & Brasen	1962
Viorst, J.	I'll Fix Anthony	Har-Row	1969
Viorst, J.	My Mama Says There Aren't Any Zombies . . .	Lothrop	1975
Viorst, J.	The Tenth Good Thing About Barney	Atheneum	1973
Waber, Bernard	Nobody is Perfect	N H.M.	1971
Waber, Bernard	Ira Sleeps Over	H.M.	1972
Waber, Bernard	You Look Ridiculous Said the Rhinocerus . . .	H.M.	1969
Walton, Darwin	Color Are You?	Johnson Chi	1973
Warburg, S.	I Like You	H.M.	1965
Wiese, Kurt	The Thief in the Attic	Viking	1965
Wiesner, William	Jack and the Beanstalk	School Bk. Service	1973

Wildsmith, Brian	Mother Goose	Watts	1965
Williams, Barbara	Albert's Tooth	Har-Row	1969
Williams, Margery	Velveteen Rabbit	Doubleday	1958
Wright, Blanche	The Real Mother Goose	Hall	1944
Yolen, Jane	Rainbow Rider	T.Y. Crowell	1974
Yolen, Jane	The Sultan's Perfect Tree	Parents	1977
Yolen, Jane	The Emperor and the Kite	World	1967
Young, Mirian	If I Drove a Truck	Lothrup	1967
Zemach, Harve	The Speckled Hen	Holt	1966
Zemach, Harve	Duffy and the Devil	Farrar, Straus, & Giroux	1973
Zemach, Margot	The Unfriendly Book	Har-Row	1975
Zion, Gene	Dear Garbage Man	Har-Row	1977
Zolotow, Charlotte	It Could Always Be Worse	F.S. & G.	1977
Zolotow, Charlotte	When the Wind Stops	Har-Row	1975
Zolotow, Charlotte	William's Doll	Har-Row	1972

GRADES 4-6

Adrian, Mary	Gray Squirrel	Holiday House	1955
Alger, Leclaire	Gaelic Ghosts	Holt	1964
Ames, Gerald and Wyler, Rose	The First People in the World	Harper and Bros.	1958
Asbjornsen, Peter C. and Moe, Jorgen E.	Norwegian Folk Tales	Viking	1961
Baker, Augusta	The Golden Lynx and Other Tales	Lippincott	1960
Barker, Will	Winter-Sleeping Wildlife	Harper Bros.	1958
Baum, Frank	Wizard of Oz	School Bk. Service	1967
Beim, Jerrold	Trouble After School	Har Brace	1957
Benson, Sally	Stories of Gods and Heroes	Dial	1940
Bigland, Eileen	Madame Curie	Criterion Books	1957
Blackwood, Paul E.	Push and Pull	Whittlesey House	1959
Bocke, Kees	Cosmic View	John Day Co.	1958
Branley, Franklyn M.	The Moon Seems to Change	Crowell	1960
Bridges, William	Zoo Celebrities	Wm. Morrow and Co.	1959
Brown, Vinson	How to Understand Animal Talk	Little, Brown & Co.	1958
Burton, Sir Richard	The Arabian Nights	McKay	1946
Caidin, Martin	The Winged Armada; the Story of the Strategic Air Command	Dutton	1964
Carpenter, Frances	The Elephant's Bathtub: Wonder Tales from the Far East	Doubleday	1962
Catherall, Arthur	A Zebra Came to Drink	Dutton	1967
Cetin, Frank	Here is Your Hobby: Stamp Collecting	Putnam	1962
Chenery, Janet	The Toad Hunt	Harper	1967
Church, A. J.	The Aenid for Boys and Girls, Retold	Macmillan	1962
Cleary, Beverly	Henry Huggins	Morrow	1950
Cleary, Beverly	Romona The Pest	Morrow	1968
Cleaver, Vera & Bill	Ellen Grae	Lippincott	1967
Clemens, Samuel Twain, Mark	Huckleberry Finn	G&D	1970
Clymer, Eleanor	My Brother Stevie	Holt	1967
Colby, Carroll	Annapolis: Cadets, Training and Equipment	Coward-McCann	1964

Colby, Carroll	Air Force Academy	Coward-McCann	1962
Colby, Carroll	Communications: How Man Talks to Man Across Land, Sea, and Space	Coward-McCann	1964
Colby, Carroll	West Point: Cadets, Training and Equipment	Coward-McCann	1963
Colum, Padraic	The Boy Apprenticed to An Enchanter	Macmillan	1966
Compton, Grant	What Does a Veterinarian Do?	Dodd	1964
Daeliesh, Alice	The Spirit of St. Louis	Scribner	1956
Dahl, Roald	Charlie and the Chocolate Factory	Knopf	1964
Dahl, Roald	James and the Giant Peach	Knopf	1961
Darling, Lois and Louis	Before and After Dinosaurs	William Morrow	1959
De Saint-Exupery, Antoine	Le Petit Prince	Harcourt Brace J. Inc.	1943
Dodge, Mary M.	Hans Brinker or the Silver Skates	Childrens	1969
Edmonds, I. G.	Ooka the Wise: Tales from Old Japan	Bobbs-Merrill	1961
Ekrem, Selma	Turkish Fairy Tales	Van Nostrand	1964
Estes, Eleanor	The Hundred Dresses	Harcourt	1944
Felton, Harold W.	Sergeant O'Keefe and His Mule Balaam	Dodd	1962
Feravolo, Rocco	Wonders of Sound	Dodd	1962
Fox, Paula	A Likely Place	Macmillan	1967
Friedman, Estelle	Digging into Yesterday	G. P. Putnam's Sons	1958
Galt, Thomas F.	How the United States Works	Crowell	1965
Garner, Alan	Elidor	Walck	1967
Gottlieb, Wm. P.	Space Flight and How It Works	Doubleday	1964
Grant, Madeline P.	Louis Pasteur: Fighting Hero of Science	Whittlesay House	1959
Grass, Ruth	Hansel and Gretel	School Bk. Service	1974
Grimm Brothers	The Four Clover Brothers	Harcourt	1967
Grimm Brothers	Grimm's Fairy Tales	Grosset & Dunlap	1962
Hamilton, Virginia	Zeely	Macmillan	1967
Harris, Christia	Once Upon a Totem	Atheneum	1963
Hawkinson, Lucy & John	What Is A Butterfly?	Benefic Press	1958
Hawthorne, Nathaniel	The Complete Greek Stories of the Author; from the Wonder Book and Tanglewood Tales	Watts	1963
Hawthorne, Nathaniel	A Wonder Book For Boys and Girls	G & D	1967
Hawthorne, Nathaniel	Tanglewood Tales For Boys and Girls	G & D	1967
Hazeltine, Alice I.	Hero Tales from Many Lands	Gordon Laite	1961
Henry, Marguerite	All About Horses	Random	1962
Henry, Marguerite	Brighty of Grand Canyon	Rand	1953
Henry, Marguerite	King of the Wind	Rand	1948
Hitchcock, Patricia	The King Who Rides A Tiger and Other Folk Tales From Nepal	Parnassus	1966
Hoff, Syd	Irving and Me	Harper	1967
Holbrook, Stewart Hall	The Golden Age of Railroads	Random	1960

Holsaert, Eunice & Solbert, Ronni	Outer Space	Henry Holt & Co.	1959
Hurliman, Bettina	William Tell and His Son	Harcourt	1967
Hunt, Wolf R. and Rushmore, Helen	The Dancing Horses of Acoma (Southwest Indian)	World	1963
Hyde, Wayne	What Does a Forest Ranger Do?	Dodd	1964
Hyde, Wayne	What Does a Secret Service Agent Do?	Dodd	1962
Jacobs, Joseph	English Folk and Fairy Tales	Putnam	1967
Johnson, Gerald W.	The Supreme Court	Morrow	1962
Kipling, Rudyard	Jungle Book	G & D	1950
Konigsberg, E. I.	From the Mixed-Up Files of Mrs. Basil E. Frankweiler	Atheneum	1967
Konigsberg, E. I.	Jennifer, Hacate, Macbeth, William McKinley and Me, Elizabeth	Atheneum	1967
Krumgold, Joseph	And Now Miguel	Crowell	1953
Lee, Robert	The Iron Arm of Michael Glenn	Little	1965
L'Engle, Madeleine	A Wrinkle in Time	Dell	1973
Lenski, Lois	Cotton in my Sack	Dell	1966
Lester, Julice	Black Folktales	Grove	1970
Lester, Julice	To Be A Slave	Dial	1968
Liars, Emil E.	A Beaver's Story	Viking Press	1958
Lovett, Margaret	The Great and Terrible Quest	Holt	1967
Mann, Peggy	The Street of the Flower Boxes	Coward	1968
McDermott, Gerald	Arrow To The Sun	Viking	1974
McGovern, Ann	Why It's a Holiday	Random	1960
Milne, Lorus & Margery	The Crab That Crawled Out of the Past	Atheneum	1965
Moody, Ralph	Wells Fargo	Houghton	1961
North, Sterling	Young Tom Edison	Houghton	1958
O'Brien, Robert C.	Mrs. Frisby and the Rats of Nimh	Anthenum	1971
O'Faolain, Eileen	Irish Sagas and Folktales	Walch	1954
Olds, Elizabeth	Deep Treasure	Houghton-Mifflin	1958
Parkinson, Ethelyn	The Operation That Happened to Rupert Piper	Abingdon	1968
Perrouet	French Fairy Tales	Knopf	1968
Picard, Barbara Leonie	Celtic Tales	Criterion	1965
Picard, Barbara	German Hero-Sagas and Folktales	Walch	1958
Picard, Barbara Leonie	The Faun and the Wood-cutter's Daughter	Criterion	1964
Pine, Tillie	The Indians Knew	Whittlesey House	1957
Porter, George	A Papa Like Everyone Else	Follett	1968
Renault, Mary	The King Must Die	Bantam	1974
Reidman, Sarah R.	Clang! Clang! The Story of Trolleys	Rand McNally	1964
Robertson, Dorothy L.	Fairy Tales From Viet Nam	Dodd	1968
Robinson, Veronica	David in Silence	Lippincott	1968
Rollins, Charlemae	Christmas Gift	Fellett	1963
Schulz, Charles	Charlie Brown All Stars	New Amer. Library	1973

Sewell, Anna	Black Beauty	G & D	1971
Shapiro, Irwin	Heroes in American Folklore	Messner	1962
Sheppard Jones, Elizabeth	Welsh Legendary Tales	Nelson	1960
Siebert, Jerry	Amelia Earhart: The First Lady of the Air	Houghton Mifflin	1960
Simpson, Jacynth Hope	A Cavalcade of Witches	Walck	1967
Stevenson, Augusta	Daniel Boone, Boy Hunter	Bobbs	1961
Stirling, Nora B.	Wonders of Engineering	Doubleday	1966
Stolz, Morna	Marassa and Midnight	McGraw-Hill	1967
Spyri, Johanna	Heidi	Penguin	1971
Tannebaum, Beulah and Stillman, Myra	Understanding Time	Whittlesey House	1958
Tashjian, Virginia	Once There Was and Was Not	Little	1966
Tolkien, J.R.R.	The Hobbit	Haughlon Mifflin	1938
Treece, Henry	Further Adventures of Robinson Crusoe	Criterion	1958
Updike, John and Chappell, Warren	The Magic Flute Music by Wolfgang Amadeus Mozart	Knopf	1962
Updike, John	The Ring. Music by Richard Wagner	Knopf	1964
Veglahn, Nancy	The Spider of Brooklyn Heights	Scribner	1967
Verrill, A. Hyatt	The Strange Story of Our Earth	Grossett & Dunlap	1958
Varney, Joyce	The Magic Maker	Bobbs-Merrill	1967
Wadsworth, Wallace C.	Paul Bunyan and His Great Blue Ox	Doubleday	1961
Weart, Edith Lucia	The Story of Your Blood	Coward-McCann	1960
Weisgard, Leonard the New Stone Age	The First Farmers in	Coward-McCann	1966
Wheeler, Opal	Ludwig Beethoven and the Chiming Tower Bells	Dutton	1942
Wheeler, Opal	Frederic Chopin, Son of Poland	Dutton	1948
Wheeler, Opal	Handel at the Court of the Kings	Dutton	1943
Wheeler & Deucher, Sybil	Mozart, The Wonder Boy	Dutton	1941
White, E. B.	Charlotte's Web	Harper	1962
Whitehead, Don	The FBI Story	Random House	1963
Whitney, Phyllis A.	Mystery of the Hidden Hand	Westminster	1963
Wiggin, Kate D.	Rebecca of Sunnybrook Farm	MacMillan	1962
Wuorio, Eva-Lis	October Treasure	Holt	1966
Wyatt, Isabel	The Golden Stag and Other Folk Tales from India	McKay	1962
Wyss, Johann	Swiss Family Robinson	Collins-World	1972

GRADES 7-12

Adamson, Joy	Born Free	Pantheon	1960
Alcott, Louisa May	Little Women	Little	1968
Allen, Betty and Briggs, Mitchell P.	Mind Your Manners	Lippincott	1964
Andrews, Roy Chapman	Beyond Adventure	Duell	1954
Armstrong, Williams	Velveteen Rabbit	Doubleday	1958
Arnold-Foster, F. D.	The Madagascar Pirates	Lathrop	1957

Arnott, Kathleen	African Myths and Legends	Walck	1963
Baumann, Hans	Gold and Gods of Peru	Pantheon	1963
Beals, Carlton	John Eliot: The Man Who Loved the Indians	Messner	1957
Beebe, Burdetta Faye and Johnson, James Ralph	American Wild Horses	McKay	1964
Berganst, Erik	Space Stations	Putnam	1962
Best, Allena (Champlin)	You Have To Go Out	McKay	1964
Bixby, William	Waves: Pathways of Energy	McKay	1963
Brennan, Louis A.	The Buried Treasure of Archaeology	Random	1964
Buck, Pearl	The Big Wave	Day	1948
Byars, Betsey	The Summer of the Swans	Viking	1970
Carrol, Lewis	Alice in Wonderland	Grossett & Dunlap	1974
Chase, Mary Ellen	Sailing the Seven Seas	Houghton	1956
Commager, Henry Steele	Crusaders for Freedom (civil rights)	Doubleday	1962
Cooke, David Coxe	Flights That Made History	Putnam	1961
Copper, Susan	The Grey King	Antheneum	1975
Gordon, S.	Girls are Girls & Boys are Boys	Jon Day	1974
Crist, Eda and Richard	The Secret of Turkeyfoo Mountain	Abelard	1957
Crowther, James Gerald	Radioastronomy and Radar	Criterion	1964
Denniston, Elinore	America's Silent Investigators	Dodd	1964
Dutton, Wm. Sherman	One Thousand Years of Explosives from Wildfire to the H-Bomb	Winston	1960
Etcher, James	Law	Watts	1963
Eifert, Virginia L.	Delta Queen: The Story of a Steamboat	Dodd	1960
Epstein, Samuel and Epstein, Berry (Wm.)	All About Engines and Power	Random	1962
Footman, David	The Russian Revolution	Putnam	1964
Fox, Paula	The Slave Dancer	Bradbury	1973
Frazier, Meta	Rawhide Johnny	Longmans	1957
Froman, Robert	Wanted: Amateur Scientists	McKay	1963
Garst, Shannon	Amelia Earhart	Messner	1947
George, Jean C.	Julie of the Wolves	Harper and Row	1972
Graves, Robert	Greek Gods and Heroes	Doubleday	1960
Hamilton, Virginia	M.C. Higgins, the Great	Macmillan	1974
Harris, Warren, H. B.	Dive!	Harper	1960
Harrison, C-William	Conservation, the Challenge of Reclaiming Our Plundered Land	Messner	1963
Harrison, C-William	Forest Fighters and What They Do	Watts	1962
Hitch, Allan S. and Sorenson, Marian	Conservation and You	Van Nostrand	1964
Hodnett, Edward	So You Want To Go Into Industry	Harper	1960
Hughes, Langston	Famous Negro Heroes of America	Dodd	1958
Hyde, Margaret O.	Medicine in Action: Today and Tomorrow	Whittlesey	1964
Irving, Washington	The Legend of Sleepy Hollow	Walts	1966
Janson, Horst W. and Janson, Dora Jane	The Story of Painting for Young People	Abrams	1962

Johnson, Gerald W.	Communism: An American's View	Morrow	1964
Keith, Harold	Rifles for Watie	Crowell	1957
Kelly, Frank	Reporters Around the World	Little	1957
Keller, Helen	The Story of My Life	Doubleday	1954
Kennedy, John	Profiles in Courage	Harper	1958
Kingsley, Charles	The Heroes	MacMillan	1954
Kjelgard, Jim	The Black Fawn	Dodd	1958
Lens, Sidney	Working Men: The Story of Labor	Putnam	1961
Lindberg, Charles	Spirit of St. Louis	Scribner	1956
Lomax, John	American Ballads and Folk Songs	MacMillan	1934
Lomax, John	Cowboy Songs and Other Frontier Ballads	MacMillan	1938
McKown, Robin	Seven Famous Trials in History	Vanguard	1963
McGrady, Mike	Crime Scientists	Lippincott	1961
McNeer, May	Armed With Courage	Abingdon	1957
Paradis, Adrian	Business in Action	Messner	1962
Paradis, Adrian	Labor in Action	Messner	1963
Parker, K. Lanloh	Australian Legendary Tales	Viking	1966
Paust, Gilbert	How a Jet Flies	Sterling	1962
Perlman, Helen (Harris)	So You Want To Be A Social Worker	Harper	1962
Piper, Roger	The Big Dish? The Fascinating Story of Radio Telescopes	Harcourt	1963
Porter, Eleanor	Pollyanna: The Glad Book	Farrar, Straus & Giroux	1912
Rogers, Frances	Painted Rock to Printed Page	Lippincott	1960
Rolfe, Douglas	Airplanes of the World 1490-1962	Simon and Schuster	1962
Ross, Frank Xavier	The World of Medicine	Lothrop	1963
Roswell, Gene	The Yogi Berra Story	Messner	1958
Sandburg, Carl	The American Songbook	JJ Har Brace	1927
Scott, Jim	Bob Mathias	Prentice	1957
Scholastic Magazine	What You Should Know About Communism	McGraw-Hill	1962
Serraillier, Ian	Beowulf	Walck	1961
Silverberg, Robert	Scientists and Scoundrels A Book of Hoaxes	Crowell	1965
Stevenson, Robert Lewis	Treasure Island	Scribner	1911
Thomas, John	Leonardo Da Vinci	Criterion	1957
Turngren, Ellen	Listen, My Heart	Longmans	1956
Harris-Warren, H. B.	Dive!	Harper	1960
Harrison, C-William	Conservation, The Challenge of Reclaiming Our Plundered Land	Messner	1963
Harrison, C-William	Forest Firefighters and What They Do	Watts	1962
Hitch, Allan S. and Sorenson, Marian	Conservation and You	Van Nostrand	1964
Hodnett, Edward	So You Want To Go Into Industry	Harper	1960
Hughes, Langston	Famous Negro Heroes of America	Dodd	1958

Hyde, Margaret O.	Medicine in Action: Today and Tomorrow	Whittlesey	1964
Irving, Washington	The Legend of Sleepy Hollow	Walts	1966
Janson, Horst W. and Janson, Dora Jane	The Story of Painting for Young People	Abrams	1962
Johnson, Gerald W.	Communism: An American's View	Morrow	1964
Keith, Harold	Rifles for Watie	Crowell	1957
Kelly, Frank	Reporters Around the World	Little	1957
Keller, Helen	The Story of My Life	Doubleday	1954
Kennedy, John	Profiles of Courage	Harper	1958
Kingsley, Charles	The Heroes	MacMillan	1954
Kjelgard, Jim	The Black Fawn	Dodd	1958
Lens, Sidney	Working Men: The Story of Labor	Putnam	1961
Lindberg, Charles	Spirit of St. Louis	Scribner	1956
Lomax, John Lomax, Alan	American Ballads and Folk Songs	MacMillan	1934
Lomax, John Lomax, Alan	Cowboy Songs and Other Frontier Ballads	MacMillan	1938
McKown, Robin	Seven Famous Trials In History	Vanguard	1963
McGrady, Mike	Crime Scientists	Lippincott	1961
McNeer, May	Armed With Courage	Abingdon	1957
Paradis, Adrian	Business in Action	Messner	1962
Paradis, Adrian	Labor in Action	Messner	1963
Parker, K. Langloh	Australian Legendary Tales	Viking	1966
Paust, Gilbert	How a Jet Flies	Sterling	1962
Perlman, Helen (Harris)	So You Want To Be A Social Worker	Harper	1962
Piper, Roger	The Big Dish? The Fascinating Story of Radio Telescopes	Harcourt	1963
Porter, Eleanor	Pollyanna: The Glad Book	Farrar, Straus & Giroux	1912
Rogers, Frances	Painted Rock to Printed Page	Lippincott	1960
Rolfe, Douglas	Airplanes of the World 1490-1962	Simon and Schuster	1962
Ross, Frank Xavier	The World of Medicine	Lothrop	1963
Roswell, Gene	The Yogi Berra Story	Messner	1958
Sandburg, Carl	The American Songbook	JJ Har Brace	1927
Scott, Jim	Bob Mathias	Prentice	1952
Scholastic Magazine	What You Should Know About Communism	McGraw-Hill	1962
Serraillier, Ian	Beowulf	Walck	1961
Silverberg, Robert	Scientists and Scoundrels A Book of Hoaxes	Scribner	1965
Stevenson, Robert Lewis	Treasure Island	Scribner	1911
Thomas, John	Leonardo Da Vinci	Criterion	1957
Turngren, Ellen	Listen, My Heart	Longmans	1955
Twain, Mark	Tom Sawyer	Wash. Square Press	1972
Wacks, Theodore	Careers in Research Science	Coward-McCann	1964
Weaver, Warren	Making Our Government Work	Coward-McCann	1964

Welch, Ronald	Ferdinand Magellan	Criterion	1956
Warnecke, Heubert H.	Celebrating Christmas Around the World	Westminster	1962
Whipple, A. B.	Famous Pirates of the World	Random	1958
White, Dale	John Wesley Powell	Messner	1958
William, J. R.	Tame the Wild Stallion	Prentice	1957
Wyss, Johann	Swiss Family Robinson	Dutton	1957
Zindel, Paul	The Pigman	Dell	1968

Index

Anderson, Hans C., 30, 65, 71
animism, 2
Armer, Alberta, 30
attention, 64, 66
audibility, 124
audience adaptation, 67–68

ballads, 25, 26, 33
Bandura, Albert, 57
Bettelheim, Bruno, 38
biographical material, 13, 31–33, 41, 42
Blake, William, 177
body, 66
Bontemps, A., 32
Boston, L.M., 48
box or object puppets, 155
Braley, Berton, 177
breathing control, 176
Breck, Vivian, 43
Brodsky, Mimi, 30
Brown, Ray, 45
Browning, Robert, 26, 78
Bryan, William Jennings, 133
building mood, 68–69
Burgdorf, Arlene, B., 42

casting a story, 85, 86
characters, life-like, 26, 48–49, 60, 119
child participation, 122–123, 125–131
children and literature, 44–48
choral reading, 98–104
Cinderella story, 4
climax, 70–71
comprehension level, 54, 60
conclusion, 33, 35
conflict, 65–66, 70–73
cosmologist, 3
creative drama, 81
criticism, 125
critique, storytelling, 183–185
cue cards, 71–72
cutting, 72–73

de la Mare, Walter, 58

delivery, 73–75
dialogue, 39
Dickens, Charles, 30
dissemination of stories, 4–6
dramatic play, 89–92
Ducket, A., 32

emotions, 31, 56–59, 60
epic, 2, 29–30, 33
Estes, Eleanore, 31
evaluation, 87–89
expression, 124

fables, 13–15
fairy tale, 15–16, 38, 48
fancy, age of, 37–40
fear, 58
finger puppets, 150–151
fist puppets, 151
flannel board construction, 145
flannel board pictures, 145
flannel boards and colorforms, 143–145
folktales, 1, 15–16, 33
folk literature, 13–21, 33
follow up after a story, 78–79, 80
Forbes, Esther, 59
Frost, Robert, 68

Garthwaite, Marion, 41, 47
Geeslin, D. H., 45, 46
Gessell, Arnold L., 36, 41
gesture, 75
glove puppets, 151–152
Goldman, Harriet, 45
Graham, Lorenz, 59
Grimm, William and Jacob, 1–2, 5, 37, 51, 64

hand puppets, 153–155
Harte, Bret, 30
Henley, William, 178
hero worship, age of, 40–42
Herzberg, Max, 16
Hess, Robert D., 45
Hoff, Syd, 45

idealism, age of, 42–43
identification with the story, 53–54
impromptu stories, 115–116
improvization, 117–118
inattentiveness, 134–135
individualism, 43–44
inflectional pattern, 98, 100–2, 146
Ingersoll, Robert G., 133
interrogation, 104–110
introduction, 64–66
Irving, Washington, 73

Jacobs, Joseph, 2
Jataka tales, 5, 37

Keightley, Thomas, 5
key situations, 70–71
Kingsley, W. H., 56
Kipling, Rudyard, 76

legends, 18–19
listening, 86–87, 132
listening and telling, 135–136
listening habits, 133–134
listening improving, 136–138
listening testing, 138
literary worth, 48–53, 60
logical plot, 51
Lomax, Louis, 30
London, Jack, 30
Longfellow, Henry W., 55, 182

Marionettes or string puppets, 159–161
Masefield, John, 182
McDonnell, V., 32
memorizing, 76
Milton, John, 68
Mirsky, R.P., 32
mood, 64, 68–69
Muller, Max, 2
Mulock, Dinah, 84
myths, 13, 16–18, 33, 48

narration, 39
narrative poetry, 13, 21–30, 33
nature, effect on stories, 2
Nicholson, Elsie Mae, 55
nursery rhymes, 21–25, 33

origin of stories, 1–3

pantomime, 95–98
paper bag puppets, 156–158
papier mache puppets, 155
participation stories, 73, 125–131

pause, use of, 69
Peltola, Bette Jean, 42, 45
Peterson, Barbara G., 49
physical arrangement, 66–67
picture stories, 129–130
pictures and chalkboards, 142
Pierce, Lt. Col. Philip, 32
pitch, 181–182
plot, 51, 52
Poe, Edgar Allan, 68
posture, 124
preparation, 63
process of storytelling, 6–8
producing a puppet story, 149–150
puppet stories, 147–148
puppet theatre, 148–149
puppet values, 146–147
puppetry, 145–161
puppets, types of, 150–161
purpose of story, 54

quality, exercises, 176–179

rate, 124
reading levels, 54–55
reading stories, 76–78
realism, 30
realistic stories, 13, 30–31
relaxation, bodily, 175
Remus, Uncle, 5
repetition, age of, 36–37
Rhodopis, 4
Robinson, J., 32
rod puppets, 152–153
role playing, 92–95
Rush, Earl M., 49

sagas, 19–21, 33
Schuon, K., 32
Scott, Sir Walter, 76
setting, 51–52, 60
shadow puppets, 153
Shakespeare, William, 181
Sheehy, 55
sock puppets, 158–159
Spock, Benjamin, 38
staging, 105
Stanchfield, Jo M., 43
Steinbeck, John, 30
Steirt, Katherine, 42
stick puppets, 152
stories for dramatization, characteristics, 84–85
stories for puppets, 147–148

story choice, 35, 126–131, 123
story dramatization, 81, 104–114
story dramatization, values, 84–85
story follow-up, 78–79
story index, 186–197
story poems, 26–29, 33
storyacting, 115
storytellers, 2, 3, 5–6, 33–7, 41–2, 43, 49, 54, 60, 73–75
storytelling grid, 59
storytelling model, 8–9
storytelling, values, 8–11, 118–121
strength, voice, 179–181
Sun-Myth position, 2
Swift, Hildegarde, 59

teacher assistance, 125
television, influence of, 30, 44–45
Tennyson, Alfred, 180
themes, adult and child, 55
time of day, 67
time limits, 123

transmigration of souls, 2
Twain, Mark, 30, 44

unity, 51
universal truth, 31, 48, 52, 60

Van Dyke, Henry, 177
variety, 54
visual aids, 124–125, 140
visual aids, choice of, 140–141
visual aids-objects, 142–143
visual aids-purpose, 140
visual aids-rules, 141
visual aids-types, 141–161
voice improvement, 175–182

Wiksell, Wesley, 135
Wilson, Frank T., 45, 46
Witty, Paul, 44
Wordsworth, William, 50
word scramble, 129
word usage, author's, 50–51, 52, 60